Essential Islamic Knowledge

A Handbook on Ḥanafi Fiqh

Qāḍī Thanā'ullāh Pānīpatī

UK ISLAMIC ACADEMY

ISBN 978 1 872531 34 2

General editor: Iqbal Ahmad Azami

Translation from Persian: Yusuf Talal De Lorenzo

Published by

UK Islamic Academy
PO Box 6645
Leicester
LE5 5WT
United Kingdom
Website: www.ukiabooks.com

British Library Cataloguing in Publication Data

A catalogue record for this book is available from the British Library.

Typeset by Muhammad al-Madani

Back cover image: Arial view of the famous *Darul ʿUlūm* in Deoband, India

Printed in Turkey by Imak Ofset

CONTENTS

بسم الله الرحمن الرحيم

PREFACE

The best of knowledge for a person is knowledge of his Creator, Allāh, glory be to Him, of His attributes, and the fundamentals of Islamic belief, and after that, knowledge of what Allāh has made lawful for him and what He has prohibited him; knowledge of His *Sharī'ah* which He has revealed to us and the *jinns* and the way He should be worshipped. The purpose, after all, behind the creation of mankind and the *jinn* is only worship of Allāh. Allāh, the Glorified and Exalted, says in the Holy Qur'ān:

وَمَا خَلَقْتُ الْجِنَّ وَالْإِنسَ إِلَّا لِيَعْبُدُونِ ﴿٥٦﴾

"*I only created mankind and jinn, that they should worship Me.*" [*adh-Dhāriyāt* 51: 56]

Since the purpose for man's creation is worship of Allāh, then knowledge of each and every major and minor rule of worship becomes an important duty for a believer. For example, a man once came from Syria to Madīnah Munawwarah in the time of Sayyidunā 'Umar ibn al-Khaṭṭāb, the second Caliph, may Allāh be pleased with him, and 'Umar, may Allāh be pleased with him, asked him: "What has brought you here from that far away place." He replied: "I have only come to learn how to read *tashahhud* in the Prayer." Upon hearing this, 'Umar wept and said: "By Allāh, I believe with certainty that Allāh will never punish you in the Hereafter." The Prophet, may the peace and blessings of Allāh be upon him, said: "No one can worship Allāh with anything better than his learning and deep understanding of his religion," and he, may Allāh bless him and grant him peace, also said: "A person who has deep understanding of *din* is more severe against Satan than a thousand worshippers without proper understanding."

In this respect, and – praise be to Allāh, the Glorified and Exalted, – who guided me to *Mālā Budda Minhu – The Essentials of Islamic Knowledge* by *Qāḍī* Thanā'ullāh Pānīpatī, who was a student of Shah Waliyyullah *Muḥaddith* Dehlawī, one of the most renowned Islamic scholars and reformers of the Indian subcontinent. He was also the greatest disciple (*khalīfah*) of Mirzā Maẓhar Jāne Jānān the famous *Shaikh* of the Naqshbandī Ṣufī order in Muslim India, who was himself a widely respected author, *muḥaddith*, exegist, *faqīh*, linguist, poet and who, above all, is known as one of the *'ulamā' ar-rabbāniyyīn.*

As for *Qāḍī* Thanā'ullāh, he was himself a great scholar, exegist, *muḥaddith* and jurist who wrote several great books on *tafsīr*, *ḥadīth* and *fiqh* while all the while leading the life of a *mujāhid*. In presenting *Mālā Budda Minhu* to the reader, he did not deprive the common Muslim masses and youth from also benefiting from his vast knowledge.

Essentially, the book gives a detailed explanation of the creed held by the *ahl-as-sunnah-wal-Jamā'ah*. Specifically, *'aqīdah*, *ṭahārah*, *ṣalāh*, *zakāh*, *ṣawm* and *ḥajj*. In addition, some basic aspects on what is prohibited and what is disliked, together with some instructions on elements of social conduct.

He deals with the issues which everyone ought to know for the correct performance of these devotions and of which, people generally, have little knowledge. While *Ḥanafī fiqh* is followed, there are occasional references to other schools of *fiqh*. However, a few intricate matters are also covered. One chapter is devoted to God-fearing behaviour; and another to individual and collective dealings; sales and purchases, highlighting their correct and distorted forms. Another deals with social behaviour; one's duties to others and prohibits the unIslamic customs and traditions which were in vogue during *Qāḍī* Thanā'ullāh's time and which are still prevalent today. Another examines *tazkiyah* and *Iḥsān*; the sincere worship of Allāh and attaining to the true spirit of faith; although this chapter is brief, it omits nothing of importance.

The original publication of this work in Persian has been taught in religious institutes across the Indian subcontinent and also Persian-speaking countries for over 300 years. I am one of those fortunate students who was taught this during my youth. It is hoped that its modern translation into English will be equally beneficial for schools and *madrasahs* the world over.

This edition has been translated and edited by brother Yūsuf Ṭalāl De Lorenzo, an American Muslim, himself an *ʿālim* and student of *Shaikhul-ḥadīth*, Maulānā Muḥammad Yūsuf Bennorī and *Muftī* Walī Ḥasan Taunkī, from among those well-known Islamic scholars of the subcontinent. De Lorenzo has also been assisted by another American brother, Yūsuf Chaudhury. May Allāh bless and reward them for their efforts.

In addition, I have also revised the work thoroughly and made important and useful alterations, and the addition of the chapter on *Ḥajj* with the assistance of my children, especially my daughter Suʿād, Sister Anis and Dr. Daud Matthews. It has been my great desire to prepare for my own children who are growing up in the West and also for my brothers and sisters whose fortunes have brought them to these countries, to present some simple instructive materials on the essentials of Islam.

May Allāh reward all the people who have participated in its production and make it a useful addition to the knowledge of Islam. To Allāh belongs all good and by His favour all righteous deeds come into existence.

Iqbal Ahmad Azami

Rabīʿ al-Awwal, 1424
Leicester, United Kingdom

Translator's Note

Essential Islamic Knowledge is a modified translation of the original Persian text *Mālā Budda Minhu.* While I have attempted in the translation to be as faithful as possible to the original, I have also made a number of improvements which I hope will make the book more readable and understandable to the modern reader.

Alterations which appear most frequently involve the inclusion in square brackets of explanatory words throughout the text. These are, for the most part, intended to clarify what might otherwise have been an obscure or ambiguous passage in the original or as a result of translation.

There are also a number of instances where I have used footnotes to discuss or include matters of contemporary relevance. At any rate, the important thing to note is that the translator or revisers have appended everything in brackets. I would like to thank Sister Besa Maẓhar Krasniqi for her valuable comments on the chapter on *ṭahārah* which the reader can find as footnotes; may Allāh reward her and keep her in the best of *Īmān.*

Another feature of this work is its specification, in cases where more than one legal opinion has been presented in the text of the original, of the *fatāwā* of later Ḥanafī scholars. In this, I have relied almost exclusively on Ibn 'Ābidīn's '*Radd al-Muḥtār,*' more popularly known as '*Shāmī*'.

Other changes have also been made for the purpose of making the text more fluid and readily understood such as the use of numbers, titles, subtitles and minor textual rearrangements. Finally, I have provided the reader with a Glossary of Technical Arabic Terms at the end of the book.

I can only hope that what I have done will prove to be useful. May Allāh, most High, accept this effort and lead us by means of it to the way of His Pleasure. *Amīn.*

Yūsuf Ṭalāl De Lorenzo

Chapter 1

Īmān

1.1 Allāh سبحانه وتعالى

Praise and glory be to Allāh, who is Self-existent while all things receive their existence from Him. They have need of Him for their origination and continuation while He has no need of anything.

He is one; in His essence, His attributes, and His acts.

No one has partnership with Him in any matter. His existing and His living are not of the same category as the existing and living of created things. His knowledge bears no resemblance to their knowledge. His seeing, hearing, power, will, and speech are not similar to, and share nothing with the seeing, hearing, power, will, and speech of creation. Aside from the similarity of sharing these names, there is no similarity or sharing.

His acts and His attributes, like His essence, are both without mode and without compare. The attribute of knowledge possessed by the Almighty, for example, is an eternal attribute. It is a non-composite, active awareness such that every piece of information from the beginning to the end of time, along with its similar and contrary states, in whole and in part, each in its particular time, is known to Him all at once. Thus, for example, He knows that so and so is to be living at a certain time, and that at a certain time he is to die, and so forth. In a similar manner, His speech is a non-composite speech, the particulars of which are the revealed books.

Allāh most High is above bodily incarnation, *ḥulūl*, and likewise, there is nothing capable of becoming incarnate in Him.

Allāh most High encompasses all things and is in the company of, and is close to, everything that exists by an encompassing, accompanying, and closeness of His own; not the sort that we can comprehend in our limited minds, as that is not worthy of His Sacred Being.

Creation [shaping and bringing into being] is an attribute especially His own.

All beings, their senses, actions and attributes are all created by Him, exalted is He. He has veiled His acts with causes and means yet, at the same time, these are the proofs that everything is of His doing. It is the way of Allāh, whenever one of His servants makes an intention to perform a certain act, that He creates that act and brings it into existence. On the basis of this semblance of will and power, the individual is called an earner, *kāsib*, and it is on this basis that he or she is praised or criticised, rewarded, or punished. It is disbelief, *kufr*, to suppose that something other than Allāh is the true creator of any part of creation.

Allāh most High is above whatever visions the *Ṣufīs* may have of Him in their meditations. Thus, it is essential to have faith in the Unseen, *ghayb*. What the *Ṣufī* sees in his meditations is only an image or representation. It is the teaching of the *Ṣufīs* themselves that all such visions should be understood as coming under and being nullified by the negative particle '***lā***' [corresponding to the word '**No**' in the testament of faith, *kalimah*, '***Lā*** *ilāha illa'llāh*, There is **no** god but Allāh'].

Then, it is our belief that the Almighty encompasses all things, and that He is indeed close by, even though we do not comprehend the full significance of these matters. Similarly, the Almighty's settling Himself on the Throne, *'arsh*, His presence in the heart of every believer, His descent to the lowest heaven in the latter part of the night, and other such things, like the mention of His hand or face, as have come to us in the Qur'ān and *aḥādīth*, must not be understood in their literal (physical) sense. Neither should we attempt to find interpretations, *ta'wīl*, for them.

We should simply have faith in these things; and in order to protect ourselves from believing to be true that which is in fact false, we should entrust their interpretation to the knowledge of the Almighty. Man's lot in these matters, is no more than ignorance and confusion. To deny the texts (of the Qur'ān and the *Sunnah*) is *kufr*, and to try to explain them by our own imagination is compound ignorance.

Those at the Lord's court acknowledged as seers,
Venture no further than saying that, 'He is.'

There is another kind of accompanying and closeness to the Almighty which is of a separate category and which bears no relation, other than that they both share the same name, to the closeness and accompanying that was mentioned above. This is the lot of His special servants; the angels, the prophets, and the *Ṣufī* saints. Still, the ordinary Muslim is not without a share of closeness either, as the degrees of closeness to Allāh are infinite. No matter how close one comes to Allāh, there will always be room for an even closer approach.

Maulānā Rūmī has written:

Brother, the court of the Lord is an endless one.
The closer you approach, the further you find you have to go…

1.2 Angels

We believe that the angels are the servants of Allāh; that they are innocent, free of either masculine or feminine gender, and in no need of food or drink. They are the messengers of Divine revelation, *waḥy*, and the bearers of the Throne, *'arsh*. They perform everything they are ordered to do.

In spite of their being the most noble of all creation, and their position as special servants at the court of the Lord Almighty, the prophets and the angels are no different from the rest of creation in that they possess no knowledge or power other than the knowledge and power granted to them by the Almighty. They perform the duties of their offices to the best of their abilities and give thanks to Allāh for the favour He has shown them.

The angels have faith in the Divine essence and attributes in the same way that all Muslims have faith in these things, and they admit their inability to comprehend His essential being.

1.3 The Prophets and the Revealed Books

Many thousands of blessings be showered upon the prophets, for, had they not been sent, no one would ever have seen the light of guidance, *hidāyah*, or attained to true knowledge.

All the prophets, peace be upon them, came in the way of truth.

The first prophet was Ādam, peace be upon him. The most excellent of them all was Muḥammad, may the peace and blessings of Allāh be upon him, the Last of the Prophets, *khātam-un-nabīyīn*. Any and all claims to prophethood after the Prophet Muḥammad, may the peace and blessings of Allāh be upon him, are false. The prophets, upon whom be peace, are *maʿṣūm*, protected from major and minor wrongdoing.

The Heavenly Ascension, *miʿrāj*, of the Messenger of Allāh, the peace and blessings of Allāh be upon him, and his Night Journey, *isrā'*, from the *Masjid al-Ḥarām* in Makkah to the *Masjid al-Aqṣā* in Jerusalem, and from there to the seven heavens and the Lote tree of the utmost boundary, *sidrat-ul-muntahā*, are all true.

The Heaven-sent Books revealed to the prophets include the Torah (*Tawrāt*) given to Mūsā, peace be upon him, the Gospel (*Injīl*) of ʿĪsā, peace be upon him, the Psalms (*Zabūr*) of Dā'ūd, peace be upon him, the Glorious Qur'ān given to Muḥammad, may the peace and blessings of Allāh be upon him, the Scrolls of Ibrāhīm, peace be upon him, and others, peace be upon all the prophets, all of them were true.*

We have faith in all of the prophets of Allāh. Although with regard to belief in the exact number of the prophets and the books of Allāh, we need not have a specific number in mind, as their exact numbers are not known with any kind of certainty. We believe about Muḥammad, may the peace and blessings of Allāh be upon him, whatever has been established by means of authentic proof.

1.4 Shirk – Associating Partners with Allāh سبحانه وتعالى

It is as much an act of disbelief to suppose that the special servants of Allāh share with Him some of His exclusive attributes as it is to worship them as His partners.

In the same way that certain disbelievers gave voice to their disbelief by denying the prophets, the Christians expressed theirs by claiming that Jesus (ʿĪsā), upon whom be peace, was the son of God. Similarly, the pagan Arabs became disbelievers when they took the angels to be the daughters of Allāh and supposed them to be in possession of knowledge of the Unseen, *ʿilm al-ghayb*. Furthermore, in the same way that the prophets and angels must not be understood as sharing in the Divine attributes, those other than the prophets must not be understood as sharing in the prophetic attributes.

Aside from the prophets and angels there are none who are protected from wrongdoing, *maʿṣūm*; not the Companions, not *Ahl al-Bayt*, the family of the Messenger of Allāh, may the peace and blessings of Allāh be upon him, and not the *ṣūfī* saints.

Only the Prophet, may the peace and blessings of Allāh be upon him, is to be followed. We may not arbitrarily assume that

* At the time of their revelation, all of these books were true. Over time, however, the texts were either lost or corrupted except the Qur'ān which remained in its pristine and original form. (Trans.)

obedience to someone else is required of us. The adoption, however, of a particular Imām's *madhhab* or way of interpreting the *Sharīʿah* is not of the latter but the former category of obedience; i.e., of obedience to the Prophet, may the peace and blessings of Allāh be upon him, as the four Imāms, [Abū Ḥanīfah, Mālik, Shāfiʿī and Aḥmad ibn Ḥanbal], were merely guides on the way of the Prophet, may the peace and blessings of Allāh be upon him. We follow an Imām as we follow a guide, inasmuch as he is more familiar with the landmarks along the way of the *Sunnah.* In doing so, we are actually following the way of the Messenger, may the peace and blessings of Allāh be upon him.

1.5 The Teachings of the Prophet ﷺ

Whatever the Messenger of Allāh, may the peace and blessings of Allāh be upon him, taught us concerning the articles of faith must become a part of our beliefs. We are to perform whatever he, may the peace and blessings of Allāh be upon him, ordered us to do, and refrain from whatever he forbade. Furthermore, we must reject the words and actions of whoever differs even a hair's breadth from the words and actions of the Messenger, may the peace and blessings of Allāh be upon him.

The Prophet, may the peace and blessings of Allāh be upon him, has informed us of the truth on the following matters:

1. The questioning in the grave by the two angels, Munkar and Nakīr.
2. The torment of the grave for the unbelievers and some of the disobedient believers.
3. The physical resurrection after death, and the Day of Judgement.
4. The first blowing of the Horn for the annihilation and destruction of the earth, and then the second blowing of the Horn for the reanimation of every living thing, the coming forth of mankind from their graves, and the re-creation of the physical world.

5. The cleaving of the skies.
6. The scattering of the stars.
7. The flying apart of the mountains.
8. The reckoning on the Day of Judgement.
9. The weighing of mankind's deeds on the scales, *mīzān*.
10. The testimony of man's limbs.
11. The crossing over the bridge, *ṣirāṭ*, set over the Hellfire that will be sharper than the blade of a sword and thinner than a hair. Some will pass over like lightning, some like the wind and some like war horses. Others will pass over slowly, and still others will fall from it into the Hellfire.
12. The intercession, *shafāʿah*, of the prophets, saints, and pious Muslims.
13. The pool of *kawthar* whose waters are whiter than milk and sweeter than honey, and whose cups are as shining and as numerous as the stars. Indeed, the Messenger of Allāh, may the peace and blessings of Allāh be upon him, said that whoever drinks of its waters will never thirst again.
14. The Almighty, if it be His will to do so, will forgive the commission of an act of major wrongdoing, *kabīrah*, from one who did not repent and will deal out punishment for the commission of even an act of minor wrongdoing, *ṣaghīrah*. Yet whosoever makes sincere repentance, *tawbah*, according to the Divine promise, will surely be forgiven.
15. Disbelievers will undergo eternal torment in the Hellfire. The wrongdoing Muslims, however, even if they should enter Hell, will, after a long or short duration, be released from Hell and be allowed to enter Paradise, *jannah*, where they will remain for eternity.
16. A believer does not automatically become a disbeliever, *kāfir*, by committing a major sin, *kabīrah*; nor can he be said to have left the faith of Islam.
17. All the various torments of the Hellfire like the snakes, scorpions, chains and shackles of fire, boiling water, *zaqqūm*, and *ghislīn*, as well as the pleasures of Paradise, like the food and drink, the *houris*, the palaces, and so forth, which the Qur'ān and

the Messenger of Allāh, may the peace and blessings of Allāh be upon him, have informed us about, are true.

18. The greatest of all pleasures to be enjoyed by the believers in Paradise will be their witnessing of the Almighty. There they will see Him directly [unveiled], though this witnessing will be unique, without direction and without reference to the how.

True faith consists of the inner conviction and assent of the heart, and the formal affirmation by the tongue. The formal profession of belief with the tongue is understood to be essential to *īmān*, though in times of necessity it can be dispensed with.

1.6 The Companions of the Prophet ﷺ

All of the Companions of the Prophet, may Allāh be pleased with them, were righteous. If, at one time or another, one of them committed a transgression, he repented of it and was forgiven. There is a great deal of absolutely sound, *mutawātir*, evidence from the Qur'ān and the *Sunnah* that is full of praise for the Companions. They are characterised in the Qur'ān: أَشِدَّآءُ عَلَى ٱلْكُفَّارِ رُحَمَآءُ بَيْنَهُمْ as being loving and merciful among themselves; yet severe with, and hostile to the disbelievers, [*al-Fath* 48: 29].

Whoever supposes that the Companions hated each other, or that they could not get along with each other, has denied the Qur'ān. Whoever is an enemy to them has had the word 'disbeliever' used to describe him in the Qur'ān,

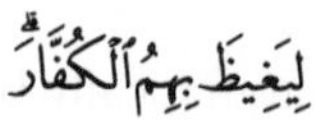

"*that through them He may enrage the disbelievers.*"
[*al-Fath* 48: 29]

The Companions were the carriers of revelation, *waḥy*, and transmitters of the Qur'ān. Whoever would deny the Companions could not possibly have faith in the Qur'ān or any of the other essential articles of faith.

It has been established through the consensus of the Companions and other textual evidences that Abū Bakr, may Allāh be pleased with him, was the most excellent of the Companions. The Companions knew him to be the best among them and accordingly gave him their oath of allegiance for the office of caliphate, *Khilāfah.* At Abū Bakr's suggestion, they accepted 'Umar, may Allāh be pleased with him, as their *Khalīfah* after him and came to a consensus about his being second in excellence. After 'Umar, the Companions conferred among themselves for three days until they determined 'Uthmān, may Allāh be pleased with him, to be the best among them. When they reached a consensus on his *Khilāfah,* they all pledged their allegiance to him. After 'Uthmān, all of the Emigrants, *muhājirīn,* and Helpers, *anṣār,* in Madīnah pledged their allegiance to 'Alī, may Allāh be pleased with him. Those who disputed with him were in the wrong, but we should not think ill of any of the Companions. Rather, we should try to view their dispute in a favourable light while having love for, and believing in them all.

CHAPTER 2

Ṭahārah

2.1 Purification*

Ṭahārah, purification, is a part of faith. A Muslim must be outwardly pure and clean in addition to having true belief and keeping oneself inwardly pure. Furthermore, purity and cleanliness are necessary prerequisites to the prayer, *ṣalāh*, the best and most rewarding of all kinds of worship. Therefore it becomes necessary to know what constitutes impurity, *najāsah*, and the actions necessary to remove it, or to lift one out of a state of impurity. Impurity is categorised as described below.

2.2 Ḥukmī or Legal Impurity

This kind of impurity [not necessarily an actual substance] comes about owing to one's having done something that the *Sharīʿah* views as causing one to become impure. This means that

* This paragraph, along with the following sections on Actual and Legal Impurity, have been added by the revisers for clarification and is not part of *Mālā Budda Minhu*.

the impure state is brought about by conditions rather than actual physical impurity being on one's person. This is further categorised as either:

(a) *ḥadath aṣghar* (minor ritual impurity); or
(b) *ḥadath akbar* (major ritual impurity).

One is in a state of minor ritual impurity when one does anything to invalidate one's ablution, *wuḍū'*, or does not have *wuḍū'* and one is in a state of major ritual impurity when one does anything to invalidate one's purificatory bath, *ghusl*, is menstruating, or experiencing post-childbirth bleeding or *janābah* intercourse or had a wet dream. Consequently, a person in a state of major impurity is also in a state of minor impurity.

The reason for this is that actions which render *ghusl* void also, subsequently, render *wuḍū'* void.

2.3 *Ḥaqīqī or Actual Impurity*

This is any substance with vulgar characteristics deemed impure by the *Sharī'ah*, such as urine. This is further categorised as either:

(a) *Najāsah khafīfah* (light impurity);
(b) or *Najāsah ghalīẓah* (gross impurity).

2.3.1 *Najāsah khafīfah* – Light impurity

All of the following substances are impure, *najāsah*, though only to the degree that they are called light impurities, *khafīfah*:

1. The urine of animals whose flesh is *ḥalāl*;
2. the urine of horses;
3. droppings of birds whose flesh is *ḥarām* [or of those whose flesh is *ḥalāl*, if the droppings give off an offensive odour].

The droppings of birds whose flesh is *ḥalāl*, with the exception of chickens and ducks [whose droppings give off an offensive odour], are [legally] pure.

2.3.2 *Najāsah ghalīẓah* – Gross impurity

The following are *najāsah ghalīẓah*, gross impurity:

1. human and baby urine;
2. the urine of an ass or other animals whose flesh is *ḥarām*;
3. the excrement of humans and four-legged beasts;
4. the blood [of men and beasts];
5. grape wine [and other liquid intoxicants];
6. the flesh of dead animals [whether they die naturally or are not properly slaughtered according to *Sharīʿah*,[1] even if it is an animal that is generally *ḥalāl* to eat, like chicken] which has flowing blood and its untanned hide;*
7. the milk of animals whose flesh is *ḥarām*;
8. the sweat and saliva of animals whose leftover food is considered impure like pigs, elephants, and ferocious quadrupeds whose flesh is *ḥarām* [except for cats whose leftovers are *makrūh*];
9. those things which come out from the human body which nullifies *wuḍū'*, such as flowing blood, semen,[2] *madhī*, *wadī*,[3] vaginal fluid,[4] blood of *istiḥāḍah*, *ḥayḍ*, and *nifās*, pus, and vomit.

2.4 *Excusable Amounts of Gross Impurity*

A spot of *ghalīẓah* impurity the size of a *dirham*, or the area of the inner palm of the hand, when the *ghalīẓah* impurity is thin [and spreads out], or of the weight of $3^5/_7$ grams when it is thick, is excusable [and one may perform one's prayer in clothes soiled by

* Points 6 and 9 have been added to this list by the revisers from *Marāqī al-Falāḥ*.

that amount]; though, were that same amount [or less] to fall into a small amount of water it would render the water unusable for the purposes of purification.[5]

2.4.1 Excusable amounts of lesser impurity

A spot of lesser impurity, if it should fall on and cover over less than a quarter of the total area of a section [a sleeve, collar, etc.] of clothing, will not prevent one from making prayer in those clothes [as that amount is so slight]. Though, if that same amount were to fall into a small amount of water it would render the water unusable for the purposes of purification such as ablution, *wuḍū'*, and the purificatory bath, *ghusl.*

However, any amount of lesser impurity above the excusable amount on one's person or clothing will prevent one from performing prayer.

2.4.2 Leftover food of other animals and humans

The leftovers [food or drink which has come into contact with the saliva] of humans, even disbelievers, horses, and animals whose flesh is *ḥalāl,* are pure. Their perspiration, and the perspiration of donkeys and mules, is pure. The leftovers of cats, mice, and other household animals and pests, like lizards, and the leftovers of birds whose flesh is *ḥarām* [like falcons and vultures] is disliked, or *makrūh.* The leftovers of pigs, dogs, elephants, and quadrupeds, whose flesh is *ḥarām,* [except for the cat and those like it, as was mentioned above] is *najis,* impure.

2.4.3 Excusable traces of urine

Flecks of urine, [when all but invisible] like the head of a pin, are excusable [as long as the total area covered by them does not exceed that of a *dirham,* as was mentioned previously].[6]

2.5 The Removal of Actual Impurity

2.5.1 Removal of dried semen

When dried and congealed semen is scratched off a garment [so that nothing of it remains visible] the garment is considered pure.

2.5.2 Cleaning solid objects

Swords and similar things [like mirrors] may be made pure by no more than wiping away the impurity.

2.5.3 Removing impurity from the ground and the like

If the ground should become impure, and then the impurity dries up so that no trace remains of it, the ground will be considered to have become pure and prayer may be performed at the very same place. However, it will not be permissible to use that earth for dry ablution, *tayammum*. The same will apply to walls, brick patios, trees, and leaves [i.e., they will become pure by the impurities drying up and disappearing]; though if the leaves are separated from the tree [or the bricks from the wall or patio], they will not be pure until they have been washed.

2.5.4 *Istinjā'* – Removing impurities after relieving oneself*

After passing urine, a person must make sure the leakage of urine has stopped and one's mind is at ease concerning the issue. It is not permitted to start the performance of *wuḍū'* without being sure that the leakage of urine has ceased. It is *Sunnah mu'akkadah* to clean the filth which comes out of the anus or genitals provided it has crossed the boundary of the orifice.

* This section has been added by the revisers from *Marāqī al-Falāḥ*.

If it has crossed the orifice and covers an area equal to the size of a *dirham*, it is *wājib* to remove it, but if it exceeds the area of a *dirham* it is *farḍ* to remove the filth by washing it with water.

When making *ghusl* to remove the state of major ritual impurity after the end of menstruation, *ḥayḍ*, or post-childbirth bleeding, *nifās*, it is *farḍ* to wash with water the filth which is at the orifice even though it is small in quantity.

Istinjā' is to be accomplished by wiping the filth with a clean stone using the left hand[7] or something similar which is clean [like toilet paper], and is not precious or honourable.[8] To wash the filth with water is better. Best of all is to use both stone and water, i.e. to wipe the filth with the stone first and then to wash with water. It is, however, correct to use either water or stones.

It is *ḥarām* to uncover, in the presence of others, the *'awrah* for the purposes of *istinjā'*.

If the filth has crossed the orifice, and the place over which it has spread is more than the measure of a *dirham*, and it is not removed despite having water available or other objects with which it can be removed, prayer is invalid.

It is *makrūh* to defecate or urinate in standing water, in the shade where people sit, in a hole where an animal might live and cause harm, on the road or walkway, or under a fruit tree. It is *makrūh* to urinate while standing, however it is permissible if a real excuse exists.

2.5.5 Perceptible impurity

All impurity must be removed until purity is attained for the thing one is trying to purify. Impurity which is perceptible to the eye when washed with water, to the degree that not a trace of the impurity remains, will become pure, according to Imām Abū Ḥanīfah. According to some Imāms, after the removal of what was perceptible the surface must be washed with water three times and, if possible, wrung out, or if not, then allowed to dry [before washing it again] until it no longer drips.

Impurity which is imperceptible to the eye must be washed at least three times and wrung out [or allowed to dry] each time between washings.

Animal hides, when tanned [chemically or in the sun] become pure, [the hide of a pig, however, does not become pure by any means of tanning].

2.6 *Permissible Water for Purification*

Purification cannot be achieved from legal, *ḥukmī*, states of minor or major impurity [i.e. through ablution, *wuḍū'*, or the purificatory bath, *ghusl*] except by the use of:

- pure water which has fallen from the sky [rain];[9]
- or welled up water from the earth like sea water, well water, or spring water.[10]

Then the water [juice] of trees and fruits, [for example, water-melon, grapes, bananas, etc.] is of no use in bringing something impure to the state of purification. These same properties of water apply for removing actual, *ḥaqīqī*, impurity where water is called for to purify.

If a foreign substance, which is pure, like sand, soap, saffron, etc., should fall into water, it will be considered permissible to make ablution, *wuḍū'*, or the purificatory bath, *ghusl*, with that water. Unless, however, the consistency of the water is affected so that it loses its thinness or becomes equal in proportion to that with which it was mixed.[11] Or if the water becomes so overwhelmed by the other substances that it loses the name 'water' and is instead called broth, rose-water, vinegar, etc. The consensus, *ijmā'*, of the scholars has it that it is neither permissible to make the purificatory bath, *ghusl*, nor ablution, *wuḍū'*, with the liquid resulting from such mixtures. According to Imām Abū Ḥanīfah, such liquids may be used to wash [and purify] clothes. The Imāms Muḥammad and Shāfi'ī, however, are of the opinion that they may not.

2.6.1 Definition of Large and Small Quantities of Water

According to most Imāms, a large amount of water is a *qullatayn* [two *qullas* or a *qullatayn* are about 210 litres]. According to Imām Abū Ḥanīfah, a large amount of water is that which when agitated on one side [bank] will not immediately become agitated on the other side. The later scholars of the *Ḥanafī* school of jurisprudence have [for the sake of simplicity] delineated this [saying of the Imām] by the ten by ten *dhirāʿ*, hand-span formula.[12]

2.6.2 Purity of Large and Small Quantities of Water

Flowing water, or water in great amounts [like water in a lake, pond, or large pool, often roughly estimated to be at least ten square *dhirāʿ* or ten by ten] will not become impure if impurity falls into it, or by the water's flowing over impurity. Unless the impurity effects a change in the taste, colour, or smell of the water [for then the water will be considered impure], it will be considered pure and usable for purification.

When impurity falls into a small amount of water, the water becomes impure and cannot be used for purification.

2.6.3 Impurity in Flowing Water

If a dog[13] sits in a current of flowing water, or if something dead falls in the flow, or if some impurity lodged in a gutter is passed over by water [on its way to the sewer below]; then in each case, if the greater part of the water comes into contact with the impurity, the water will become impure. If a lesser part of the water comes into contact with the impurity, the water will be considered pure and usable for purification.

2.6.4 Purity of wells

If an animal should fall into a well and die, then, if the carcass swells up or bursts open, all the water in the well will be unusable for purification and will have to be pumped out. If the carcass does not swell up, then, if the animal is large, [the size of a cat or larger] all of the water will have to be removed also. The same rule applies if three or more mid-sized animals [or birds] fall in. If the animal is small like a mouse or a sparrow, then, on its death, twenty to thirty buckets of water will have to be drawn from the well. If something mid-sized [like a pigeon] should die in a well, then forty to sixty buckets of water will have to be drawn from it before the well water can be used for purification. Three sparrows [are considered legally] equal to one pigeon.[14] And Allāh knows best.

2.7 *Wuḍū' – Ablution*[15]

2.7.1 The *fard* elements of *wuḍū'*

The performance of the following is obligatory in *wuḍū'*:

1. washing the face from the hairline to below the chin, and from ear to ear, once;
2. If one's beard is thick, it is not necessary to force water through the hairs [to beneath the skin when washing the face];
3. washing both hands up to and including the elbows, once;
4. wiping [with a wet hand] a fourth part of the head;
5. and washing both feet up to and including the ankles, once.

If even so much as the area of a fingernail should remain dry on the surface of any of the four parts of the body which are *farḍ* in *wuḍū'*, the *wuḍū'* will be invalid.

According to Imāms Shāfiʿī, Mālik, and Aḥmad, *niyah* [making intention] and *tartīb* [performing *wuḍū'* in a set order] are also *farḍ*.

Furthermore, according to Imām Mālik, it is *farḍ* to perform the *wuḍū'* as one continuous process, *muwālāh*. This means that one may not pause so long that the water on the last limb to be washed dries before one begins washing the next limb.

According to Imām Aḥmad, it is also *farḍ* to begin with the name of Allāh, and to rinse the nostrils and mouth with water.

Imāms Mālik and Aḥmad consider it *farḍ* to wipe the entire head.

Clearly, prudence dictates that one should perform all of these [regardless of which Imām one follows].

2.7.2 THE *SUNNAH* ELEMENTS OF *WUḌŪ'*

The performance of the following is *Sunnah* in *wuḍū'*:

1. the intention, *niyah*;
2. beginning by saying, "*Bismillāh ir Raḥmān ir Raḥīm*";
3. [to wash the right before the left, except for the hands, face, head, and ears which are washed simultaneously];
4. washing the hands up to the wrists and between the fingers three times;
5. using *miswāk*, a tooth-stick [or otherwise cleaning the teeth];
6. rinsing the mouth out three times with water, [using the right hand to draw the water];
7. rinsing the nostrils three times with water [using the right hand to draw the water] and cleaning the nostrils [using the left hand];
8. washing the entire face, three times;
9. washing both arms up to and including the elbows and hands, three times;
10. wiping, the entire head, the ears [and the nape of the neck, all with the same stroke]; It is not necessary to rewet the hands in between [the wiping of the head and the wiping of the ears];
11. washing both feet, up to and including the ankles, and between the toes, three times;
12. [*tartīb* or making *wuḍū'* in the prescribed sequence;]

13. [and *muwālāh*, or making *wuḍū'* in a continuous process without break.]

2.7.3 The *Du'a'*, supplication after completing *wuḍū'*

أَشْهَدُ أَن لاَّ إِلَهَ إِلاَّ اللَّهُ وَحْدَهُ لاَ شَرِيْكَ لَهُ ، وَأَشْهَدُ أَنَّ مُحَمَّدًا
عَبْدُهُ وَرَسُولُهُ. اللَّهُمَّ اجْعَلْنِي مِنَ التَّوَّابِينَ وَاجْعَلْنِي مِنَ الْمُتَطَهِّرِيْنَ.
سُبْحَانَكَ اللَّهُمَّ وَبِحَمْدِكَ، أَسْتَغْفِرُكَ وَأَتُوبُ إِلَيْكَ.

Ash-hadu a(n) lā ilāha illallāhu waḥdahū lā sharīka lahū, wa ash-hadu anna Muḥammadan 'abduhū wa rasūluh. Allāhumma! (I)j'alnī min attawwābīna wa (i)j'alnī min al–mutaṭahhirīna. Subḥānaka (A)llāhumma wa biḥamdika, astaghfiruka wa atūbu ilayka. (I bear witness that there is no god except Allāh. He is One and has no partner. And I bear witness that Muḥammad is His servant and messenger. O Allāh! Make me of those who often repent; and of those who are purified. Glory be to You, O Allāh, and all praise! I seek Your forgiveness and repent to You.)

Thereafter, two cycles, *rak'ats*, of supererogatory, *nafl*, prayer, called *taḥiyyat-ul-wuḍū'*, should be offered.

2.7.4 Conditions that render *wuḍū'* void

The following conditions nullify *wuḍū'*:

- Excretion from the private parts;
  [This includes urine, faeces, wind, pre-sexual fluid of both sexes, semen, and female sexual fluid.]
- That impurity which comes out from any part of the body and then flows to a place [on the body] which must be washed [in either *wuḍū'* or *ghusl*];[16]

[Then, blood or pus which oozes to the surface of a wound and congeals without flowing out over the surface will not break *wuḍū*ʾ.]

- More than a mouthful of vomit;

  [That is to say, however much is too much to hold in] regardless of whether it be solid, liquid, bile, or blood; except for phlegm. According to Imām Abū Yūsuf, if a mouthful of phlegm comes from the stomach it also makes *wuḍū*ʾ void. If blood should mix with saliva and then fill the mouth and run over, and the blood has changed the colour of the saliva to red, the *wuḍū*ʾ becomes void.[17]

  If one should vomit a number of times, a little amount each time, [less than a mouthful] then, according to Imām Muḥammad, if there should be [for all the instances of vomiting] only one cause, [nausea for example], the amount should be added together. While according to Imām Abū Yūsuf, if the cause of vomit was not once but it happened in one place then the total amount of vomit will be considered.

- Loss of consciousness regardless of the cause;
- Insanity, intoxication, and sleeping invalidate one's *wuḍū*ʾ. Sleeping, either on one's back or side, or propped up against something which if removed would lead to one's falling, breaks *wuḍū*ʾ.[18] However, sleeping in the standing or sitting position without any kind of prop, or in the prescribed *Sunnah* positions of *rukū*ʿ or *sajdah* will not break *wuḍū*ʾ.
- Laughter in prayer;

  [If it is audible to others] by a mature person, and in the prayers comprised of *rukū*ʿ and *sajdah*.[19]
- and *al-mubāsharah al-fāḥishah*, lustful, direct, skin-to-skin contact of a man with his wife, while they are in one garment, in which position usually pre-sexual fluid comes out, also makes one's *wuḍū*ʾ void.

However, neither the direct handling of one's own private parts, nor a man's directly touching a woman's skin will break *wuḍū*ʾ. Both of these things, however, according to other Imāms, cause *wuḍū*ʾ to be broken.

In addition, in the opinion of Imām Aḥmad, the eating of camel flesh breaks *wuḍū'*.

Observing prudence is the best way. Therefore, one should renew his *wuḍū'* if any of the above-mentioned situations occur.

2.7.5 What is *Makrūh* in *Wuḍū'* *

It is disliked in *wuḍū'*:

1. to use excess water;
2. to use too little water so that washing becomes like wiping;
3. to violently splash water on the face instead of with ease;
4. to talk, saying things other than glorification and supplication to Allāh;
5. to ask others for help without excuse;
6. and wiping the head three times.

2.7.6 Wiping over footgear – *Khuffayn*[20]

If the one performing *wuḍū'* is wearing *khuffayn* that one put on while in the state of purification [i.e. having *wuḍū'*] then, [from the time the *wuḍū'* breaks] for a period of 24 hours in the case of the non-traveller, and for 72 hours in the case of a traveller, it is permitted to keep one's *khuffayn* on and to wipe over them, *masaḥ*, when making *wuḍū'* during this period.

If the *khuffayn* should have a hole in them of a size such that three toes could fit into it, then it is not permitted to wipe over them.

If a person with *wuḍū'* should pull one of the *khuffayn* down to the point where the greater part of one's foot fills that part of the *khuff* that fits on one's calf, or if the period of *masaḥ* has expired, then, in both cases, one need only remove the *khuffayn* and wash one's two feet. It will not be necessary to perform a whole new *wuḍū'*, except in the opinion of Imām Mālik.

* This section has been added by the revisers.

2.7.7 The *Farḍ* and *Sunnah* elements of wiping on socks

It is *farḍ* to wipe the back [top] of the *khuffayn*, an area three fingers wide, once while it is *Sunnah* to draw all five fingers from the toes over the back of the foot to above the ankles at the beginning of the calf. According to Imām Aḥmad, this much is *farḍ*. Clearly, the most prudent course is to make *masaḥ* in this way.

2.8 Ghusl – The Purificatory Bath

The purificatory bath, *ghusl*, is the necessary physical means of purification when one is in a state of major impurity.

2.8.1 The *Farḍ* elements of *ghusl*

The performance of the following is obligatory in *ghusl*:

1. pouring water on the entire body;
2. rinsing the mouth out with water;
3. and rinsing the nose out with water.

It is obligatory, *farḍ*, for a woman with braided hair to wet the roots of her hair, though it is not necessary for her to undo her braids. If a man braids his hair, he will have to undo them for the *ghusl* and wash all of his hair from the ends down to the roots.

2.8.2 The *Sunnah* elements of *ghusl*

The performance of the following is considered *Sunnah* in *ghusl*:

1. to make intention, *niyah*;
2. washing the hands;

3. cleansing the body of all actual impurity;
4. *wuḍū'*;
5. washing the entire body three times;
6. and when the *ghusl* is performed in such a place where the used water gathers at the feet of the one making the *ghusl* [i.e., where there is no drain or sloped surface], it is *Sunnah* to wash the feet after making *ghusl.*

2.8.3 Things that necessitate *ghusl*

The purificatory bath, *ghusl*, is necessary when the following situations exist or occur:

- sexual intercourse, regardless of whether or not there is an emission;
- emission [i.e. semen or female sexual fluid]; when accompanied by ejaculation or orgasm in either sleep or a wakeful state [i.e. emission of a sexual nature]. The dream of a sexual nature when not accompanied by an emission does not necessitate *ghusl.*
- And the termination of the periods of menstruation, *ḥayḍ*, and post-childbirth bleeding, *nifās*.

2.8.4 Things that do not necessitate *ghusl**

The purificatory bath, *ghusl*, is not needed when the following situations exist or occur:

- the emission of *madhī*;
- the emission of *wadī*;
- the dream of a sexual nature when not accompanied by an emission;
- giving birth to a child without any signs of blood;
- having an injection;
- and inserting a finger or similar object in the anus or vagina.

* This section has been added by the revisers from *Marāqī al-Falāḥ*.

2.8.5 Things forbidden in the state of impurity

It is not permitted for one without *wuḍū'* [i.e. in the state of minor impurity or *ḥadath aṣghar*] to:

- touch the Qur'ān, [unless the Qur'ān is wrapped or encased in something that is not a part of the Qur'ān]. One may, however, read from it or recite from memory;
- perform circumambulation, *ṭawāf*, of the Ka'bah;
- or perform the prayer, the *janāzah* prayer, and the *sajdah* of *tilāwah.*

A person in a state of major impurity [one for whom *ghusl* has become necessary], menstruation, *ḥayḍ*, post-childbirth bleeding, *nifās* or *janābah*, may neither touch nor recite the Qur'ān. One may also not enter a *Masjid.*[21]

2.9 Tayammum – Dry Ablution

If the person intending to make prayer should be unable to use water [for *wuḍū'* or *ghusl*]:

- owing to its distance [over one mile];
- due to fear of illness;
- due to fear of a delay in one's recovery;
- due to the fear of worsening one's condition;
- due to one's fear of an enemy [lurking near the supply of water] or of an animal;
- due to thirst or fear of it;
- or owing to one's not having a bucket or rope [with which to draw the water].

Then, in each case, that person will have permission to make *tayammum*, instead of *wuḍū'* or *ghusl* [as the case may be] with any earth related substance, whether it be dust, sand, lime, mortar, or marble; provided that it be free of impurity, *najāsah.*

2.9.1 The *fard* of *tayammum*

The performance of the following is obligatory in *tayammum*:

1. to make the intention, *niyah*;
2. to gently beat one's hands on the earth, and then to wipe them over the entire face;
3. and to gently beat one's hands on the earth and wipe them over both arms, up to and including the elbows and the hands.

If the slightest area like that of even a fingernail on the face or arms should remain untouched, the *tayammum* will be invalid. So if a ring is worn, it will have to be twisted; [or removed]. It is also necessary to rub between the fingers.

If the body or clothing of the one intending to make prayer is impure, and one is unable to obtain water, then one will be permitted to make prayer with the impurity on one's body or clothing after performing *tayammum*. One may use impure clothing as long as there is no clean clothing large enough to cover one's private parts.[22]

2.9.2 Timing of *tayammum* with respect to prayer

It is permitted to both make *tayammum* before the coming in of the time for prayer, and to perform with that one *tayammum* any number of *farḍ* and *nafl* prayers.

2.9.3 When *tayammum* becomes invalidated

At the time of one's becoming able to use water, one's *tayammum* will be broken; even if one should be engaged at the time in reciting prayer. But if one is able to use water for purification after completing the prayer, one does not have to repeat the prayer; the prayer with *tayammum* will suffice.

That which breaks *wuḍū'* or calls for the performance of the *ghusl* also breaks *tayammum*.

2.10 *Ḥayḍ – Menstruation*

2.10.1 *Ḥayḍ* (Menstruation) and *Nifās* (Post-childbirth bleeding)

Legally, the period of menstruation, *ḥayḍ,* lasts no fewer than three days and no more than ten days. Post-childbirth bleeding, *nifās*, lasts no longer than forty days, and there is no limit to the least amount of time post-childbirth bleeding may last. During this period, with the exception of that which is pure white, blood of any colour is considered blood of menstruation or post-childbirth bleeding.

The shortest legal period for *ṭuhr,* purity between two separate periods of menstruation is fifteen days.

2.10.2 *Istiḥāḍah* (Non-menstrual bleeding)

The blood which comes for fewer than three days, or more than ten, and that which continues to come after the forty days of post-childbirth bleeding, *nifās*, is called non-menstrual bleeding, *istiḥāḍah*, and does not prevent a women from performing prayer, *ṣalah*, or fasting, *ṣawm*.[23]

If a woman's menstruation should last longer than her normal period but no longer than ten days, all of these will be counted as menstrual bleeding and it will not be called non-menstrual bleeding, *istiḥāḍah*, and she will not be responsible for making any prayer, *ṣalāh*, or fast, *ṣawm*, in those days, though she will have to make up the fast at some other time. When her period lasts longer than ten days, then all of that which exceeds her normal period will be considered non-menstrual bleeding, *istiḥāḍah*, and she will have to make up, as *qaḍā'*, whatever prayer or fast she missed in the days beyond her normal period.[24]

A young woman who has only begun to menstruate and who has no monthly period on her own if she experiences bleeding for more than ten days, her menstruation will be ten days. Any blood that continues to come after ten days will be considered non-menstrual bleeding, *istiḥāḍah.*

2.10.3 A new *wuḍū'* is needed for every prayer

Since a continuous blood flow is considered *ḥadath*, impurity that comes out of one part of the body and then flows to another part, *wuḍū'* becomes invalid. Therefore, it is necessary for a woman with non-menstrual bleeding, *istiḥāḍah*, to perform a new *wuḍū'* [as well as to wash away any blood on her person] before every new prayer.[25]

2.10.4 Prayer during the flow periods

During the periods of menstruation, *ḥayḍ*, and post-childbirth bleeding, *nifās*, prayer is suspended and its make up, *qaḍā'*, is not necessary. Similarly, menstruation, *ḥayḍ*, and post-childbirth bleeding, *nifās*, will prevent a woman from fasting. However it is compulsory, *wājib*, to make up, as *qaḍā'*, all fasts which are missed because of menstruation or post-childbirth bleeding.

2.10.5 Sexual relations during the flow periods

Sexual intercourse during the periods of menstruation, *ḥayḍ*, or post-childbirth bleeding, *nifās* is forbidden, *ḥarām*, but not during the time of non-menstrual bleeding, *istiḥāḍah.*

If the discharge of menstruation should stop at some time before the completion of ten days then, before the woman makes *ghusl*, intercourse will not be permissible, *ḥalāl*, unless the time of one complete prayer should go by.

It is, however, permitted for her to have intercourse before taking a *ghusl*, at the termination of the ten-day period according to Imām Abū Ḥanīfah. Most other Imāms are of the opinion that without first having a *ghusl* she may not engage in intercourse.

2.10.6 NOT FULFILLING A VOW TO PRAY OR FAST BECAUSE OF *ḤAYḌ* OR *NIFĀS*

If a woman makes a vow to offer a certain number of *rakʿats* of voluntary prayer on the morrow, or to fast, and then on the next day finds that her monthly period, *ḥayḍ*, has begun, she will have to make *qaḍāʾ* [of whatever she vowed to do] when her *ḥayḍ* is over.

Notes

1. If an inedible animal, such as a lion, is slaughtered Islamically, the skin of the animal is rendered pure but not its meat. The meat of an inedible animal is not purified in any way. (Besa Mazḥar Krasniqi)
2. According to Imām Shāfiʿī and others, semen is not *najasah*, but pure. (Trans.)
3. *Madhī* is a white, thin, sticky, watery fluid that is emitted through the genitals upon sexual arousal. *Wadī* is a thick white fluid that is emitted after urinating or lifting something heavy. The emission of either does not call for the performance of *ghusl*, but renders *wuḍūʾ* void. (Revs.)
4. Vaginal fluid is a white discharge occurring in the period of purity between menstruations. The *fatwā* of the school is the position of Abū Ḥanīfah that it is pure, even though it breaks *wuḍūʾ*. See the *Bulāq* Edition of *Radd al-Muḥtār*, Vol. 1, p. 112 and p. 233. (Besa Mazḥar Krasniqi)
5. However, any amount of gross impurity above the excusable amount on one's person or clothing will prevent one from making ritual prayer. (Revs.)
6. Flecks of urine the size of the head of a pin are excusable on clothing for the acceptability of the prayer, even if the total amount exceeds a *dirham*. See *Marāqi al-Falāḥ*. The same is mentioned in Ibn ʿĀbidīn's *Radd al-Muḥtār*, Vol. 1, p. 214. However, if such a garment is put into water, or the flecks of urine themselves fall into a small quantity of water, it renders the water impure. (Besa Mazḥar Krasniqi)
7. It is *makrūh* to use the right hand for *istinjāʾ* except when there is an excuse for not using the left hand. (Revs.)
8. It is *makrūh* to make *istinjāʾ* by the use of bone, food, baked brick, coal, glass, or anything worthwhile such as cotton or jewels. (Revs.)
9. This includes melted snow, ice, and hail. (Revs.)
10. The water that has already been used for purification, such as in *wuḍūʾ*, is legally pure but can no longer be used for purification purposes. The water is considered to be 'used' as soon as it separates from the body. (Revs.)

11. For example, a half gallon of fruit juice and a half gallon of water. (Trans.)

12. The *fatwā* of the *Ḥanafī* school is that a small quantity of water is defined as ten *dhirāʿ* by ten *dhirāʿ* and a *dhirāʿ* is a hand's span from the tips of the finger to the elbow. (Besa Mazḥar Krasniqi)

13. Dogs are essentially impure as are pigs, but are rather considered in the category of non-edible animals and are not absolutely impure. Therefore, the saliva, milk, and meat of dogs are impure, not its hair and skin. In the above example, the dog sitting in a current of flowing water will only make the water impure if its saliva touches it, not its skin or hair. (Besa Mazḥar Krasniqi)

14. A large animal is the equivalent of a human being, sheep, or dog. As for an animal the size of a cat or chicken, all the water does not need to be drawn out, but rather 40 buckets, with 60 buckets being recommended. (Besa Mazḥar Krasniqi)

15. *Wuḍūʾ* is a physical act of purification that is necessary to lift one out of a state of minor impurity, *ḥadath aṣghar*, and is an essential precondition to ritual purification for prayer. (Revs.)

16. Like blood which wells to the surface of the skin from a cut and then flows out over the skin. Furthermore, menstruation, *ḥayḍ*, and post-childbirth bleeding, *nifās*, break *wuḍūʾ* and also make it necessary to take the purificatory bath, *ghusl*, at the termination of the bleeding. (Revs.)

17. If one vomits blood, the consideration is whether it fills the mouth, or rather cannot be contained as when one is normally overcome by vomit. As for blood from the mouth itself, the consideration in the nullification of *wuḍūʾ* is whether the blood has overtaken the phlegm. Yellow means the phlegm is dominant, while pink and red indicate that blood is prevalent. (Besa Mazḥar Krasniqi)

18. The legal position of the *Ḥanafī* school is that if one is firmly seated on the ground, one's *wuḍūʾ* is not broken if one falls asleep, even if one is leaning against something that if removed would cause one to fall down. The legal position that it breaks *wuḍūʾ* is that of Qudūrī and Ṭaḥāwī, though in the opinion of the majority of scholars in the *Ḥanafī* school it does not. See *Marāqi al-Falāḥ*. (Besa Mazḥar Krasniqi)

19. Laughter, then, outside of prayer or in the funeral prayer, *janāzah*, will not break *wuḍūʾ*. (Trans.)

20. The *khuffayn* are a particular type of tight-fitting, leather sock which covers the entire foot including the ankle, and in which one may walk a distance of three miles without fear of their wearing through. *Khuffayn* means two socks, and the singular form of the word is *khuff*. Cotton, woollen, or nylon socks are not acceptable substitutes for the *khuffayn* in the matter of *masah* or wiping [which will be discussed further on]. *Khuff* made from other than

leather are permissible provided they fulfil the conditions of a *khuff*. Owing to the fact that most shoes nowadays are cut below the ankles they, also, are not acceptable as substitutes. The calf or ankle high boot, however, since it covers both the foot and ankle, if it is clean, tight-fitting, and made of non-absorbent materials (which means only that water doesn't penetrate while wiping, not that they are a 100% waterproof) is an acceptable substitute. This is the opinion of most *Ḥanafī* scholars. There are those, however, who feel that the shoes and socks mentioned here are acceptable as *khuffayn* as they have the properties required by the traditional definition, including the ability to hold up under a three mile walk. And Allah knows best. (Trans.)

21. Being in a state of ritual impurity does not prevent a person from saying '*Bismillāh*,' '*Alḥamdu lillāh*', and other *dhikr*, or from making *du'a'*. (Trans.)

22. An explanation of how much of the body must be covered will be given in the Chapter on Prayer (*Ṣalāh*). (Trans.)

23. Such a woman may recite the Qur'ān, enter a *Masjid*, and engage in sexual relations with her husband. Nor will she need to perform the purificatory bath for attaining purity, as a person after menstruation, *ḥayḍ*, or post-childbirth bleeding, *nifās*, would. *Wuḍū'* will suffice. (Trans.)

24. For example, if a woman has a regular period of six days and then, unexpectedly, one month she has a period of nine days, then the discharge of the entire period will be considered menstruation. If, however, the period extends to twelve days, then the normal period of six days will be considered menstruation, and the other six days will be considered non-menstrual bleeding.

25. One *wuḍū'* will be sufficient for the *Sunnah* and *farḍ* of a particular prayer, for example, *ẓuhr*, but she must make a new *wuḍū'* for the prayer of *'aṣr*, and so on. (Trans.)

Chapter 3

Ṣalāh

3.1 The Importance of Prayer

After adherence to correct belief the most rewarding worship is *ṣalāh*. Jābir, may Allāh be pleased with him, related that the Prophet, may the peace and blessings of Allāh be upon him, said, "The link between a Muslim and disbelief, *kufr*, is his or her neglect of prayer." (Muslim)

The meaning of this *ḥadīth* is that a Muslim who continually neglects prayer will eventually fall into the state of disbelief.

Buraydah, may Allāh be pleased with him, related that the Messenger of Allāh, may the peace and blessings of Allāh be upon him, said, "The bond between us that separates us from the rest of humankind is prayer. Whoever neglects it will become a disbeliever, *kāfir*." (Aḥmad, Tirmidhī and Nasā'ī)

Abū Dardā', may Allāh be pleased with him, is reported to have said, "My friend, may the peace and blessings of Allāh be upon him, counselled me, saying, 'Do not associate partners with Allāh even if you are threatened with death or burning. Do not disobey your parents, even if they were to order you to give up your wife, children, and wealth. Do not intentionally neglect an obligatory, *farḍ*, prayer. For indeed, whoever intentionally neglects *farḍ* prayer, Allāh the Exalted withholds all responsibility to him.'" (Ibn Mājah)

ʿAmr ibn al-ʿĀṣ reported that the Prophet, may the peace and blessings of Allāh be upon him, said, "Whoever takes care to regularly perform one's *farḍ* prayers will have light, status, and success on the Day of Judgement. And whoever was neglectful will have no light, no status, and no success. Instead, one will be joined with Firʿaun, Hāmān, Qārūn, and Ubayy ibn Khalaf." (Aḥmad, Dārimī and Baihaqī)

ʿAbdullāh ibn Shaqīq related that the Companions of the Messenger of Allāh, may the peace and blessings of Allāh be upon him, knew nothing which, if neglected, would lead to disbelief, except prayer. (Tirmidhī)

On the basis of these *aḥādīth*, Imām Aḥmad ibn Ḥanbal reached the conclusion that whoever intentionally neglects even one prayer will become a disbeliever, *kāfir*.[1] In the opinion of Imām Shāfiʿī, such a person is to be given the death penalty, though one's death will be that of a Muslim, and one will not die a disbeliever. According to Imām Abū Ḥanīfah, such a person is jailed indefinitely or until he or she repents. And Allāh knows best.

3.1.1 Who must perform prayer

Prayer becomes obligatory upon every person in the state of [having accepted or been born into] Islam when:

1. the time for the prayer arrives;
2. the individual is sane;
3. the individual has reached the age of discretion [puberty];
4. and a woman is free of menstrual bleeding, *ḥayḍ*, and post-childbirth bleeding, *nifās*.

If a disbeliever becomes Muslim, or a child reaches maturity, or a madman regains his sanity moments before the passing of a time of prayer such that there is enough time only to make *takbīr taḥrīmah* [to begin the prayer, with the words *'Allāhu Akbar'* while raising the hands to the level of the ears], then [the performance of] that [outgoing] prayer becomes *farḍ* on that person.

Similarly, after the termination of a period of *ḥayḍ* or *nifās*, if there remains enough time to make *ghusl* and make *takbīr taḥrīmah*, prayer becomes *farḍ*.

3.2 The Timings of Prayers

3.2.1 The daily *farḍ* prayers

Fajr – Dawn Prayer

The time for performing *fajr* is from the appearance of the true dawn until the actual rising of the sun.

Ẓuhr – Midday Prayer

The time for performing *ẓuhr* is from after the declining of the sun [from its zenith at midday] to the time when the shadow of everything [upright] becomes equal in length to the height of that which is standing, with an allowance made for the original shadow.[2]

The above is the teaching of the Imāms Abū Yūsuf and Muḥammad, and the majority of the Imāms of *fiqh* [including Imāms Mālik, Shāfiʿī and Aḥmad ibn Ḥanbal], and, according to one source, this was also the opinion of Imām Abū Ḥanīfah.

Nonetheless, the teaching of the Imām upon which the *fatwās* are given is that the time for *ẓuhr* remains until the length of the shadows of every upright object becomes equal to double the height of those objects, when allowance is made for the length of their "original shadows".

ʿAṣr – Late-Afternoon Prayer

The time for *ʿaṣr* prayer comes in with the passing of the time for *ẓuhr* [whichever one of the two it may be as outlined above], and remains as long as the sun does not pale or lose its rays, for after that there comes a *makrūh* time for *ʿaṣr* [which lasts] until the setting of the sun. It is, however, permitted to perform that day's *'aṣr* prayer [not a make up, *qaḍā'*, prayer] in that time, though it is extremely *makrūh*. Other prayers, be they *farḍ* or *nafl*, may not be performed during this *makrūh* period.

Maghrib – Sunset Prayer

The time for performing *maghrib* is from after the setting of the sun until, according to most Imāms, the time when the dominant colour of the horizon is red. According to Imām Abū Ḥanīfah, however, the time for *maghrib* lasts beyond the time of the red horizon to the time when the dominant colour on the horizon is white but when the stars come out in multitudes, the performance of *maghrib* becomes *makrūh tanzīhī*.

'Ishā' – Nightfall Prayer

The time for performing *'ishā'* comes in with the passing of the time for *maghrib* and remains, according to the majority of the Imāms of *fiqh* until halfway through the night.[3] According to Imām Abū Ḥanīfah, however, though the time of *'ishā'* remains until dawn it is considered to be *makrūh taḥrīmī* if it is delayed after midnight.

3.2.2 *WITR* PRAYER[4]

The time for *witr* prayer is from after the performance of *'ishā'* prayer until (before) the dawning of the day.

3.2.3 *MUSTAḤAB* TIMES OF PRAYER

It is *mustaḥab* to:

1. delay the performance of *ẓuhr* prayer a little during the hot season;
2. perform *'ishā'* [shortly] before the first third of the night has passed;

3. and finish performing *fajr* prayer in the first light of day when enough time remains before the actual rising of the sun. To re-read the entire prayer in a *masnūn* manner should something happen to invalidate the first [attempt at] prayer.

As for other prayers, this humble writer considers it best to perform them soon after their beginning time, except if it is delayed for a bigger congregation.

3.2.4 Times when prayer is forbidden

Prayer is forbidden when:

1. the sun is rising;
2. the sun is at its midday zenith;
3. and the sun is setting.

No prayer, except for the *ʿaṣr* prayer of the same day [not *qaḍāʾ* of some other day's *ʿaṣr*], may be performed during the sun's setting; neither the *sajdah of tilāwah* (prostration of recitation) nor the funeral prayer, *janāzah*.

3.2.5 *Makrūh* times of *nafl* prayer

During the time of:

1. *fajr* [except for the *Sunnah* of *fajr* before the *farḍ*, or any make up prayer];
2. after [the performance of] *ʿaṣr*; and before the sun pales;
3. and before the *farḍ* of *maghrib*,

it is *makrūh* to make any *nafl* prayer. *Sajdah* of *tilāwah*, however, may be performed during any of these periods.

3.3 *The Number of Rakʿats that are Farḍ in Daily Prayers*

The performance of the following number of *rakʿats* is obligatory:

1. two *rakʿats* of *fajr*;
2. four *rakʿats* of *ẓuhr*, *ʿaṣr*, and *ʿishāʾ*;
3. three *rakʿats* of *maghrib* and *witr*.

3.4 *Adhān – Call to Prayer*

It is *Sunnah* to recite the *adhān* and *iqāmah* before the performance of prayer, whether it is made in its proper time, or postponed and performed as a make up, *qaḍāʾ*.

It is *makrūh* for a traveller, *musāfir*, to leave out the *adhān*.

For a person who performs prayer at home, the *adhān* of the city Masjid is sufficient. But if he lives far away from the masjid he should perform *adhān* for himself.

To perform the *adhān*,* one must face the *qiblah*, while standing with his index fingers in his ears, and call out the *adhān* in a moderately paced, loud and beautiful manner. When he comes to the words, "*Ḥayya ʿalaṣ Ṣalāh*, حَيَّ عَلَى الصَّلَاة" the *muʾadhdhin* turns his head to the right; and when he comes to the words, "*Ḥayya ʿalal Falāḥ*, حَيَّ عَلَى الْفَلَاح" he turns his head to the left. One must make sure not to move the chest away from the direction of the *qiblah*.

One may perform the *adhān* without *wuḍūʾ*; however it is *makrūh* to do so, and better for one to make *wuḍūʾ* before calling the *adhān*.

One listening to the *adhān* should repeat the text of the *adhān* after the *muʾadhdhin* finishes each sentence. One should also say,

---

* From this sentence on in this section, an *adhān* has been added by the revisers and is not part of *Mālā Budda Minhu*.

"*Lā Ḥawla walā Quwwata Illā Billāh,* لاَحَوْلَ وَلاَ قُوَّةَ إِلاَّ بِاللّه" after the words, "*Ḥayya ʿalaṣ Ṣalāh*" and "*Ḥayya ʿalal Falāḥ*" are called out.

When the *muʾadhdhin*, in the *fajr* prayer calls outs "*Aṣ-ṣalātu khayrum min an-nawm*" one listening should say "*ṣadaqta wa bararta*".

Text of the Adhān

اللّهُ أَكْبَر اللّهُ أَكْبَر اللّهُ أَكْبَر اللّهُ أَكْبَر

أَشْهَدُ أَن لاَّ إِلَهَ إِلاَّ اللّه أَشْهَدُ أَن لاَّ إِلَهَ إِلاَّ اللّه

أَشْهَدُ أَنَّ مُحَمَّدًا رَّسُولُ اللّه أَشْهَدُ أَنَّ مُحَمَّدًا رَّسُولُ اللّه

حَيَّ عَلَى الصَّلاَه حَيَّ عَلَى الصَّلاَه

حَيَّ عَلَى الْفَلاَح حَيَّ عَلَى الْفَلاَح

Allāhu Akbar	– Allāh is the Greatest (4 times).
Ashhadu anlā Ilāha Illallāh	– I testify that there is no god but Allāh (twice).
Ashhadu anna Muḥammadar Rasūlullāh	– I testify that Muḥammad is the Messenger of Allāh (twice).
Ḥayya ʿAlaṣ-Ṣalāh	– Come to prayer (twice).
Ḥayya ʿAlal-Falāḥ	– Come to success (twice).

الصَّلاَةُ خَيْرٌ مِّنْ النَّوْمْ الصَّلاَةُ خَيْرٌ مِّنْ النَّوْمْ

Aṣ-Ṣalātu Khayrum min an-nawm	– Prayer is better than sleep (twice);

(added to the *adhān* for *fajr* only and one listening should say: *Ṣadaqta wa bararta* صَدَقْتَ وَبَرَرْتَ, You said the truth and you are purified).

اللّهُ أَكْبَر اللّهُ أَكْبَر

لاَ إِلَهَ إِلاَّ اللّه

Allāhu Akbar	– Allāh is the Greatest (twice).
Lā Ilāha Illallāh	– There is no god but Allāh (once).

3.4.1 The *Iqāmah*

The *iqāmah* is performed the same way, but with the addition of the words, "*Qad qāmati'ṣ Ṣalāh,* قَدْ قَامَتِ الصَّلاَةُ، قَدْ قَامَتِ الصَّلاَه" repeated twice after saying, "*Ḥayya 'alal-Falāḥ*". One does not have to place one's hands to the ears when calling the *iqāmah*. Nor does one need to turn one's head to the right and then left for "*Ḥayya 'ala'ṣ-Ṣalāh*" and "*Ḥayya 'alal-Falāh.*" The *iqāmah* should be recited with haste, but not so fast as to not understand what is being said.

3.5 The Preconditions of Prayer

The following conditions must be observed before approaching the prayer:

- bodily purification, *ṭahārah*, from both actual, *haqīqī*, and ritual conditions, *hukmī*, of impurity, *najāsah*;
- purification of clothes;
- purity of location [the place where prayer is to be performed];
- ascertaining the time of prayer has arrived; prayers after the time of prayer expires must be prayed as a make up, *qaḍā'*;
- covering [at least] one's nakedness, *'awrah.*

A man must cover from the navel to below the knees. A woman must cover her entire body except the face, hands, and feet. If a fourth part of any limb [from among those which must be covered] on the body of a man or woman should become uncovered, then the prayer will become invalid. The hair that hangs down from a woman's head is legally considered a separate limb and, as such, if a fourth part of it should remain uncovered [during prayer], the prayer will be invalid.

3.5.1 Women's voices

A woman's voice is also a part of her *'awrah*. Therefore, if a woman should [in the presence of a *non-maḥram*] read her prayer aloud, the prayer will be invalid.[5]

3.5.2 Prayer of one with no clothes

A person who has no clothing [no clean clothes, or none at all, or not enough to cover all that which must be covered] may make one's prayer without them, [or with as much as one has] facing the *qiblah*.

3.5.3 When the *qiblah* is unknown

If the direction of the *qiblah* is unknown or uncertain [and there is no way to ascertain it with any accuracy] an estimation is to be made, and prayer may be performed in the direction thus determined. It is not permitted to make prayer [in such a situation] without first making an estimation.

Should a person be unable to face the *qiblah* due to fear of an enemy, or to sickness, then one may perform one's prayer while facing in any direction that is convenient.

A mounted person, while in the desert [or wilds of any description], may perform *nafl* [but not *farḍ*] prayer [while mounted] in whichever direction his mount is headed.

Intention, *niyah*; for *nafl* prayer [like *Sunnah* and *tarāwīḥ*] an unspecified intention will suffice; though for *farḍ* and *witr* a specific intention will have to be made before the opening *takbīr*. One praying behind an imām in a congregation must include in the intention that one is following the imām. It is not necessary when making the intention to specify the number of *rak'ats* to be made.

3.6 The Pillars of Prayer[6]

1. The first pillar is the opening *takbīr at-taḥrīmah*; saying, "*Allāhu Akbar*," for which like all other pillars all of those things which are preconditions to prayer itself are preconditions; like *tahārah*, covering the *ʿawrah*, facing the *qiblah*, and making intention, *niyah*;
2. standing, *qiyām*;
3. recitation of the Qur'ān, *qirā'ah*;

   According to Imām Abū Ḥanīfah, recitation of the Qur'ān is *farḍ* while standing in the first two *rakʿats* in each of the five daily *farḍ* prayers, and in all the three *rakʿats* of *witr* prayer, and in each of the two *rakʿats* of *nafl* prayer.

   According to Imāms Shāfiʿī and Aḥmad, recitation of the Qur'ān, *qirā'ah*, is *farḍ* in every *rakʿah* of *farḍ* and *nafl* prayer.

   The amount of recitation that is *farḍ* is one verse, [regardless of how short it may be]. According to Imāms Abū Yūsuf and Muḥammad the *farḍ* recitation is three small *āyats* like of *Sūrah Kawthar*, or one large *āyah* equal to three small *āyats*.

   According to Imāms Shāfiʿī and Aḥmad, the recitation of *Sūrah Fātiḥah* is also a *farḍ* of each *rakʿah*; and according to them, *bismillāh* is an *āyah* of *Sūrah Fātiḥah*.

   However, when praying behind an imām [in congregation], the follower is absolutely prohibited from making recitation of the Qur'ān, according to Imām Abū Ḥanīfah.[7]

   According to Imām Shāfiʿī, recitation of *Fātiḥah* is *farḍ* for both the *Imām* and *Muqtaḍī* but other Imāms do not see it as *farḍ* for *Muqtaḍī*.
4. bowing, *rukūʿ*;
5. both prostrations, *sajdah*;

   In *sajdah* it is *farḍ* to place the nose and forehead on the ground, though, when necessary, it is enough to place only one or the other.

According to Imāms Shāfiʿī and Aḥmad, it is necessary in *sajdah* to place not only the nose and forehead on the ground, but the hands, knees and toes of each foot as well.

6. and the final sitting, *qaʿdah akhīrah.*

   The first *qaʿdah* and the recitation of the *tashahhud*, the recitation of the *tashahhud* in the second *qaʿdah* are *farḍ* according to Imām Aḥmad. Imām Abū Ḥanīfah, however, considered these things to be *wājib*.

The recitation of *ṣalāt-ʿalan-nabī*, *darūd* in the final *qaʿdah* after *tashahhud* is *farḍ* according to Imāms Aḥmad and Shāfiʿī.

To say "*salām*" [*As-Salāmu ʿAlaikum Wa Raḥmatullāh* at the end of prayer while in the final *qaʿdah*] is a pillar of prayer and *farḍ* according to the three Imāms [Mālik, Shāfiʿī, and Aḥmad]. According to Imām Abū Ḥanīfah, it is *farḍ* for a *muṣallī* to come out of the prayer with intention as he started it, as for saying *salām* to end the prayer it is *wājib*.

The *takbīrs* at each raising and lowering of the head [in other words, when changing positions in prayer]; reading, "*Subḥāna Rabbiyal-ʿAẓīm*," once, in *rukūʿ*; reading, "*Subḥāna Rabbiyal-Aʿlā,*" once, in *sajdah*; reading "*Samiʿallāhu li man Ḥamidah*" when returning [briefly] to the standing position [after *rukūʿ*]; reading, "*Rabbighfir lī,*" between the two *sajdahs*; all of these things, according to Imām Aḥmad ibn Ḥanbal, are *farḍ*. Yet, according to the same Imām, if the one praying forgets to recite one of these things, one's prayer will not become invalid.

Tartīb, the performing of each pillar of prayer in order, is *farḍ* except for the second *sajdah* in a *rakʿah*, *tartīb* in its performance is considered *wājib*, not *farḍ*.

If one performs one *sajdah* in a *rakʿah* and forgets to do the second *sajdah* his prayer will not be invalidated. He should make up the missed *sajdah* in the next *rakʿah* and offer *sajdah sahw* in the end to rectify the mistake of delaying the second *sajdah* from its original place.

3.7 *Wājib Elements of Prayer*

The performance of the following is *wājib* in prayer according to Imām Abū Ḥanīfah:

1. recitation of *Fātiḥah* in every *rakʿah* of prayer [before reciting any other *sūrah*];
2. the additional recitation of a *sūrah*, or one long *āyah*, or three short *āyahs*, in every *rakʿah* of *nafl* and *witr*, and in the first two *rakʿats* of *farḍ* prayer;
3. the designation of the first two *rakʿats* for recitation;
4. attention to the sequence of [one] *sajdah* [coming after the other];

   Thus, if in the first *rakʿah* the one praying makes one *sajdah* and forgets the second, the prayer will not become void, if in the second *rakʿah* one makes three *sajdahs* and performs the prostration of forgetfulness.
5. holding, *ṭumānīnah* [after assuming] each position [for a while before assuming the next position];
6. the resumption of standing position [after *rukūʿ*], which is called *qawmah*;

   In the *fatāwā* of Qāḍī Khān it is written that if the one praying, having made *rukūʿ*, should then go into *sajdah* without resuming the standing position, one's prayer, according to Imāms Abū Ḥanīfah and Muḥammad, will not be invalidated, though one will have to make *sajdah sahw.*
7. sitting between the two *sajdahs*, known as *jalsah*;
8. the first sitting, *qaʿdah ʾūlā*;

9.–10. the recitation of the *tashahhud* while in the first and final sittings, *qaʿdah,* position;

11. performing the pillars of prayer without unnecessary breaks, *muwālāh*;

    Thus, if one makes a second *rukūʿ* [after making the first *rukūʿ* and rises] or if one makes three *sajdahs*, or invokes blessings on the Prophet after the first *tashahhud* so that it caused delay in going to *qiyām* for the third *rak'ah*, in each of these instances, one will have to make *sajdah sahw.*

12. recitation of the Qur'ān by the imām, aloud, in the first two *rak'ats* of *fajr*, *maghrib*, *'ishā'*, *jumu'ah*, and the two *'Īd* prayers; and silently in *ẓuhr*, *'aṣr*, and *nafl* prayer;
13. completion of prayer with *salāms* by turning the face to the right and saying, "*As Salāmu 'Alaikum Wa Raḥmatullāh*," and then to the left,[8] repeating the *salāms*;
14. recitation of *du'a' al-qunūt* in *witr* prayer;
15. and the [extra] *takbīrs* in the two *'Īd* prayers.

There is a difference between *farḍ* and *wājib* in the *fiqh* of Abū Ḥanīfah.[9] If a *farḍ* element is left out, prayer will become invalid. However, if a *wājib* element is left out, prayer will not become invalid. The prostration of forgetfulness, *sajdah sahw*, however, becomes necessary. If *sajdah sahw* is then performed, the prayer will be acceptable. If, however, the prostration of forgetfulness is not performed, or if anything *wājib* is omitted intentionally, then the prayer will need to be performed over again. The other Imāms make no distinction between the two [*farḍ* and *wājib*], though they do require a *sajdah sahw* to be made when certain things, the performance of which is either *wājib* or *Sunnah*, are omitted.

3.8 Sajdah Sahw – Prostration of Forgetfulness

Any omission or forgetting of a *wājib* element of prayer requires one to rectify one's mistake by making a prostration of forgetfulness, *sajdah sahw.*

If in one prayer a number of different *wājib* elements are omitted, then, nonetheless, one *sajdah sahw* will be sufficient.

The Description of Sajdah Sahw

Sajdah sahw is [to be performed in the following way]; after [completing prayer by saying] the *salāms* [preferably after saying only one *salām,* though it does not matter if two are said], two more *sajdahs* are to be made, followed by the *tashahhud, darūd,* and *duʿaʾ*. Then [prayer is to be completed by again saying] *salāms.*

If before making any *salāms* the one praying makes *sajdah sahw*, it will be regarded as correct.

3.8.1 *Sajdah Sahw* of the Latecomer to the Congregational Prayer

One who joins the congregational prayer late must follow the imām in making *sajdah sahw*, [even if the imām's error occurred before one joined the congregation]. If, on the other hand, the latecomer to the congregational prayer makes an error while finishing one's prayer after the imām has completed prayer with the congregation, one will have to make *sajdah sahw* on one's own.

3.8.2 Situations in Which *Sajdah Sahw* Applies[10]

If the one praying should remember, while in *rukūʿ* or *sajdah,* that one neglected to make *sajdah* for example in the first *rakʿah*, or that one failed to make a *sajdah* of *tilāwah,* one should either make up the missed *sajdah* immediately or at the close of prayer by means of *sajdah sahw.* And if one chooses to make it up immediately with regard to the missed *sajdah* in which one was engaged, [when one remembered missing the other *sajdah*] it is *mustaḥab* that one make it up [directly upon making up the remembered *sajdah*]; though it is not absolutely necessary that one do so.

If, after performing two *rakʿats*, one rises forgetfully for the third *rakʿah* without having made the first *qaʿdah* then, if he is still close to the ground when he realises his mistake, he may at once assume the *qaʿdah* position, there will be no need for making *sajdah sahw*. But, if one is closer to the standing position [when one remembers], then by returning to a sitting position the [*farḍ*, not *nafl*] prayer will become invalid. Instead, one will have to continue with the prayer and, at the end, make *sajdah sahw*.[11]

If, after performing four *rakʿats*, the one praying rises for a fifth, then as long as he has not made *sajdah* he may, immediately upon realising the error, reassume the final *qaʿdah* position, give *salām*, and make *sajdah sahw*. If, however, he has gone to the point of making *sajdah* in the fifth *rakʿah*, the *farḍ* prayer will become invalid, now one may continue with a sixth *rakʿah*, give *salām*, and make *sajdah sahw*. Or one may, if he chooses, assume the final *qaʿdah* without making a sixth *rakʿah*, and then make *salāms*, in which case the four *rakʿats* will be counted as *nafl* and the fifth as *fāsid* or void.[12]

3.9 The Importance of Congregational Prayer

The performance of the five daily *farḍ* prayers in congregation is *farḍ* according to Imām Aḥmad; though the prayers will be valid if not performed in congregation. According to Imām Shāfiʿī, it is *farḍ kifāyah*.[13] According to Imāms Abū Ḥanīfah and Mālik, prayer in congregation is *Sunnah muʾakkadah*, rather almost *wājib*. Prayer in congregation is so strongly recommended that in a case where there is a possibility of missing the *fajr* prayer in congregation [when time is short], the [two *rakʿats* of] *Sunnah* before *fajr*, the most emphasised of the *Sunnah* prayers, may be omitted to catch up with the congregation of *fajr*.

If the [Muslim] inhabitants of a city [governed under Islamic Law] altogether give up the performance of prayer in congregation, then, [if necessary], they should be engaged in battle [until they agree to start behaving like Muslims again by honouring and upholding this institution of Islam].[14]

A congregation composed solely of women is *makrūh*, according to Imām Abū Ḥanīfah. The other Imāms hold it to be *mubāḥ*, or permitted.[15]

3.10 The Most Suitable Imām

The most suitable imām is a person who has memorised more of the Qur'ān and who knows the legal rulings concerning prayer. Secondly comes the person who best knows the *Sharīʿah* [not simply the legal rulings of prayer] and knows enough of the Qur'ān to read the prayer. This is the opinion of Imām Abū Yūsuf. Most Imāms, however, [including Abū Ḥanīfah] consider the reverse [that the one most learned in the *Sharīʿah* is preferable] to be correct.[16]

It is permitted, but *makrūh*, for a [known and habitual] wrong-doer to perform the duties of an imām.

A mature male capable of performing the prayer may not do it as a follower, *muqtadī*, in the congregational prayer behind a child, woman, or an illiterate [one who neither reads nor remembers anything of the Qur'ān]. Similarly, a person who is performing *farḍ* prayer may not become the follower in prayer of an imām who is leading *nafl* [or *Sunnah*] prayer.

If an illiterate performs prayer as the imām for a reader of the Qur'ān and another illiterate, the prayer of all three will be invalid.

Prayer behind someone who is without *wuḍū'* is not permitted and is invalid.

If an imām does something which spoils his prayer, the prayer of the followers in the congregation will also be invalidated.

The prayer of a standing congregation behind a sitting imām, and the prayer of one who has made *wuḍū'* behind one who has made *tayammum* are both permitted.

A person who is able to make *rukūʿ* and *sajdah* is not permitted to pray behind an imām who is incapable of making *rukūʿ* and *sajdah.*

If there is only one person performing prayer with an imām, he is to stand [together] to the right of the imām.[17] If there are two or more followers in the congregation, they are to stand behind the imām.

If someone stands alone behind a row of people praying in congregation and performs the prayer there, then his prayer will be *makrūh*. According to Imām Aḥmad, it is *ḥarām* to perform prayer in this way.

If a follower in the congregational prayer performs the prayer while standing ahead [even a few inches] of the imām, the follower's prayer will be invalid.

Ibn Mājah related on the authority of Anas ibn Malik, may Allāh be pleased with him, that the Messenger of Allāh, may the peace and blessings of Allāh be upon him, said: "A man's prayer in his own home carries with it the blessings of one prayer; his prayer in the local Masjid carries the blessings of twenty-five prayers; his prayer in a Masjid where the *Jumuʿah* is read carries the blessings of five hundred prayers; his prayer in the *Masjid al-Aqṣā* carries the blessings of a thousand prayers; his prayer in the *Masjid Nabawī* in Madīnah carries the blessings of fifty thousand prayers, and his prayer in the *Masjid al-Ḥarām* in Makkah carries the blessings of one hundred thousand prayers."

3.11 The Description of the Performance of Prayer

The way to perform the prayer according to the *Sunnah* is as follows:

3.11.1 *Takbīr Taḥrīmah* – Entering the prayer

Every prayer should be performed with concentration and humility. It is *Sunnah* to first say the *adhān* and *iqāmah,* even when praying alone. After fulfilling all the prayer's preconditions, while standing, one raises both hands to the height of the soft [lower] part of one's ears with the palms facing the *qiblah* and says the *takbīr:* "*Allāhu Akbar* اللّٰهُ أَكْبَر," this is essential to enter the prayer. After the opening *takbīr*, one brings the hands to the navel and folds the right hand over the left. This is the opinion of Imām Abū Ḥanīfah.

The hands of a woman [at the time of *takbīr*] should be raised only as high as her shoulders. She should thereafter clasp them together right over left at her breast.

When in the standing position, the eyes of the one in prayer should be on the ground where one's forehead touches in prostration, *sajdah.*

[In congregational prayer,] after the *adhān* has been called and the *mu'adhdhin* reaches, while giving the *iqāmah* the words:

"*Ḥayya 'alaṣ-Ṣalāh*", the imām will rise, and so will the followers. When the *mu'adhdhin* calls out the words:

"*Qad Qāmatiṣ-Ṣalāh*", the imām will make *takbīr* and [at the same time or a little before] make his intention, *niyah,* and raise his two hands to the height of the soft [lower] part of his ears.[18]

After the imām has made *takbīr*, the congregation will then say their *takbīr* [to themselves]. The followers may not assume any of the positions in prayer before the imām has assumed them, otherwise the prayer is void.

Qiyām – Standing

1. Opening Praise[19] – *Thanā*

   Thereafter, one [including the imām and the followers in the group prayer] will silently recite *thanā*:

   سُبْحَانَكَ اللَّهُمَّ وَبِحَمْدِكَ، وَتَبَارَكَ اسْمُكَ، وَتَعَالَى جَدُّكَ، وَلَا إِلَهَ غَيْرُكَ.

   Subḥānaka (A)llāhumma wa bi-Ḥamdika, wa Tabāraka(i)smuka, wa Ta'ālā Jadduka wa lāilāha Ghairuka. (Glory be to you, O Allāh!, and I praise You. Blessed is Your name, and Exalted is Your majesty. There is no god other than You.)

2. *Ta'awwudh* (Seeking refuge in Allāh from satan.)

   Then the one praying will silently say: "*A'ūdhu billāhi Minash-shayṭān ir Rajīm,* أَعُوذُ بِاللهِ مِنَ الشَّيْطَانِ الرَّجِيمْ." (I seek refuge in Allāh from the accursed Satan.)

3. *Tasmiyah* (Beginning with *Bismillāh-ir-Raḥmān-ir-Raḥīm.*)

Then one recites silently: "*Bismillāh-ir-Raḥmān-ir-Raḥīm,* بِسْمِ اللّٰهِ الرَّحْمٰنِ الرَّحِيْمِ." (In the name of Allāh, the Most Gracious, the Most Merciful.)

In congregational prayer, the imām [but not the followers] will silently read *ta'awwudh* and the *bismillāh.* The latecomer to the group prayer, when making *qaḍā'* [by standing after the imām has completed the prayer and making up the number] of whatever *rak'ats* he missed, will also read *ta'awwudh* and *bismillāh.*

4. *Fātiḥah* (The Opening *Sūrah* of the Qur'ān.)

Next, one recites the first chapter of the Glorious Qur'ān, the *Fātiḥah.* At its completion, one will say in a less than audible voice, "*Āmīn.*" In the third and fourth *rak'ats* of *farḍ* prayer there is to be no more than the silent recitation of *bismillāh* and *Sūrah Fātiḥah.*

In congregational prayer, the imām will recite *Sūrah Fātiḥah* aloud in the prayers of *fajr*, *maghrib*, and *'ishā'* in the first two *rak'ats*, and silently in *ẓuhr* and *'aṣr* prayers. The congregation must remain silent and listen to the recitation of the imām. When the prayer has reached the third or fourth *rak'ah* of *farḍ* prayer, [where the imām is silently reading *Fātiḥah*], the followers in the group prayer are to remain silent [throughout the prayer] and are not to recite any verses of the Qur'ān.

5. *Qirā'ah* (Recitation of the Qur'ān.)

One will next recite a *sūrah*, three short verses or one long verse from the Qur'ān.

In congregational prayer, the imām will recite aloud in the first two *rak'ats*, during the *fajr*, *maghrib*, and *'ishā'* prayers, and silently in the *ẓuhr* and *'aṣr* prayers. The congregation are to remain silent [throughout the prayer] and are not to recite any verses of the Qur'ān, giving their attention to the recitation of the imām.

The *Sunnah* with regard to recitation in prayer under normal conditions when not on a journey or in fear [of an enemy attack, etc.] is to recite, in the *fajr* and *ẓuhr* prayers, from the "*ṭiwāl mufaṣṣal,*" or any of the *sūrahs* from *Sūrah Ḥujurāt* to *Sūrah Burūj.* In *ʿaṣr* and *ʿishāʾ* prayers, from the "*awsāṭ mufaṣṣal,*" or any of the *sūrahs* from *Sūrah Burūj* to *Sūrah Bayyinah.* And in *maghrib*, to recite from the "*qiṣār mufaṣṣal,*" or any *sūrah* from *Sūrah Bayyinah* to the end of the Qurʾān.

It is not, however, *Sunnah* to hold to this rule without exception, because the Messenger of Allāh, may the peace and blessings of Allāh be upon him, sometimes recited *al-muʿawwidhatain* the last two *sūrahs* of the Qurʾān in *fajr* prayer, and *Sūrah Ṭūr*, *Sūrah Najm*, or *Sūrah Mursalāt* in *maghrib* prayer.

The Messenger of Allāh, may the peace and blessings of Allāh be upon him, used to often recite *Sūrah Alif Lām Mīm Sajdah* and *Sūrah ad-Dahr, Hal atā ʿalaʾl insani ḥīnum min ad-dahr* on *jumuʿah* at *fajr* prayer.

In congregational prayer, if it should be that the followers are both ready and willing to stand for a long time, then the imām may recite from the Qurʾān at length. The *Khalīfah,* Abū Bakr Ṣiddīq, may Allāh be pleased with him, is known to have recited *Sūrah Baqarah* in one *rakʿah* of *fajr* prayer. The Messenger of Allāh, may the peace and blessings of Allāh be upon him, recited *Sūrah al-Aʿrāf* in two *rakʿats* of *maghrib* prayer. The *Khalīfah,* ʿUthmān, may Allāh be pleased with him, often read *Sūrah Yūsuf* in *fajr* prayer.

Again, however, it is imperative that the condition of the followers be taken into consideration. When the Companion, Muʿādh ibn Jabal, may Allāh be pleased with him, read *Sūrah al-Baqarah* in *ʿishāʾ* prayer, one of the followers complained about it to the Messenger of Allāh, may the peace and blessings of Allāh be upon him. The Messenger of Allāh then called for Muʿādh ibn Jabal and said, "Muʿādh! What are you? A trouble-maker? Read something like '*sabbiḥiʾsma*' [*Sūrah al-ʿAlā*] or '*wash-shams*' [*Sūrah ash-Shams*; both from the *awsāṭ mufaṣṣal*]."

One must always be careful to observe the wishes of the congregation in such situations.

In *nafl* prayers it is *Sunnah* to [quietly] make *du'a'* when reciting verses in which there is mention of the finer things, and asking for forgiveness, *istighfār*, when reciting verses in which there is mention of the baser things; to seek refuge at the mention of Hell, and pray for admission at the mention of Paradise.

Rukū' – Bowing

After finishing one's recitation, one makes *takbīr* [by saying, "*Allāhu Akbar*"] and bows down with both hands, with the fingers spread wide, grasping the knees firmly with eyes focused on the space between one's feet. The head and back should be on the same level as the buttocks [i.e. the back should be parallel with the ground].

An amount of time consistent [not necessarily commensurate] with the amount of time spent standing, *qiyām*, should be spent in *rukū'*.

It is not *Sunnah*, according to Imām Abū Ḥanīfah, to raise the two hands when making *takbīr* at the time of [leaving the standing position to go down into] *rukū'*, or at the time of lifting the head from *rukū'*. There are, however, many Imāms of *fiqh* and *ḥadīth* scholars who consider this to be *Sunnah*. In *rukū'*, the words: "*Subḥāna Rabbi al-'Aẓīm*, سُبْحَانَ رَبِّيَ الْعَظِيْم" (Glory be to my Lord the Great) should be read an odd number of times. The least number, according to the *Sunnah*, is three times.

Qawmah – Standing after Rukū'

Then, after *rukū'*, one will lift one's head and resume a standing position for a short time, *qawmah*, while saying, "*Sami' Allāhu Li Man Ḥamidah*, سَمِعَ اللّٰهُ لِمَنْ حَمِدَه" (Allāh hears those who praise Him); and then say, "*Rabbanā Laka'l Ḥamd*, رَبَّنَا لَكَ الْحَمْد" (O Lord, praise is only for You).

The people in the congregational prayer must follow the imām when going into *rukū'* and *sajdah*.

After *rukū'* in congregational prayer, the imām and, afterwards, the followers will lift their heads and, according to Imām Abū

Ḥanīfah, the imām will say, "*Samiʿ Allāhu Li Man Ḥamidah,*" and the followers will afterwards only say, "*Rabbanā Lakal-Ḥamd,* رَبَّنَا لَكَ الْحَمْدُ." A person praying alone will recite both *duʿa's* and according to Imāms Abū Yūsuf and Muḥammad the Imām will also recite both.

Sajdah – Prostration

Then, having made *takbīr*, prostration, *sajdah* will be made in such a way that first the knees and then the hands are placed on the ground. The nose and forehead should be placed between the hands, the fingers of which should be brought together and pointed in the direction of the *qiblah.* The arms are held away from the ribs, and the stomach away from the thighs. Similarly, the forearms and the shins should be held away from [and not allowed to rest on] the ground.

The posture of a woman in *sajdah* should be low to the ground, and all of her limbs should be brought close together.

The duration of *rukūʿ* and *sajdah* should be consistent with the time spent in *qiyām.*

In *sajdah* the words: "*Subḥāna Rabbi al-Aʿalā,* سُبْحَانَ رَبِّيَ الْأَعْلَى" (Glory be to my Lord, the most high) should be read an odd number of times silently and without haste, at least three times, according to the *Sunnah.*

Jalsah – Sitting Back Between Two Sajdahs

Then, having made another *takbīr*, the sitting position or *jalsah* is to be assumed briefly. [In *nafl* prayer] the words,

اللَّهُمَّ اغْفِرْ لِي وَارْحَمْنِي، وَاهْدِنِي وَارْزُقْنِي، وَارْفَعْنِي وَاجْبُرْنِي.

Allāhumma'gh fir lī, wa'rhamnī, wa'hdinī, wa'rzuqnī, wa'rfaḥnī, wa'jburnī, (O Allāh! Forgive me, have mercy on me, guide me, provide for me, elevate me and set my affairs right), may be recited in this position. Then, after making *takbīr*, the *sajdah* will again be performed in the same way as before. After the second *sajdah* one *rakʿah* has been completed.

3.11.2 Beginning the second *rakʿah*

After making *takbīr*, one will then rise from the second *sajdah*, first lifting the head, then the hands, then the knees, and perform a second *rakʿah* just like the first; except that the *thanā* and *taʿawwudh* will be omitted and only *bismillāh*, *Fātiḥah*, and some verses of the Qurʾān will be recited.

When beginning the second *rakʿah* behind the imām in congregational prayer, one leaves the recitation of *thanā*, *taʿawwudh*, and *bismillāh* and stands in silence, [while the imām recites *bismillāh*, *Fātiḥah*, and some verses of the Qurʾān].

Qaʿdah ʾUlā – The First Sitting

Upon completing the second *rakʿah* one will sit for the first *qaʿdah*. The left foot should be set on its left side on the ground and sat on, while the right foot is allowed to stand on end on its toes with the heel in the air. The toes of both feet should be pointed in the direction of the *qiblah*.[20] [While in this sitting position], the two hands should be allowed to rest on the thighs close to the knees [and their fingers should be pointed towards the *qiblah*].

Tashahhud

In the first *qaʿdah*, nothing more than the *tashahhud* is to be read. The *tashahhud* is:

التَّحِيَّاتُ لِلّٰهِ وَالصَّلَوَاتُ وَالطَّيِّبَاتُ. السَّلَامُ عَلَيْكَ أَيُّهَا النَّبِيُّ
وَرَحْمَةُ اللّٰهِ وَبَرَكَاتُهُ. السَّلَامُ عَلَيْنَا وَعَلَى عِبَادِ اللّٰهِ الصَّالِحِينَ.
أَشْهَدُ أَن لَّا إِلَٰهَ إِلَّا اللّٰهُ، وَأَشْهَدُ أَنَّ مُحَمَّدًا عَبْدُهُ وَرَسُولُه.

Atta ḥiyyātu lillāhi waṣ-ṣalāwātu waṭṭayyibāt. As-salāmu ʿalayka ayyuha'n-Nabiyyu wa raḥmatullāhi wa barakātuh. As-salāmu ʿalainā wa ʿalā ʿIbādillāhiṣ-ṣāliḥīn. Ash-hadu alā-Ilāha Illa'llahu wa ash-hadu anna Muḥammadan ʿabduhu wa Rasūluh. (All worship, through words, actions, and wealth is for Allāh. Peace be on you, O Prophet, and the mercy of Allāh and His blessings. Peace be on us and on those who are righteous servants of Allāh. I testify that there is no god but Allāh and I testify that Muḥammad is His servant and Messenger.)

While reciting the *tashahhud* the little and ring fingers of the right hand should be brought together and the middle finger and the thumb brought to join and form a ring. The index finger should be left pointing towards the *qiblah* while resting on the knee.

In the opinion of the four major Imāms, it is *Sunnah* to [in some way] gesture with the index finger when reading *tashahhud.* According to the famous opinion of Imām Abū Ḥanīfah, one should not gesture with one's finger but rather put them on one's thighs, pointing towards the *qiblah.*[21]

After reciting the *tashahhud*, one begins the third *rakʿah* [in prayers with three or more *rakʿats*] or one finishes the prayer [as indicated below] when the first sitting, *qaʿdah*, is the final sitting, such as in *fajr* prayer and prayers with only two *rakʿats.*

3.11.3 Beginning the third *rakʿah*

After making *takbīr* [saying "*Allāhu Akbar,*"] one will rise from the sitting position, *qaʿdah*, for the third *rakʿah* [without the assistance of one's hands pushing off the ground]. At this point it is *Sunnah*, according to some Imāms, but not to Imāms Abū Ḥanīfah and Shāfiʿī, to raise the two hands. In the third and fourth *rakʿats* [of *farḍ* prayer] there is to be no more than the silent recitation of *bismillāh* and *Sūrah Fātiḥah.*[22]

When in the third or fourth *rakʿah* of congregational prayer, the imām will recite *bismillāh* and *Fātiḥah* silently and the followers will stand in silence.

3.11.4 THE FINAL SITTING *QAʿDAH AKHĪRAH*

When the third and fourth *rakʿats* are completed [in prayers of that many *rakʿats*] or in the second *rakʿah* of prayers with only two *rakʿats*, the final sitting will be assumed and, after the *tashahhud* is recited, *Aṣ-ṣalātu ʿalaʾn-Nabī* blessings and peace (*darūd*) will be invoked on the Prophet.

Aṣ-ṣalātu ʿalaʾn-Nabī – Darūd

Blessings may be invoked as follows:

اللّٰهُمَّ صَلِّ عَلَى مُحَمَّدٍ وَّعَلَى آلِ مُحَمَّدٍ، كَمَا صَلَّيْتَ عَلَى إِبْرَاهِيمَ وَعَلَى آلِ إِبْرَاهِيمَ، إِنَّكَ حَمِيدٌ مَّجِيْدٌ. اللّٰهُمَّ بَارِكْ عَلَى مُحَمَّدٍ وَّعَلَى آلِ مُحَمَّدٍ، كَمَا بَارَكْتَ عَلَى إِبْرَاهِيمَ وَعَلَى آلِ إِبْرَاهِيمَ، إِنَّكَ حَمِيدٌ مَّجِيْدٌ.

Allāhumma! Ṣalli ʿalā Muḥammadin wa ʿalā āli Muḥammadin, Kamā Ṣallayta ʿalā Ibrāhīma wa ʿalā āli Ibrāhīma innaka Ḥamīdum Majīd. Allāhumma Bārik ʿalā Muḥammadin wa ʿalā āli Muḥammadin, Kamā Bārakta ʿalā Ibrāhīma wa ʿalā āli Ibrāhīma innaka Ḥamīdum Majīd. (O Allāh, have mercy on Muḥammad and the family of Muḥammad just as You have had mercy on Ibrāhīm and the family of Ibrāhīm, indeed You are the Praiseworthy, the Glorious. O Allāh, send blessings on Muḥammad and on the family of Muḥammad just as You have sent blessings on Ibrāhīm and on the family of Ibrāhīm, indeed You are the Praiseworthy, the Glorious.)

Duʿaʾ – Supplication

After the invocation of blessings, a *masnūn duʿaʾ* should be read, especially this *duʿaʾ*:

اللَّهُمَّ إِنِّي أَعُوذُ بِكَ مِنْ عَذَابِ جَهَنَّمَ، وَأَعُوذُ بِكَ مِنْ عَذَابِ الْقَبْرِ، وَأَعُوذُ بِكَ مِنْ فِتْنَةِ الْمَسِيحِ الدَّجَّالِ، وَأَعُوذُ بِكَ مِنْ فِتْنَةِ الْمَحْيَا وَالْمَمَاتِ. اللَّهُمَّ إِنِّي أَعُوذُ بِكَ مِنَ الْمَأْثَمِ وَالْمَغْرَمِ.

Allāhumma innī A'ūdhu bika min 'adhābi jahannama wa a'ūdhu bika min adhābi'l-qabri wa a'ūdhu bika min fitnati'l-masīhi'd-dajjāli wa a'ūdhu bika min fitnali'l-Maḥyā wa'l-Mamāt. Allāhumma! Innī a'ūdhu bika min al-ma'thami wa'l-maghram. (O Allāh! I seek refuge with You from the punishment of Hell and from the punishment of the grave. I seek refuge with You from the trial of dajjāl the antichrist, and from the trial of life and death. O Allāh! I seek refuge with You from sin and debt.)

The writer has given special mention to the above *du'a'*. Among the very famous *du'a's* is one which the Prophet, blessings and peace of Allāh be upon him, taught to Abū Bakr, may Allāh be pleased with him, and that is:

اللَّهُمَّ إِنِّي ظَلَمْتُ نَفْسِي ظُلْمًا كَثِيرًا، وَلَا يَغْفِرُ الذُّنُوبَ إِلَّا أَنْتَ، فَاغْفِرْ لِي مَغْفِرَةً مِّنْ عِنْدِكَ، وَارْحَمْنِي إِنَّكَ أَنْتَ الْغَفُورُ الرَّحِيمُ.

Allāhumma! Innī ẓalamtu nafsī zulman kathīrā. Wa lā yaghfiru'z-zunūba illā anta. Fa'gfir lī maghfiratan min 'indika warḥamnī Innaka anta'l-gafūru'r-Raḥīm. (O Allāh! I did great injustice to myself, and surely no one can forgive sins except You. Bestow forgiveness on me from You and have mercy on me. You are Most forgiving, the Most merciful.)

Ending the Prayer with Salāms

One then [after the *du'a'*] says,

السَّلَامُ عَلَيْكُمْ وَرَحْمَةُ اللَّه السَّلَامُ عَلَيْكُمْ وَرَحْمَةُ اللَّه

As Salāmu ʿAlaikum Wa Raḥmatullāh, (May peace be upon you and the mercy of Allāh),

first to the right, and then to the left. One should intend to address the angels at the time of giving *salāms* when praying alone. Once the *salāms* are made, the prayer has ended.

In congregational prayer, the imām and followers should make *salām* just as the person praying alone does, except that the imām should intend to address both the angels and the followers in the prayer. The followers in the congregation should intend to address the imām, the angels, and the other followers in the prayer with their *salāms*.

3.11.5 Some recommended remembrance of Allāh (*Dhikr*) after prayer

After ending the prayer with *salāms*, the one praying may recite *Āyat al-Kursī* [*al-Baqarah* 2: 255]:

ٱللَّهُ لَآ إِلَٰهَ إِلَّا هُوَ ٱلْحَىُّ ٱلْقَيُّومُ ۚ لَا تَأْخُذُهُۥ سِنَةٌ وَلَا نَوْمٌ ۚ لَّهُۥ مَا فِى ٱلسَّمَٰوَٰتِ
وَمَا فِى ٱلْأَرْضِ ۗ مَن ذَا ٱلَّذِى يَشْفَعُ عِندَهُۥٓ إِلَّا بِإِذْنِهِۦ ۚ يَعْلَمُ مَا بَيْنَ أَيْدِيهِمْ وَمَا
خَلْفَهُمْ ۖ وَلَا يُحِيطُونَ بِشَىْءٍ مِّنْ عِلْمِهِۦٓ إِلَّا بِمَا شَآءَ ۚ وَسِعَ كُرْسِيُّهُ ٱلسَّمَٰوَٰتِ
وَٱلْأَرْضَ ۖ وَلَا يَـُٔودُهُۥ حِفْظُهُمَا ۚ وَهُوَ ٱلْعَلِىُّ ٱلْعَظِيمُ ﴿٢٥٥﴾

"*Allāh! There is no god but He, – the Living, the Self-subsisting, Supporter of all. No slumber can seize Him nor sleep. His are all things in the heavens and on earth. Who is there can intercede in His presence except as He permitteth? He knoweth what (appeareth to His creatures as) Before or After or Behind them. Nor shall they compass aught of His knowledge except as He willeth. His Throne doth extend over the heavens and the earth, and He feeleth no fatigue in guarding and preserving them for He is Most High, the Supreme (in glory).*" [*al-Baqarah* 2: 255] once, "*Subhānallah,* سُبْحَانَ اللهِ" thirty-three times, "*Al-Ḥamdu li'llāh,* اَلْحَمْدُ لِلّٰهِ" thirty-three times, "*Allāhu Akbar,* اَللّٰهُ أَكْبَرُ" thirty-four times, and "*Lā Ilāha Illa'llāh Muḥammad-ur-Rasūlullāh,* لَا إِلٰهَ إِلَّا اللّٰهُ، مُحَمَّدٌ رَّسُولُ اللّٰهِ" once.[23]

3.12 Breaking Wuḍū' in Prayer

If, while performing prayer, one's ablution, *wuḍū'*, should break, he will have to [leave off prayer and] go and make *wuḍū'*. Thereafter, one may begin where one left off. With regard to one praying alone, however, it is better that one begins all over again.

A member in the congregation [in this situation], after remaking his *wuḍū'*, should return to his former place [in the congregation]. Upon returning, he should first perform whatever the imām had performed during his absence, though without making any recitation, and then join in the prayer of the imām.

When the follower in the congregational prayer returns, if the imām has completed the prayer, then he will have a choice; either return to his former place, or complete the prayer near to where he made *wuḍū'*. If [before the *tashahhud*] he intentionally breaks *wuḍū'*, then one's prayer will become invalid.

If one's *wuḍū'* should break after he has recited the [final] *tashahhud*, he may, after remaking *wuḍū'*, complete his prayer by [assuming the final *qa'dah* position and simply] making *salāms.*

If it should happen that the imām breaks his *wuḍū'*, he will have to signal someone [among the followers in the congregation] to come forward and take his place. Thereafter he may go and make *wuḍū'*. When the imām returns he is to join the [line of] followers of the congregation [if the congregation is still standing].

If an imām, after his *wuḍū'* breaks, should give over the responsibility of completing the prayer to someone who joined the prayer late, then the latecomer is to complete the prayer of the imām. Thereafter, however, the latecomer must motion for a person from the congregation who joined the prayer on time to come forward and read *salāms* [thus completing the prayer for the congregation which started with the imām]. Then, the latecomer will rise and finish his own prayer.

If the imām should find himself unable to recite, he may motion for a follower from the congregation to become his *khalīfah*; on condition that he [the imām] has not already recited enough as is sufficient for prayer [for, if that is the case, he need only make *rukū*ʿ].

If one's *wuḍū*ʾ should break while he is in *rukū*ʿ or *sajdah*, then when he returns [after remaking *wuḍū*ʾ] to complete the prayer, he will have to repeat the *rukū*ʿ or *sajdah* [and then continue from there, until the prayer is complete].

If the one praying should, while in prayer:

- become insane;
- have a seminal emission;
- laugh out loud;
- become splattered by enough impurity, *najāsah*, as would prevent one from making prayer in the first place; or
- receive an injury [from which blood begins to flow], or
- leave the Masjid [or, if outside, leave the congregation] thinking that one's *wuḍū*ʾ had broken only to discover that it had not;

then his prayer will become invalid. If, however, thinking that the *wuḍū*ʾ is broken, he [breaks off one's prayer but] does not leave the Masjid or his place in the congregation, then he may rejoin the prayer [on discovering his *wuḍū*ʾ did not break] and take up the place he had left.

3.13 Joining the Prayer Late

If someone joins the congregation [late] it is considered that he began from the *rukn*–pillar in which the imām [is engaged in].

For example, if one joins [while the imām is in] *rukūʿ*, then one will be considered to have joined the imām for the entire *rakʿah* [even though one missed the *qiyām* and recitation, etc.]. If one should join after the [imām has given *takbīr* for rising from] *rukūʿ*, however, one will have missed the *rakʿah*. Then, when the imām completes his prayer, the latecomer, *masbuq*, will complete whatever remains of his prayer.

The two basic principles to be observed by a latecomer when completing prayer on his own are as follows:

- with regard to recitation; [whatever remains of] the latecomer's prayer should be performed as if from the beginning;
- And with regard to *qaʿdah* [when and which: it is the end of prayer that will determine that matter].

Thus, upon the imām's completion of prayer, when the latecomer rises to complete his or her own prayer, one should first recite *thanā, taʿawwudh* and *bismillāh*.

Further, if the latecomer has performed with the imām, one *rakʿah* of *fajr*, two *rakʿats* of *maghrib*, or three *rakʿats* of any prayer in which there are four *rakʿats*, then, in performing the final *rakʿah* alone, one will recite the *Fātiḥah* and another *sūrah*.

If one has performed with the imām one *rakʿah* of *maghrib*, or two of a prayer in which there are four *rakʿats*, then in each of the final two *rakʿats* one will recite the *Fātiḥah* and another *sūrah*.

If one has performed with the imām only one *rakʿah* of a prayer in which there are four *rakʿats*, then in the first two of the three *rakʿats* that he will perform alone, he will recite the *Fātiḥah* and another *sūrah*. But, in the last *rakʿah* he will recite only the *Fātiḥah*.

One example should serve to illustrate the principle having to do with sitting, *qaʿdah*, in the prayer of a latecomer. If a latecomer to congregational prayer makes one *rakʿah* of *maghrib* with the imām, he will sit for what will be the imām's last *qaʿdah*. Afterwards, when completing prayer alone, a latecomer will make two more *qaʿdahs*. This is because the end of the prayer will be two *rakʿats* away, and in each of the last two *rakʿats* of *maghrib* there is a *qaʿdah*.

If the latecomer to the prayer had not known this principle, he or she might have reasoned that since *maghrib* prayer has two *qaʿdahs*, of which one has already been performed with the imām, there should remain only one more *qaʿdah*.

3.14 Qaḍāʾ – Making Up Missed Prayers

If the time for prayer should elapse, a make up prayer, *qaḍāʾ*, will have to be performed with *adhān* and *iqāmah,* as if the prayer is being performed on time.

The *qaḍāʾ* of a prayer which is recited aloud when performed in congregation should be recited aloud and, when performed by oneself, may be recited quietly [or aloud, as the one praying wishes. It is best, however, to recite it aloud].

It is *farḍ* to perform *qaḍāʾ* of omitted prayers in chronological order. According to Imām Abū Ḥanīfah, the same rule applies to *witr* which though it is only a *wājib* prayer, when performed as *qaḍāʾ*, must be performed after *ʿishāʾ* as the sequence between the prayers is *farḍ.*

If, in spite of one's remembering that he must perform *qaḍāʾ* of an omitted prayer, he performs the prayer of the time, then that prayer even though it is performed on time will be nullified [because it was not performed in sequence].

If, after omitting a prayer, like *fajr*, and then performing a prayer, like *ẓuhr, qaḍāʾ* is made of an omitted prayer [*fajr*] before performing a second [*ʿaṣr*] chronological prayer, then the *farḍ* status of the first chronological prayer [*ẓuhr*] will be nullified.[24]

If, before making *qaḍāʾ* of a prayer, five prayers are performed, each in its own proper time, then those five prayers will be subject to nullification. If a sixth prayer is made before making up the omitted prayers, then all six prayers, according to Imām Abū Ḥanīfah, will be considered correct.

If, out of forgetfulness, someone should perform *ʿishāʾ* without *wuḍūʾ*, and then perform the *Sunnah* and *witr* with *wuḍūʾ*, then, according to Imām Abū Ḥanīfah, he will have to again perform his *Sunnah*, not *witr*, after making *qaḍā'* of *'ishā'*. According to his two Companions, Imāms Abū Yūsuf and Muḥammad, he has to pray *witr* again.

3.14.1 What abrogates making up prayers in chronological order

There are three things which cancel [the necessity of making up and performing prayers in] sequence:

- lack of time for [anything but the proper performance of] the scheduled prayer;[25]
- forgetfulness;[26]
- or the state of being responsible for six or more, old or new omitted prayers [i.e. not being a '*ṣaḥib at-tartīb*' as in the technical terms of *fiqh*].

Later, when all the omitted prayers have been made up, it will again be necessary to perform all prayers in sequence. If someone is responsible for six or more omitted prayers, and then makes up a few, but not all, of them so that one still remains responsible for less than six prayers, then, according to some *fuqahā'*, it will again become necessary for one to observe sequence in one's prayers. The *fatwā*, however, is that it will not again become necessary to observe sequence until all of the omitted prayers are made up.

3.15 Elements Which Nullify or Detract From Prayer

The following elements may nullify or detract from one's prayer:

1. speech;

   Any speech, regardless of whether it comes out accidentally or while the one praying is momentarily asleep.

2. *du'a'* for something one might just as easily ask of another person;[27]
3. lamentation, or moaning;
4. crying or wincing aloud in pain or because of some worldly trouble; though not if brought on by mention of Paradise or Hellfire;
5. coughing without reason;
6. answering someone who sneezes by saying, "*Yarḥamukallāh,*" May Allāh have mercy on you, for example;
7. answering good news with the words, "*Al-Ḥamdu lillāh,*" Praise belongs to Allāh, for example;

   Answering amazing news with the words, "*Subḥān allāh,*" Glory be to Allāh, or "*Lā ḥawla wa lā quwwata illā bi'llāh,*" There is no strength nor power except with Allāh, for example;

   Answering bad news with the words, "*Innā li'llāhi wa innā ilaihi Rāji'ūn,*" To Allāh we belong and to Him is our return;
8. If a person praying [on his own or in a different congregation] prompts an imām [other than one's own imām, who has forgotten a verse], the prayer will become invalid. If someone is praying and prompts his own imām, the prayer will not be affected.[28]
9. intentionally responding to someone's *salāms* with, "*Wa 'Alaikumus-Salām,*" and upon you be peace, or giving *salāms*;

   However, if one should make *salāms* [not a greeting but] mistakenly [thinking that one may now bring his prayer to a close], the prayer will not become invalid.
10. reciting directly from a copy of the Qur'ān;
11. eating and drinking during prayer;
12. excess movement;

    This is anything which requires both hands to do. According to some *'ulamā'*, excess movement is that which when witnessed by another causes one to think that the person making those movements is not performing the prayer. According to others, it is that which the one in prayer himself considers to be excessive;
13. if *sajdah* is made on impurity, *najāsah*, prayer will become invalid;

14. if prayer is performed on a large piece of cloth, part of which is worn by the one in prayer and part of which is impure, then, if by one's moving the part of the cloth that is worn the impure part also moves, the prayer will be nullified; but if it does not move, the prayer will be proper;
15. and turning the chest away from the *qiblah*.

3.15.1 That which does not detract from prayer

The performance of the following do not detract from one's prayer:

1. if, while in prayer, the one praying starts into another prayer by making *takbīr*, then the first prayer will be invalid. If, however, one starts the same prayer over again, then the [*rakʿahs* one made in the] first prayer will not be invalid;
2. if the one in prayer works some food loose with one's tongue from between one's teeth and then swallows it, the prayer will be valid if the amount swallowed is less than a chickpea; however, if it is greater in size, the prayer will be invalid;
3. if the one praying looks at and takes in the meaning of some writing on the wall etc., one's prayer will be valid;
4. if one passes in front of someone making prayer in the open or in a shop, the person's prayer will be valid. The passer-by, however, if he or she is sane, will have committed a wrong action, unless the place where prayer is being performed is higher than the head of the passer-by;

   Sutrah (Restrictive Barrier), the *Sunnah*, when making prayer in the open, is for the one praying to implant a *sutrah* [any kind of rod or staff, i.e. a barrier], measuring at least one span [nine inches] in height [when stuck into the ground] in front and one finger in breadth, though a little off centre of wherever one intends to make prayer. Merely placing the *sutrah* on the ground [rather than standing it upon end], or drawing a line in the dust, is of no benefit.

   One *sutrah* in front of the imām will suffice for the entire congregation.

A person praying, when there is no *sutrah* before him, may ward off the passer-by by making a sign [with his head or eyes] or by saying, "*Subḥānallāh*," but not by both [which is *makrūh*].

5. and if prayer is performed on a piece of cloth which has been spread on the ground, and of which one part [off to the side] is impure, the prayer will be proper regardless of whether or not the impure side moves when the opposite side is moved.

3.15.2 What is *Makrūh* in Prayer

The performance of the following is *makrūh* in prayer:

1. fidgeting with one's clothes or body; as long as the movement is not excessive [in which case the prayer will be nullified];
2. to clear gravel from the place of *sajdah*, except that *sajdah* be impossible without the one in prayer clearing the ground once or twice;
3. finger popping, knuckle cracking, and fidgeting with the hand on the stomach;
4. turning the face to the right or left, as long as the chest remains directed towards the *qiblah* [for moving the chest to another direction will nullify the prayer];
5. to sit [instead of the *iftirāsh* style of sitting in *qa'dah*] like a dog [with the buttocks and the hands on the ground and the knees up against the chest];
6. placing the forearms on the ground during *sajdah* [except if the one praying is a woman in which case it is desirable];
7. answering someone's *salām* or greeting with a motion of the hand;
8. sitting cross-legged in *farḍ* prayer without any kind of excuse;
9. gathering up one's clothes in order to protect them from getting dusty;
10. dangling an article of clothing [such as a necktie, scarf, or shawl] by wearing it on the head or shoulders without fastening the ends [so that they hang from the body of the one in prayer];
11. yawning;

12. stretching the body in order to ward off fatigue;[29]
13. keeping the eyes closed;

    The one praying should train his eyes [while standing] on the place where he [puts his head when he] makes *sajdah.*
14. twisting the hair of one's head into curls while performing prayer. It is *sunnah*, if one has long hair to leave it open, so that the hair could also do *sajdah*;
15. performing the prayer bare-headed, except that it be done out of humility and self-abasement;
16. counting on the fingers the number of verses or *tasbīḥs* recited; though according to Imāms Abū Yūsuf and Muḥammad, this is not *makrūh*;
17. the imām's standing alone in the *miḥrāb* of the Masjid while those behind him stand outside it; or his standing above them on [a platform];
18. In a congregational prayer standing alone in a row of his own when there is room in the row before him.

    If there is no room, then he may pull someone out of the last row [on the supposition that the other person knows this particular ruling] and start [the two of them in] a new row.[30]
19. and wearing clothing on which there are pictures of animals or human beings.

    Prayer in a place where a picture of a living being is kept in a place of honour, such as on the wall, regardless of whether it be to the right or to the left or directly in front of the one praying, is *makrūh.* If the picture is not in such a place, but is under one's feet or behind the one praying, then the prayer will not be *makrūh.* Similarly, if the picture is only a landscape, or of a living thing without its head, then the prayer will not be *makrūh.*

3.15.3 What is not *Makrūh* in Prayer

The performance of the following is not considered *makrūh* in prayer:

1. to kill a snake or scorpion, [even if it requires excess motion];
2. for the imām to make *sajdah* in the prayer niche, *miḥrāb,* of the Masjid, if he stands outside the *miḥrāb* while making prayer;
3. and to perform prayer while facing the back of someone who is engaged in conversation, or toward a Qur'ān, or a suspended sword, or a candle, or a lamp.

3.16 Prayer of the Sick

If a sick person is unable to stand, or fears that by doing so the illness will grow worse, then one may perform one's prayer from a sitting position, making *rukūʿ* and *sajdah* in more or less the usual way.

If a sick person is unable to make *rukūʿ* and *sajdah* but is able to stand, then, according to Imām Abū Ḥanīfah, the *fatwā* on that is that it is better for one to sit and perform the prayer than to stand. Then, when performing the prayer in the sitting position one may, by motioning with his head, make *rukūʿ* and, by nodding one's head a bit lower, make *sajdah.* One may, however, if he prefers, stand and perform one's prayers by motioning [for *rukūʿ* and *sajdah*].

In my humble opinion, if one is able to pray standing, it is better for him to offer his prayer to gain the reward of standing though he is allowed to pray while sitting.

If a sick person does not have the strength to either stand or make *rukūʿ* and *sajdah,* then he may perform the prayer sitting, by motioning with his head. Furthermore, if a sick person is unable even to sit then one may perform the prayer on his back, arranging one's two feet so that they face the *qiblah* or, if one prefers, one may perform it lying on one's side with one's face towards the *qiblah,* motioning with one's head for *rukūʿ* and *sajdah.*

If a sick person is unable even to motion with his head, then he may put off making prayer until such a time as he is able to motion. If, during this period [of offering no prayers due to disabling illness], he dies, he is excused and will not die a wrongdoer.

If the one praying should become ill while performing prayer, he may complete the prayer in whatever way he can.

If, while a sick person is performing the prayer from a sitting position, [making *sajdah* and *rukū*ʿ in more or less the usual way] and should suddenly become able to stand, then he should do so, and thus complete the prayer from the standing position in the usual way. According to Imām Muḥammad he should start the prayer anew.

If, while a sick person is performing prayer, making *sajdah* and *rukū*ʿ by motioning with his head, he becomes able to make *sajdah* and *rukū*ʿ, then according to all the *ʿulamā*ʾ, he must start the prayer over again.

3.16.1 The make up prayer of the insane

If a person should lose consciousness or go temporarily insane for a period of less than 24 hours, he will be responsible for *qaḍā* of the prayers missed in that period. If his disability should last even a moment longer than 24 hours, he will not be responsible for making up those prayers. According to Imām Muḥammad, [and the *fatwā* is given here on his opinion] such a person will be responsible for *qaḍā* until the time of the sixth prayer.[31]

3.17 Prayer of the Traveller – Musāfir

3.17.1 The legal distance for shortening the prayer

A person who goes out from his permanent residence to beyond the city limits with the intention of journeying [at least] 48 miles [is legally considered a traveller, *musāfir*, and] is to perform his *farḍ* prayers with two instead of four *rakʿats*.[32]

If a traveller makes four *rakʿats*, and makes *qaʿdah* after the first two *rakʿats*, the first two will be considered to have been one's *farḍ* prayer, and the second two will be *nafl*. However, owing to his mixing the *nafl* with the *farḍ*, he will be a wrongdoer.

If, out of forgetfulness, one should do the same thing, then, owing to one's delay in making *salām*, one will have to make *sajdah sahw*.

If a traveller makes four *rakʿats* without assuming the *qaʿdah* position at the end of the first two *rakʿats*, then one's *farḍ* will be lost. However, the four *rak'ats* [which one did perform] will be considered *nafl*; one will also have to make *sajdah sahw*.

3.17.2 *Niyah* – Intention

In matters of journeying and residing, the intention of the one who is followed, like an officer or a husband, is to be considered, and not the intention of the one who is a follower, such as a common soldier, child, [or other dependants].

3.17.3 How long one may remain a traveller

A person will remain a traveller [and is subject to the various laws concerning *musāfirs*] until he returns to the place he has made his residence, or to the place where [having arrived at some city or town on his way] he makes the intention to stay [as a temporary resident] for a period of at least fifteen days. His intention, however, to stay at some place in the desert [or any uninhabited place] will not have any effect on his status as a *musāfir*. A nomad, however, who is constantly wandering in the wilds, will always perform prayer as if he were at home except when he makes the intention of undertaking a journey of 48 miles or more.[33]

3.17.4 A traveller praying behind a resident

If a traveller should join in the prayer of a resident, non-traveller, *muqīm*, as a follower, *muqtadī*, in the congregational prayer, when the prayer is being performed in its proper time, then one will have to perform all four *rakʿats* [with the imām]. If, however, the prayer is not being performed in its proper time, but rather as *qaḍā*, the traveller will not be permitted to be a part of the congregation of an imām who is a resident.

3.17.5 A resident praying behind a traveller

A resident, non-traveller may become a follower in the congregational prayer of a traveller imām both when the prayer is on time and when it is late, being read as a make-up. A traveller imām will give *salāms* at the end of the two *rakʿats* [thus completing his prayer] and a resident, following in the congregation will stand up and continue with his prayer until he completes four *rakʿats*.

3.17.6 The status of one's permanent residence

One's permanent residence will lose its status only [when replaced] by a new permanent residence; not by a journey. If one sets out on a journey, and lives in a temporary residence and after that returns to his permanent residence, his status as a traveller ceases and he has to offer his prayers of four *rakʿats* in full even though he does not intend to stay long.

3.17.7 The status of one's temporary residence

The temporary residence, however, will lose its status by:

1. the traveller's leaving it for another temporary residence, so that if one should return to that first temporary residence, he will continue to perform prayer as a traveller until he again makes the intention to stay there beyond fifteen days;
2. [the traveller's leaving it for] a permanent address;
3. and [merely setting out on] a journey.

3.17.8 The make up prayer of the traveller

Whatever [four *rak'ah*] prayer is missed while a person is a resident, *muqīm*, he then performs as *qaḍā'* while a traveller, he will have to pray [the full] four *rakʿats*.

However if the prayer is missed while a person is a traveller and then performs it as *qaḍāʾ* while as a resident, he will be required to pray only two *rakʿats*.

3.17.9 The journey of wrong

The "Journey of Wrong," [that which is made for the purpose of crime] according to the three Imāms (Mālik, Aḥmad ibn Ḥanbal, and Shāfiʿī) may not be taken by the [ill-intentioned] traveller as an opportunity to shorten prayer. According to Imām Abū Ḥanīfah, however, it is permitted that the traveller under such circumstances breaks his fast if he chooses to, and it is necessary that he [like any other traveller] shortens the prayer.

3.18 Jumuʿah Prayer

If *jumuʿah* prayer is to be performed properly, and [the need to perform] *ẓuhr* dispensed with, six conditions must be fulfilled:

1. it must be performed in a city;

   A population centre having a Muslim ruler and a *qāḍī*, or the suburbs of that city [which are] populated for the purpose of providing for the necessities of the city. Therefore, according to Imām Abū Ḥanīfah, it is not permitted to hold *jumuʿah* prayer in a small village. According to Imām Shāfiʿī and most other Imāms, however, *jumuʿah* is permitted, though they do not permit *jumuʿah* in the suburbs.

   According to most accepted opinion in the *Ḥanafī* school, it is permitted to hold several *jumuʿah* congregations in one city.
2. it must be performed in the presence of the sulṭān or ruler or one of his deputies;

   This is not a condition with the majority of the other Imāms.[34]
3. it must be performed at the time of *ẓuhr*;

4. it must be performed with *khuṭbah* [in Arabic];

   A *khuṭbah* [the length] of one *tasbīḥ* is sufficient, according to Imām Abū Ḥanīfah.[35] According to his two companions, Imāms Abū Yūsuf and Muḥammad, the *khuṭbah* must be as long as some lengthy *dhikr* [at least as long as the *tashahhud*].

   The *Sunnah* elements of the *khuṭbah* are:

   (a) the addressing of two [Arabic] *khuṭbahs* [between which the *khaṭīb* should sit for the time which takes to recite three verses from the Qurʾān];

   (b) including praise of Allāh, *ḥamd,* and invoking blessings on the Prophet, may the peace and blessings of Allāh be upon him;

   (c) recitation from the Qurʾān;

   (d) advice to the assembled Muslims;

   (e) and asking Allāh for forgiveness, *istighfār,* for the *khaṭīb* himself as well as for the assembled Muslims.

   Imām Abū Ḥanīfah considers all of the above-mentioned elements to be *Sunnah* and according to his two companions, Imāms Abū Yūsuf and Muḥammad, these elements are *farḍ*; however, it is *makrūh*, according to him, to leave out any of these.

5. it must be performed in congregation;

   A congregation, according to Imāms Shāfiʿī and Aḥmad, consists of forty or more persons. According to Imām Abū Ḥanīfah, three persons, other than the imām, make a congregation. According to Imām Abū Yūsuf, two persons other than the imām make a congregation.[36] If in the middle of the *jumuʿah* prayer some members of the congregation leaves, leaving fewer than are necessary for the congregation, the *jumuʿah* prayer will become invalid and those left will have to perform *ẓuhr* prayer instead;

6. and it must be performed with open admission [to the Masjid].

3.18.1 Those exempt from *Jumuʿah* prayer

The following persons are exempt from the performance of *jumuʿah*:

1. children
2. women
3. travellers
4. the sick

   If a sick person or a traveller makes *jumuʿah* prayer in the city then, since one has performed *jumuʿah*, there will no longer remain a need for him to perform *ẓuhr*;
5. and a blind man even if he has someone to guide him.

   This is according to Imām Abū Ḥanīfah; however, according to the other three Imāms, if a blind man has someone to guide him, he must attend *jumuʿah*, otherwise it is not necessary.

Anyone other than those exempted from *jumuʿah* must perform the *jumuʿah* prayer [i.e. *jumuʿah* is *farḍ* on them]. If someone outside the city limits hears the *adhān* for *jumuʿah*, he will have to present himself at the *jumuʿah* prayer. It is permitted to hold *jumuʿah* prayer in more than one place in the same city. It is permitted to take a sick man or traveller, *musāfir*, as the imām for *jumuʿah* prayer.

3.18.2 The *Jumuʿah* prayer congregation of travellers

If a group of travellers performs *jumuʿah* prayer in a city Masjid in which there is no one who is a resident, *muqīm*, [so that the whole congregation is made up of travellers], the *jumuʿah* prayer will be correct, according to Imām Abū Ḥanīfah. According to Imāms Shāfiʿī and Aḥmad, however, unless there are at least forty people present who are residents, *muqīm*, the prayer will not be correct [and they will have to perform *ẓuhr* instead].

3.18.3 Performing *Ẓuhr* before *Jumuʿah* prayer

If someone, having no excuse, performs *ẓuhr* prayer before *jumuʿah* prayer, then his *ẓuhr* will be considered to have been performed, but it will be *makrūh taḥrīmī.* Afterwards, if the same person should, in attempting to make *jumuʿah*, finds that the imām has not yet completed his prayer, then his *ẓuhr* prayer will become nullified and if thereafter he can join [the congregation for] *jumuʿah* prayer, then his *jumuʿah* prayer is proper and valid, otherwise he has to pray *ẓuhr* again. According to Imāms Abū Yūsuf and Muḥammad, however, if one is unable to join [the congregation for] *jumuʿah* on time, his *ẓuhr* will not be nullified.

It is *makrūh* for prisoners and those who are excused from attending *jumuʿah* prayer [like travellers and sick persons] to perform *ẓuhr* prayer in a congregation [in a city where *jumuʿah* prayer is held].[37]

3.18.4 Joining the *Jumuʿah* prayer late

Someone who joins *jumuʿah* prayers [or *ʿĪd* prayer] while the imām is [in the final *qaʿdah*] reading *tashahhud* or making *sajdah sahw*, is to perform, after the imām [finishes his prayer and] makes *salāms*, two *rakʿats* of *jumuʿah* prayer [according to Imām Abū Ḥanīfah]. According to Imām Muḥammad [and Imāms Mālik and Shāfiʿī], however, if someone fails to join the congregation for *jumuʿah* prayer in the second *rakʿah* [before the imām rises from *rukūʿ*], he will have to perform, with that same *taḥrīmah* [i.e. without starting over again], four *rakʿats* of *ẓuhr* prayer.[38]

3.18.5 The etiquette of *Jumuʿah* prayer

After the first *adhān* for *jumuʿah* has been made, all buying and selling is *ḥarām*, and every effort must be made to get to the Masjid. After the imām comes out for *khuṭbah* [and climbs the *minbar*] for the *khuṭbah*, all talking and performing [of *nafl* or *Sunnah*] prayer is prohibited until the *khuṭbah* is completed. Then the second *adhān* is to be called [by the *mu'adhdhin*, while standing and] facing the imām towards the *qiblah*. At that time all those in attendance are to direct their attention to the imām. When the *khuṭbah* has been completed, the *iqāmah* may be given.

It is *Sunnah* to recite *Sūrah Jumu'ah* and *Sūrah Munāfiqūn* in *jumu'ah* prayer. According to another narration, it is *Sunnah* to recite *Sūrahs A'lā* and *Ghāshiyah*.

3.19 Prayers that are Wājib

According to most Imāms, there are no *wājib* prayers, other than the daily five, which are *farḍ*. According to Imām Abū Ḥanīfah however, *Witr* prayers, *'Īd al-Fiṭr* prayers, and *'Īd al-Aḍḥā* prayers are *wājib*. The other Imāms consider these three prayers to be *Sunnah*.

3.19.1 *Witr* Prayer

Witr prayer consists of three *rak'ats* with one *salām* [at the very end], according to Imām Abū Ḥanīfah. In each of the three *rak'ats*, the *Fātiḥah* and another *sūrah* [or its equivalent in *āyahs*] are to be recited. In the third *rak'ah*, after reciting [the *Fātiḥah* and a *sūrah*] one raises his hands and makes *takbīr*, saying, "*Allāhu Akbar*," and then refolds the hands over the waist and recites *du'a' al-qunūt* before going to *rukū'*. The *du'a' al-qunūt* is as follows:

اللَّهُمَّ إِنَّا نَسْتَعِينُكَ وَنَسْتَغْفِرُكَ، وَنُؤْمِنُ بِكَ وَنَتَوَكَّلُ عَلَيْكَ،
وَنُثْنِي عَلَيْكَ الْخَيْرَ كُلَّهُ، وَنَشْكُرُكَ وَلاَ نَكْفُرُكَ، وَنَخْلَعُ وَنَتْرُكُ
مَنْ يَفْجُرُكْ. اللَّهُمَّ إِيَّاكَ نَعْبُدُ، وَلَكَ نُصَلِّيْ وَنَسْجُدُ، وَإِلَيْكَ
نَسْعَى وَنَحْفِدُ، وَنَرْجُو رَحْمَتَكَ وَنَخْشَى عَذَابَكَ، إِنَّ عَذَابَكَ
بِالْكُفَّارِ مُلْحِقْ.

Allāhumma! Innā nastaʿīnuka was nastagfiruka wa nuʾminu bika wa natawakkalu ʿalayka wa nuthnī ʿalaykal-khaira kullahū; wa nashkuruka wa lā nakfuruka wa nakhlaʿu wa natruku ma(n)y yafjuruka. Allāhumma! Iyyāka naʿbudu wa laka nuṣallī wa nasjudu wa ilayka nasʿā wa naḥfidu wa narjū raḥmataka wa nakhshā ʿadhābaka, inna ʿadhābaka bil-kuffāri mulḥiq. (O Allāh, we seek Your help and beg of Your forgiveness and affirm our faith in You and rely on You and praise You and thank You and do not withhold our gratitude from You and we cast off and leave one who disobeys You. O Allāh, You alone do we worship and to You we offer prayer and fall prostrate before You and rush towards You and hope for Your mercy and fear Your punishment. Indeed Your punishment will overtake the disbelievers.)

After reciting *duʿaʾ al-qunūt* one makes *takbīr* to go into *rukūʿ* and finishes the prayer as usual. This is to be done every day of the year. According to Imām Shāfiʿī, it is *Sunnah* to read *duʿaʾ al-qunūt* only in the last half of Ramaḍān. Furthermore, most Imāms say that *qunūt* should be read after *rukūʿ* [while the one praying is] in the *qawmah*, [brief standing position before *sajdah*]. It is *mustaḥab* to recite *Sūrah Aʿlā* in the first *rakʿah* of *witr*, *Sūrah Kāfirūn* in the second, and *Sūrah Ikhlāṣ* in the third.

Qunūt is Bidʿah at Fajr

It is *bidʿah* to perform *qunūt* at *fajr*, though, according to Imām Shāfiʿī, it is *Sunnah* to perform it at that time.

3.19.2 The *ʿĪd* prayer and its conditions

The conditions for [holding] *ʿĪd* prayer are similar to those for *jumuʿah* prayer, except that the *khuṭbah* is not *farḍ* in *ʿĪd* prayers [nor is the *ʿĪd* prayer performed during the time of *ẓuhr*]. The two *khuṭbahs*, however, after *ʿĪd* prayer has been performed are considered *Sunnah*. In these two *khuṭbahs* the laws relating to *ṣadaqah al-fiṭr* [at *ʿĪd al-Fiṭr*], *uḍḥiyyah* [at *ʿĪd al-Aḍḥā*] and the *takbīrs* made during the Days of

Tashrīq [from *fajr* on the 9th of Dhu al-Ḥijjah to *ʿaṣr* of the 13th] should be explained [to the assembly of Muslims].

The Sunnah Elements of ʿĪd al-Fiṭr

It is *Sunnah* on the day of *ʿĪd* that one:

1. use a *miswāk*;
2. make *ghusl*;
3. apply scent to the body [males only];
4. put on one's best clothes;
5. eat something [before going to the place where the *ʿĪd* prayer is to be performed];
6. and go to the place of prayer, making *takbīr* silently;
7. give *ṣadaqah al-Fiṭr* just before the *ʿĪd al-Fiṭr* prayer.

The Time of the ʿĪd Prayers

From the time the sun rises high [off the horizon], while still appearing dim to the eye [so that one may look at it without difficulty] to the time it reaches its zenith [at midday] is the time for the two *ʿĪd* prayers. No *adhān* or *iqāmah* is to be given for the *ʿĪd* prayers.

The Description of the ʿĪd Prayer

When performing *ʿĪd* prayer, which consists of two *rakʿats*, one begins with the *takbīr taḥrīmah*, and then the recitation of *thanā* (the opening praise). Then say three extra *takbīrs*, raising one's hands for each *takbīr*, and saying "*Allāhu Akbar*," and dropping them. When three *takbīrs* have been made in this way, one refolds the hands. The *tasmiyah* and *taʿawwudh* are to be read; followed by the *Fātiḥah* and some verses of the Qur'ān which will be read aloud by the imām. The rest of the *rakʿah* will be performed as usual. In the second *rakʿah*, after the recitation and before *rukūʿ*, the one praying is to read three more *takbīrs*, raising the hands for each and dropping them to one's side. Thereafter, one will make *takbīr* for *rukūʿ*. This *takbīr* [the 4th] is essential, *wājib*, to the performance of *ʿĪd* prayer. If it is not made, *sajdah sahw* will have to be made instead.[39]

Making Up the ʿĪd Prayer

There is no make up, *qaḍāʾ*, for either of the *ʿĪd* prayers in the event that one is unable to perform *ʿĪd* prayer with the imām and congregation.

If, for some reason, *ʿĪd al-Fiṭr* prayer cannot be performed on the proper day, it may be performed on the following day, but not after. *ʿĪd al-Aḍḥā*, however, may be performed [when necessary] on any day until the 12th of Dhu al-Ḥijjah.

Conditions Relating Particularly to ʿĪd al-Aḍḥā

ʿĪd al-Aḍḥā is similar to *ʿĪd al-Fiṭr* [in all particulars] except that it is *mustaḥab* after prayer [on *ʿĪd al-Aḍḥā*] to eat of one's own *uḍḥiyah* or sacrifice. It is not permitted to sacrifice before prayer of *ʿĪd al-Aḍḥā*. Another difference [between the two *ʿĪds*] is that [on *ʿĪd al-Aḍḥā*] one should recite one's *takbīrs* aloud when walking to the *ʿĪd* prayer.

Takbīrs of Tashrīq

It is *wājib* for residents [as opposed to travellers] to say the *takbīrs* of *tashrīq* [immediately] after each *farḍ* prayer performed in congregation from the morning of the day of ʿArafah to *ʿaṣr* of the *ʿĪd* day, according to Imām Abū Ḥanīfah. His two companions, however, say that the *takbīrs* should be recited from *fajr* on the day of ʿArafah to *ʿaṣr* of the 13th of Dhu al-Ḥijjah. The *fatwā* in this issue has been given in accordance with the opinion of the Imām's two companions, Imāms Abū Yūsuf and Muḥammad.

If a woman or traveller should perform the *farḍ* prayer on one of those days with a congregation whose imām is resident, then he or she, too, must say the *takbīrs* of *tashrīq*. The *takbīr tashrīq* that one says aloud is as follows:

اللّٰهُ أَكْبَرُ اللّٰهُ أَكْبَرْ لَا إِلَهَ إِلاَّ اللّٰهُ وَاللّٰهُ أَكْبَرْ اللّٰهُ أَكْبَرُ وَلِلّٰهِ الْحَمْدُ.

Allāhu Akbar, Allāhu Akbar, Lā Ilāha Illa'llah, Wallāhu Akbar, Allāhu Akbar, Wa Lillāhil-Ḥamd, (Allāh is most Great, Allāh is most Great. There is no god but Allāh, and Allāh is most Great. Allāh is most Great and for Him is all Praise.)

If the imām forgets to say the *takbīrs* of *tashrīq*, the followers in the congregation should say them anyway.

3.20 Sunnah Prayers

3.20.1 Prayers which are highly recommended – *Sunnah mu'akkadah*[40]

1. two *rak'ats* before *fajr*, reciting *Sūrah Kāfirūn* in the first and *Sūrah Ikhlāṣ* in the second;
2. four *rak'ats* with one *salām* before *ẓuhr* and *jumu'ah*;
3. two *rak'ats* after *ẓuhr*;
4. four *rak'ats* after *jumu'ah*; according to Imām Abū Yūsuf, six *rak'ats* [with two *salāms*] are *Sunnah*;[41]
5. two *rak'ats* after *maghrib*;
6. and two *rak'ats* after *'ishā'*.

3.20.2 Recommended *sunnah* prayers – *Mustaḥab* or *Sunnah ghayr mu'akkadah*[42]

1. it is *mustaḥab* that four *rak'ats* [instead of two] be performed after *ẓuhr* with two *salāms*;
2. before *'aṣr*, either two or four *rak'ats* are *mustaḥab*;
3. after *maghrib*, six *rak'ats* after the two *rak'ats* which are *Sunnah mu'akkadah*, are *mustaḥab*; This is called *Salāt al-Awwābīn*. According to another narration, this prayer is comprised of twenty *rak'ats*.
4. before *'ishā'*, four *rak'ats* are *mustaḥab* and praying another four of the above two *sunnah rak'ats* after *'ishā'* are also *mustaḥab*;
5. and after *witr* prayer, two *rak'ats*, in a sitting position are *mustaḥab*.[43] In the first *rak'ah*, one should recite *Sūrah Idhā Zulzilatl*, and in the second *rak'ah Qul yā ayyuhal kāfirun*.

3.20.3 *Tahajjud* – Night vigil prayer

It is *Sunnah mu'akkadah* to perform *tahajjud.*[44] The Messenger of Allāh, may the peace and blessings of Allāh be upon him, never neglected it. If, on occasion, the prayer went unperformed, he, may the peace and blessings of Allāh be upon him, would make twelve *rak'ats* during the day to make up the prayer.

The *tahajjud* prayer [performed by the Messenger of Allāh, may the peace and blessings of Allāh be upon him, was never less than four and there is no evidence he prayed more than twelve *rak'ats*.

The Messenger of Allāh, may Allāh bless him and grant him peace, used to always perform *witr* prayer after *tahajjud*; and this is the *Sunnah.* Therefore, anyone who can rely on oneself not to miss *tahajjud* in the last part of the night should delay it and pray after *tahajjud*, as that is the best way. However, if one cannot rely on oneself, one should perform *witr* sometime before going to sleep at night, as this is the more prudent way.

The Messenger of Allāh, may the peace and blessings of Allāh be upon him, sometimes performed *tahajjud* with *witr* in seven *rak'ats*, sometimes in eleven *rak'ats*, sometimes thirteen, and sometimes fifteen. He prayed *tahajjud* in units of two and four *rak'ats* while sometimes these *rak'ats* were performed even all at once, with only one *salām.* Sometimes the Messenger of Allāh, may the peace and blessings of Allāh be upon him, would make *wuḍū'*, use his *miswāk* after every two *rak'ats*, after which he would go to sleep; only to awaken later on and perform two more *rak'ats* [and so on until *fajr*].

The Messenger of Allāh, may the peace and blessings of Allāh be upon him, would recite all of *Sūrah al-Baqarah* in the first *rak'ah* and *Sūrah Āl 'Imrān* in the second *rak'ah, Sūrah an-Nisā'* in the third, and *Sūrah al-Mā'idah* in the fourth. His, may Allāh bless him and grant him peace, *rukū'* was consistent with [and not necessarily commensurate to his] *qiyām*; and the same applies to *sajdah, qawmah,* and *jalsah.*

Sometimes the Messenger of Allāh, may the peace and blessings of Allāh be upon him, would recite all four of these *sūrahs* in one *rak'ah*. He stood for so long, sometimes, that his feet became swollen and blistered.

'Uthmān, may Allāh be well pleased with him, once recited the entire Qur'ān in one *rak'ah* of *witr* prayer.[45]

Reciting the Qur'ān Often

[The best remembrance of Allāh is recitation of the Qur'ān.] It is *mustaḥab* to recite each day however much one thinks that one will regularly be able to recite. It is preferable that one recite in a month's time the entire Qur'ān once, twice or three times.

Most Companions of the Prophet, may Allāh be pleased with them, were in the habit of reciting the entire Qur'ān in seven nights, as follows:

- Three *sūrahs* [*Sūrahs al-Baqarah*, *Āl 'Imrān*, and *an-Nisā'* along with *Sūrah al-Fatiḥah*];
- Five *sūrahs* [from *Sūrah al-Mā'idah* to *Sūrah at-Tawbah*];
- Seven *sūrahs* [from *Sūrah Yūnus* to *Sūrah an-Naḥl*];
- Nine *sūrahs* [from *Sūrah Banī Isrā'īl* to *Sūrah al-Furqān*];
- Eleven *sūrahs* [from *Sūrah ash-Shū'arā'* to *Sūrah Yāsīn*];
- Thirteen *sūrahs* [from *Sūrah aṣ-Ṣāffāt* to *Sūrah al-Ḥujurāt*];
- and then [from *Sūrah Qāf*] to the end of the Qur'ān.

The Qur'ān should be read with *tartīl* slowly, with close attention to both proper pronunciation and [most preferably] the meaning too.

3.21 Nafl Ṣalāh – Optional Prayer

3.21.1 *Ṣalāt al-Ishrāq* – Prayer of daybreak

It is *mustaḥab* that after one performs his *fajr* prayer in congregation, he remain engaged in *dhikr* [or *tilāwah*] until the sun has risen above the horizon. At that time, if one performs two *rakʿats* of *nafl* prayer, one will bring blessings upon oneself equivalent to those of one complete *ʿumrah* and one *ḥajj*; and it is related that if one performs four *rakʿats*, in the beginning of his day, Allāh most High will suffice for his every need until sunset of that day. This prayer is called *Ṣalāt al-Ishrāq*.

3.21.2 *Ṣalāt ad-Ḍuḥā* – Prayer of midmorning

When the heat of the sun becomes intense, before the sun reaches its summit, it is related that the Messenger of Allāh, may the peace and blessings of Allāh be upon him, used to perform eight *rakʿats* of *nafl* prayer known as *ḍuḥā* prayer.

It is also related that the Messenger of Allāh, may the peace and blessings of Allāh be upon him, performed four *rakʿats* after midday and before *ẓuhr*.

3.21.3 *Dhikr* between *ʿAṣr* and *Maghrib*

It is also *Sunnah* to remain engaged in the remembrance of Allāh between *ʿaṣr* and *maghrib* prayers.

3.21.4 *Taḥiyyat al-Wuḍūʾ* and *Taḥiyyat al-Masjid*

It is *Sunnah* to perform two *rakʿats* of *nafl* after making *wuḍūʾ*. This prayer is called *Taḥiyyat al-Wuḍūʾ*. It is also *Sunnah* to perform two *rakʿats* of *nafl* upon entering a Masjid. This prayer is called *Taḥiyyat al-Masjid*.

3.21.5 *Tarāwīḥ* prayer

It is *makrūh* to perform *nafl* prayer in congregation; except in the month of Ramaḍān, when it is *Sunnah* to perform twenty *rakʿats* with ten *salāms* [every night after *ʿishāʾ* prayer]. In each *rakʿah* ten *āyats* should be recited so that by the end of the month the entire Qurʾān will have been completed. This is the minimum that should be recited, regardless of how indolent the congregation might be. Yet, if they are desirous, two, three or four *khatms* may be performed.

After every four *rak'ats* the congregation should sit for a period commensurate to that of their standing in prayer and engage themselves in *dhikr*. This is called the *tarāwīḥ* prayer.

After *tarāwīḥ*, *witr* prayer should be performed in congregation. To perform *witr* in congregation at any other time other than Ramaḍān is *makrūh*.

3.21.6 *Ṣalāt al-Istikhārah* – Prayer for Divine Guidance

When one is faced with some important matter, it is *Sunnah* that one make *istikhārah*; by first making *wuḍū'*, and then performing two *rak'ats* of *nafl* prayer. After completion, one then praises Allāh [by reciting the *Fātiḥah*], asking peace and blessings for the Prophet, and then reciting the following *du'a'*:

اللَّهُمَّ إِنِّي أَسْتَخِيرُكَ بِعِلْمِكَ وَأَسْتَقْدِرُكَ بِقُدْرَتِكَ وَأَسْأَلُكَ مِنْ فَضْلِكَ الْعَظِيمِ فَإِنَّكَ تَقْدِرُ وَلاَ أَقْدِرُ وَتَعْلَمُ وَلاَ أَعْلَمُ وَأَنْتَ عَلاَّمُ الْغُيُوبْ. اللَّهُمَّ إِنْ كُنْتَ تَعْلَمُ أَنَّ **هَذَا الأَمْرَ** خَيْرٌ لِي فِي دِينِي وَمَعَاشِي وَعَاقِبَةِ أَمْرِي – فِي عَاجِلِ أَمْرِي وَآجِلِهِ – فَاقْدُرْهُ لِي. وَإِنْ كُنْتَ تَعْلَمُ أَنَّ **هَذَا الأَمْرَ** شَرٌّ لِي فِي دِينِي وَمَعَاشِي وَعَاقِبَةِ أَمْرِي – فِي عَاجِلِ أَمْرِي وَآجِلِهِ – فَاصْرِفْهُ عَنِّي وَاصْرِفْنِي عَنْهُ وَاقْدُرْ لِيَ الْخَيْرَ حَيْثُ كَانَ، ثُمَّ رَضِّنِي بِهِ

Allāhumma! Innī astakhīruka bi'ilmika wa astaqdiruka bi qudratika wa as-aluka min faḍlika'l 'aẓīm. Fa innaka taqdiru wa lā aqdiru wa ta'lamu wa lā a'lamu wa anta 'allāmu'l-ghuyūb. Allāhumma! In kunta ta'lamu anna ***hādha'l-amra*** *khayrun lī fī dīnī wa ma'āshī*

ʿāqibati amrī – fi ʿājili amri wa ʾājilihī – faqduruhu lī wa yassirhu lī thumma bārik lī fīh. Wa in kunta taʿlamu anna ***hādhaʾl-amra*** *sharrun lī fī dīnī wa maʿāshi wa ʿaqibati amrī – fī ʿājili amri wa ʾājilihī – faʾṣrifhu ʿannī waʾṣrifnī ʿanhu waʾqdur liy al-khayra ḥaythu kāna thumma raḍḍnī bih.* (O Allāh, I ask You of Your knowledge, for guidance, for Your Power, and for Your strength – and I ask You of Your excessive generosity. Certainly You are powerful and I am not, and You are knowing and I am not, and You are the Knower of the Unknown. O Allāh! If You know this matter [here the supplicant should substitute for the words "**this matter**" whatever it is specifically that he or she has in mind. For example, "this journey" or, "marriage", etc.] to be good for my religion, my worldly life, my life in the next world, my present state of affairs or my future state, then decree it for me, and make it easy, and bless me in it. And if You know **this matter** to be detrimental to my religion, my worldly life, my life in the next world, my present state of affairs or my future state, then divert it from me, and turn me away from it, and decree for me that which is good, wherever it may be, and then make me pleased with it.)

3.21.7 *Ṣalāt at-Tawbah* – Prayer of Repentance

Whenever one commits an act of wrongdoing, he should hasten [as soon as possible] to make *wuḍūʾ*, and then perform two *rakʿats* of *nafl* prayer. Thereafter he should seek forgiveness from Allāh, and repent of whatever wrong he had committed until he feels genuine remorse at what he had done, and resolves never again to commit that particular wrong.

3.21.8 *Ṣalāt al-Ḥājah* – Prayer to fulfil one's need

Whenever one finds himself in need of something, he should make *wuḍūʾ*, perform two *rakʿats* of *nafl* prayer, invoke the praise of Allāh, read *darūd* for the Messenger of Allāh, may the peace and blessings of Allāh be upon him, and then read the following *duʿa*:

لَا إِلَهَ إِلاَّ اللَّهُ الْحَلِيمُ الْكَرِيمُ، سُبْحَانَ اللَّهِ رَبِّ الْعَرْشِ الْعَظِيمِ، الْحَمْدُ لِلَّهِ رَبِّ الْعَالَمِينَ. اللَّهُمَّ إِنِّي أَسْأَلُكَ مُوجِبَاتِ رَحْمَتِكَ، وَعَزَائِمَ مَغْفِرَتِكَ، وَالْغَنِيمَةَ مِنْ كُلِّ بِرٍّ، وَالسَّلَامَةَ مِنْ كُلِّ إِثْمٍ. أَسْأَلُكَ أَلاَّ تَدَعَ لِي ذَنْبًا إِلاَّ غَفَرْتَهُ، وَلَا هَمًّا إِلاَّ فَرَّجْتَهُ، وَلَا حَاجَةً هِيَ لَكَ رِضًا إِلاَّ قَضَيْتَهَا لِي يَا أَرْحَمَ الرَّاحِمِينَ.

Lā ilāha illa'l-lāhu'l-ḥalīmu'l-karīmu, subḥānā'llāhi rabbi'l-ʿarshi'l ʿaẓīm al-ḥamdu lillāhi rabbi'l ʿālamīn. Allāhumma! Innī as-ʾaluka Mūjibāti raḥmatika wa ʿazā'ima maghfiratika wa'l-ghanīmata min kulli birr, was-salāmata min kulli ithm. As-ʾaluka ʾalla tadaʿ lī dhanban illā ghafartahū wa lā hamman illā farrajtahū Wa lā ḥājatan hiya laka riḍan illā qaḍaytahā li, yā arḥam'ar-rāḥimīn. (There is no god but Allāh, the Clement, the Generous. I celebrate the glory of Allāh, Lord of the Magnificent Throne. All praise be unto Allāh, Lord of the Worlds. I seek of You that which will make certain [for me] Your forgiveness, as well as a share of every virtue and freedom from every offence. Do not leave me a wrong but that You have pardoned it, a worry but that You have relieved me of it, or a need that meets with Your pleasure but that You provide for it. O most Merciful of the merciful!)

3.21.9 *Ṣalāt at-Tasbīḥ*

The 'prayer of *tasbīḥ*' is performed in order that one may gain forgiveness for all one's misdeeds, major and minor, intentional and unintentional, public and private. It is related that the Messenger of Allāh, may the peace and blessings of Allāh be upon him, taught his uncle, ʿAbbās, may Allāh be pleased with him, to make *tasbīḥ* prayer in the following way: four *rakʿats*; in each *rakʿah*, after reciting the Qur'ān, the following *tasbīḥ* is to be read fifteen times:

سُبْحَانَ اللّٰهِ وَالْحَمْدُ لِلّٰهِ وَلَا إِلٰهَ إِلَّا اللّٰهُ وَاللّٰهُ أَكْبَر

Subḥānallāhi, Wal-Ḥamdu Lillāhi, Wa Lā Ilāha Illallāhu, Wallāhu Akbar. (Glory be to Allah, All Praise belongs to Allah, there is no god but Allah and Allah is most Great.)

This *tasbīḥ* is to be read again in *rukū'* ten times, then in *qawmah* ten times, then in *sajdah* ten times, then in *jalsah* ten times, then in the second *sajdah* ten times, and again, finally in the sitting position, *qa'dah,* after the second *sajdah,* ten times. In each *rak'ah,* seventy-five *tasbīḥ* will be read, and in four *rak'ats,* the total will be three hundred *tasbīḥs.*

If at all possible this prayer should be performed once every day, or, if not, then once a week, or once a month, or once a year, or at the very least once in a lifetime.

It is preferable that four of the *musabbiḥāt sūrahs* be recited in the four *rak'ats* of prayer of *tasbīḥ.* These *sūrahs* are seven in number and include *Sūrah Banī Isrā'īl, Sūrah Ḥadīd, Sūrah Ḥashr, Sūrah Ṣaff, Sūrah Jumu'ah, Sūrah Taghābun* and *Sūrah A'lā.*[46]

3.21.10 *Ṣalāt al-Kusūf* – The solar eclipse prayer

At times of solar eclipse it is *Sunnah* for the imām who leads *jumu'ah* prayer [and, according to Imāms Shāfi'ī and Mālik, any imām] to lead two *rak'ats* of prayer. Each *rak'ah,* like any other prayer, will have one *rukū'*; and the recitation should be extended and performed quietly. This recitation, according to Imāms Abū Yūsuf and Muḥammad, should be performed aloud. After the prayer, the congregation should engage themselves in *dhikr* until such time as the sun reappears.

If a congregation cannot be formed, individuals may perform two or four *rak'ats* on their own. As it is also *sunnah* to pray if a lunar eclipse, a wind storm, an earthquake, or some other event of that nature occurred.

3.21.11 *Ṣalāt al-Istisqā'* – The prayer for rain

The Messenger of Allāh, may the peace and blessings of Allāh be upon him, sometimes just made supplication for rain, and sometimes he supplicated for it standing on the *minbar* while delivering a *Jumu'ah* sermon. As 'Umar, may Allāh be pleased with him, came out and just supplicated for it asking forgiveness from Allāh.

Accordingly, Imām Abū Ḥanīfah did not consider prayer [in congregation] to be *Sunnah mu'akkadah* in the supplication for rain, saying instead that the supplication for rain consists of *du'a'* and *istigfār* [but if they performed *salāt*, they can do it individually].

There is, however, a sound *ḥadīth* in which it is recorded that the Messenger of Allāh, may the peace and blessings of Allāh be upon him, came out to the place of *'Īd* prayer [outside the populated area of the city] and performed the prayer with a congregation in his supplication for rain. For this reason Imāms Abū Yūsuf and Muḥammad, and most of the scholars [of *fiqh*] are of the opinion that the imām should lead a congregation of Muslims to a prayer ground outside the city, and there perform with them two *rak'ats* of prayer, reciting aloud in each *rak'ah*.

After the prayer, as in the *'Īd* prayer, two *khuṭbahs* should be offered, and *istighfār*, and a *masnūn du'a'* like the following *du'a'* be recited:

اللَّهُمَّ اسْقِنَا غَيْثًا مُّغِيْثًا، مَرِيْئًا مَّرِيْعًا، نَافِعًا غَيْرَ ضَارٍّ، عَاجِلاً غَيْرَ رَائِثٍ، مُمْرِعَ النَّبَاتْ. اللَّهُمَّ اسْقِ عِبَادَكَ وَبَهَائِمَكَ، وَأَنْزِلْ رَحْمَتَكَ، وَأَحْيِ بَلَدَكَ الْمَيِّتْ.

Allāhumma! Isqinā ghaythan mughīthan marī'an marī'an nāfi'an ghayra ḍārrin 'ājilan ghayra rā'ithin mumri'an-nabāti. Allāhumma! Isqi ibādaka wa bahā'imaka, wa anzil raḥmataka wa aḥyi baladaka'l-mayyit. (Allāh! Give us rain that will help us, that is good and productive, that is useful and not destructive, that will come now and not later, that will fertilize and nourish our crops. Allāh, give rain to Your slaves and Your cattle. Send down Your mercy. Give life to Your land which has become dead.)

Afterwards the imām, no one else, should reverse the fold of his cloak.[47]

3.21.12 *Nafl* prayer once started becomes *wājib*

[The least number of *rakʿah* in *nafl* is two, there is no *nafl ṣalāh* with only one *rakʿah*. Therefore it should be noted that *Farḍ rakʿats* in *nafl* are two]. *Nafl* prayer, once begun, becomes *wājib*. If a *nafl* prayer is spoiled, two *rakʿats* of *qaḍā* will have to be made.[48]

According to Imām Abū Yūsuf, if, in a situation where the intention was for four *rakʿats* of *nafl* prayer, and the prayer should be somehow spoiled before the first *qaʿdah,* four *rakʿats* of *qaḍā* will have to be made.

A similar difference is the case of the one in prayers performing four *rakʿats* of voluntary prayer without reciting in any of them or, in another case, of one's only reciting in one *rakʿah* of the second pair of *rakʿats*.[49]

If the one in [a *nafl*] prayer [of four *rakʿah*] recites:

- in only the first two *rakʿats*;
- or only in the last two *rakʿats*;
- or neglects to recite in one of the first two *rakʿats*;
- or recites in one of the last two *rakʿats*,

then, in each of these four cases, the Imāms agree [though for different reasons] that only two *rakʿats* of *qaḍāʾ* are necessary.

However if the one in prayer recites:

- in only one of the first two *rakʿats*;
- or in one of the first two *rakʿats* and one of the second two;

then, in both cases, according to Imām Muḥammad, one will be responsible for two *rakʿats* of *qaḍāʾ*. According to Imāms Abū

Ḥanīfah and Abū Yūsuf, however, one will have to make four *rakʿats* of *qaḍā'*.[50]

Neglecting to sit in the first *qaʿdah* when the one in prayer intends to perform four *rakʿats* of *nafl* prayer renders the prayer nullified according to Imām Muḥammad. According to Imāms Abū Ḥanīfah and Abū Yūsuf, however, prayer will not be void, but *sajdah sahw* will have to be made in the case where the omission took place unintentionally.[51]

Sitting for Nafl Prayer is Permitted

It is permitted, *jā'iz*, for one to perform voluntary prayer in a sitting position, even when he has the ability to perform it standing and there exists no excuse for him doing so in a sitting position. However, one's performance of the prayer in the sitting position, in the absence of any excuse, will yield only half the blessing of the performance of the same prayer while standing.

It is further permitted for a person who begins his prayer standing to sit [at some point during his performance of the prayer] and complete the prayer from that position. This, however, is *makrūh* unless there is an excuse. It is also permitted to lean up against a wall while performing *nafl* prayer. The *farḍ* prayer must be performed while standing, unless an excuse exists for someone to perform their *farḍ* prayers while sitting.

Nafl Prayer May Be Performed While Mounted

It is permissible to perform *nafl* prayer while mounted on a horse, or camel, or the like, when outside the city limits, by the use of gestures to indicate *rukūʿ* and *sajdah*, regardless of which direction the mount is facing.[52]

Getting Off One's Mount While Praying

If someone starts to perform *nafl* prayer while mounted on the back of a horse, and then dismounts, he will have to complete the prayer standing, making *rukūʿ* and *sajdah* in the usual way. According to Imām Abū Yūsuf, however, one will have to begin again. If one should begin to perform a prayer on the ground, and then mount a horse, his prayer will be rendered null, and he will have to make *qaḍā*. All Imāms are in agreement on this point.

3.22 Sajdah of Tilāwah – Prostration of Recitation

Throughout the Qur'ān there are fourteen such verses of *sajdah* which are well marked in all printed copies. *Sajdah* of *tilāwah*, becomes *wājib* upon whoever recites, hears, or even unintentionally overhears an *āyah* of *sajdah* from the Qur'ān.

The Description of Sajdah of Tilāwah

Sajdah of *tilāwah* is performed in the following way: with the preconditions of prayer [such as purification, etc.], fulfilled, the person on whom the *sajdah tilāwah* has become *wājib* should make *takbīr* and then go into *sajdah* where he will read *tasbīḥs* of prostration. As one lifts his head from *sajdah*, he will again make *takbīr* [and the whole prostration of recitation will be complete]. There is no *taḥrīmah*, *tashahhud*, or *salām* in *sajdah* of *tilawāh*.

Sajdah of Tilāwah During Group Prayer

By the imām's recitation of an *āyah* of *sajdah* it becomes *wājib* for the followers in the congregational prayer to make *sajdah*, even though the imām's recitation is silent. However, the follower in the congregational prayer's recitation of such an *āyah* will not obligate anyone to make prostration. An exception to this rule is the case of a person who happens to overhear the follower in the congregational prayer recite such an *āyah* while passing by [the congregation in which the person is standing. Then the passer-by will have to make a prostration of recitation, and the others praying in the congregation will not]. Similarly, a person's recitation of an *āyah* of *sajdah* in *rukūʿ*, *qawmah, sajdah,* or *jalsah* will not obligate anyone to make *sajdah.*

If the recitation of someone outside of the prayer should be heard by a person praying, one will have to make *sajdah* after completing prayer. If one should make *sajdah* while in prayer, it will not be proper, though the prayer will not become null.[53]

Prostration of the Latecomer to the Group Prayer

If someone hears an imām recite [while leading the prayer] a verse of prostration and then joins in the prayer [behind the same imām, then if one joins] just before the imām makes *sajdah*, one will make *sajdah* when the imām makes it; and if one joins the prayer in the same *rakʿah*, but after the imām has made *sajdah*, then he will not have to make *sajdah* at all. However, if one joins the prayer in a later *rakʿah* [other than the *rakʿah* in which the imām has made *sajdah*], then he will make *sajdah* after completing the prayer, as though he had not joined the prayer with the imām.

Making Up a Prostration of Recitation

The prostration of recitation which becomes *wājib* while one is performing the prayer may not be made up, *qaḍāʾ*, after the prayer [if it is not made during the prayer].[54]

Repetition of a Verse of Prostration

If someone repeats a verse of prostration again and again in one sitting, he will have only to make one *sajdah* which is *wājib*. However, if he changes his sitting place, or reads another *āyah*, he will have to make another *sajdah*. Further, if the sitting place of the one reciting is one, while that of the listener is varied [so that one hears a verse of prostration; even though it be the same *āyah*, in one position, and then shifts and hears it in another] the reciter will have only to make one *sajdah* and the listener two [or as many as were one's positions while listening to the *āyah* of *sajdah*]. This is reversed when the listener remains in one position and the reciter moves about.

If someone recites an *āyah* of *sajdah* outside of the prayer and then, while performing prayer, again recites the same *āyah* and then makes *sajdah* of *tilāwah*, the one *sajdah* will suffice. If, however, after reciting the *āyah* outside of the prayer, one makes *sajdah*, it will become necessary for him to make *sajdah* again if one recites the same *āyah* while performing the prayer.

Omitting a Verse of Prostration Purposely

It is *makrūh* to recite an entire *sūrah* while omitting [to recite of it only] the verse of prostration. To do the opposite, however, is not *makrūh*; though it is preferable that one or two other *āyahs* be recited with the *āyah* of *sajdah*.

It is best, while reciting a verse of prostration in the presence of others, to do so quietly so that *sajdah* does not become *wājib* on them.

Notes

1. Then, according to Imām Aḥmad, a person who does this has in effect renounced Islam. (Trans.)
2. The original shadow is the measure of the shadow as it stood when the sun was at its zenith. It therefore must be taken into account when measuring the length of the shadow. (Trans.)
3. The first third of the night is the best or the *mustaḥab* time for *'ishā'* and up to half of the night is *mubāḥ* and after that until *fajr* is *makrūh*.
4. *Witr* is a prayer that is compulsory, *wājib*, not obligatory, *farḍ*, and will be discussed later in greater detail.
5. There is nothing wrong with her reciting aloud when alone or leading a congregation of women. (Trans.)
6. The conditions (*Shurūṭ*) and pillars (*arkān*) are obligations (*farḍ*) of *salāt*. However, the jurists have called the obligations that precede the actual performance of prayer, such as ritual purity, 'conditions', whereas the obligations that are observed while performing the *salāt* are called pillars

(*arkān*). If one were to omit the performance of the following obligatory elements, one's prayer would be invalid.

7. As the Messenger of Allāh, may the peace and blessings of Allāh be upon him, said, "Whoever has an *imām*, then the recitation of the *imām* will be the recitation for him."

8. To say *salāms* to the right is *wājib* while saying it again to the left is *Sunnah*. (Revs.)

9. The reasons for this difference are attributable to differences in approaches to legal theory, *uṣūl al-fiqh*. (Trans.)

10. The following scenarios are in addition to omissions of and errors in *wājib* elements of the prayer. (Revs.)

11. If the person praying should make *salāms* after two *rakʿats* and suddenly realise that the prayer one intended to make has more than two *rakʿats* [i.e. *ẓuhr*, *ʿaṣr*, *maghrib*, or *ʿishā*], one may resume the prayer and finish the number of *rakʿats* necessary, and then make *sajdah sahw*. This is allowed provided one does not turn one's shoulders away from the *qiblah*, nor converse with anyone before realising one's mistake. (Revs.)

12. If one is in doubt with respect to the amount of *rakʿah* one has prayed, one assumes the least amount of *rakʿats* one is sure about, completes the prayer from this number of *rakʿats*, and then makes *sajdah sahw* at the end of the prayer. (Revs.)

13. In other words, it is *farḍ* that there be a congregation for the five daily prayers; not that it is *farḍ* for everyone to attend it. If no one attends, everyone in the community of the Masjid will be held responsible for non-performance of a *farḍ*. (Trans.)

14. Obviously, the order to thus engage in battle would have to come from an Islamic government. Thus, while the matter is of little relevance to Muslims today, it has to be retained in the translation to give the reader an idea of the importance of congregational prayer. (Trans.)

15. However, in this case, the woman leading the prayer should stand in the middle, parallel to other women praying with her and not ahead of them. *Radd al-Muḥtār*, Vol. I, p. 566.

16. The *fatwā* here is with Imām Abū Ḥanīfah. See Ibn ʿĀbidīn, *Radd al-Muḥtār*, Vol. I, p. 374. (Trans.)

17. It is advisable that the follower should stand some inches behind the imām and make sure that he is not ahead of the imām in any situation. However, if that one person is female she would stand behind the imām in a separate row. (Trans.)

18. The opinion of Imām Abū Yūsuf, and the *fatwā* of most scholars of the *Ḥanafī* school, is that the imām should not make *takbīr* before the *mu'adhdhin* has completed the *iqāmah*. See Ibn ʿĀbidīn, *Radd al-Muḥtār*, Vol. I, p. 322. (Revs.)

    According to authentic *aḥādīth*, the Prophet, may the peace and blessings of Allāh be upon him, and his Companions, may Allāh be pleased with them, used to ensure that the rows were straight and without gaps between the followers before starting the prayer. The majority of *Ḥanafī ʿulamā'*, therefore, give *fatwā* that the imām and the followers should stand for *ṣalāh* before the *iqāmah*. (Azami)

19. If a person joins the group prayer late, when the imām is reciting aloud, one need not read the *thanā*. (Revs.)

20. A woman, in both the first and final *qaʿdah*, should sit with her left buttock on the ground, folding both her legs side by side beneath her so that both feet emerge on her right side.

21. The *fatwā* in the *Ḥanafī* school is on making a gesture. One should lift his index finger on the word *Lā ilāh* and drop it on *illallāh.*

22. In *Sunnah* and *nafl* prayer, however, one reads *bismillāh*, *Sūrah Fātiḥah*, and a *sūrah* or some verses of the Qur'ān. (Revs.)

23. Many such formulas for recitation have been mentioned in the *aḥādīth*. The important thing to note is that they are not part of the prayer and, thus, not essential to the proper performance of prayer. (Trans.)

24. Instead, the four *rakʿats* will be considered *nafl*, *qaḍā'* will have to be made of *ẓuhr*, and afterwards *ʿaṣr* may be performed on time. (Trans.)

25. For example, if one went to sleep at night without making *ʿishā'* and then awoke minutes before the rising of the sun, so that there remained only enough time to perform the scheduled *fajr* prayers, then one may forego the sequential performance of *ʿishā's qaḍā'* and then *fajr*; performing *fajr* directly instead. (Trans.)

26. If one should perform *ʿaṣr* forgetting that one had not performed *ẓuhr*, then one's *ʿaṣr* prayer will be correct and one will be responsible for the *qaḍā'* of *ẓuhr* only. (Trans.)

27. For example, "O Allāh, give me a new pair of shoes." On the other hand, a *duʿa'* for something which only Allāh has the power to grant, like forgiveness, will not nullify prayer. (Trans.)

28. It is better to prompt the imām only when he has recited less than is necessary for prayer. (Trans.)

29. If a person is tired, it is better that one rests. (Trans.)

30. Most of the later *Ḥanafī ʿulamā'* recommended that one simply stand alone, as to do otherwise is likely to cause misunderstandings. (Trans.)

31. In other words, the times of five prayers will have had to pass completely. For example, if a person loses consciousness at 10 a.m. and does not regain it until 11 a.m. the next day, one will not be responsible for *qaḍā*, according to the other Imāms. According to Imām Muḥammad, however, one will be responsible for *qaḍā*'. According to Imām Muḥammad and all the later *Ḥanafī* '*ulamā*', one will have to remain unconscious until the coming of the time of the sixth prayer, [in this case, the beginning of the time of *ẓuhr*] before one will be absolved of the responsibility of making *qaḍā*'. See Ibn 'Ābidīn, *Radd al-Muḥtār*, Vol. I, p. 512. (Trans.)

32. *Fajr* and *maghrib* are to be read as their usual number. Unlike the Shāfi'ī school, it is not permissible in our school to combine the prayers of *ẓuhr* and '*aṣr* in either time or *maghrib* and '*ishā*' in either time. Each prayer must be performed in its respective time and cannot be combined for any excuse such as rain or travelling. Combining prayers is only permissible to the person on *ḥajj* in *iḥrām* at 'Arafāt praying the *ẓuhr* and '*aṣr* prayers in the time of *ẓuhr*, provided he or she performs them with the imām of *ḥajj*. The pilgrim should combine the *maghrib* and '*ishā*' prayers in the time of '*ishā*' in Muzdalifah. However, one on a journey to combine the prayers by delaying the *ẓuhr* prayer so that it is performed just before the time of '*aṣr* comes in is permissible as is delaying *maghrib* until the onset of the time of '*ishā*', since each prayer is performed in its respective time. (Revs.)

33. In other words, such a person may not avail himself of the traveller's license to shorten his prayers. (Trans.)

34. In countries under non-Muslim rule, Muslims may choose one of their members to lead *jumu'ah* prayer. Even in Muslim countries, according to the author of *Jami' al-Rumūz*, if it is not possible to contact the ruler for his permission to hold *jumu'ah*, the prayer may still be held legally. (Trans.)

35. Just the *khaṭīb's* saying, "*Subḥānallāh*," *or* "*Allāhu Akbar*," the condition will be fulfilled. (Trans.)

36. The *fatwā* is with Imām Abū Ḥanīfah. See *Marāqi al-Falāḥ*. (Revs.)

37. Imāms Mālik, Shāfi'ī and Aḥmad consider it *Sunnah* for them to do so. On the question of prisoners holding their own *jumu'ah* prayer, it is evident from the work of later *Ḥanafī* scholars, among them Ibn 'Ābidīn, that there is permission for their doing so. Muftī 'Azīz-ur-Raḥmān of Deoband has indicated his preference for this opinion in the fifth volume of his collected *fatāwā*, page 211. On page 95 of the same volume of *fatāwā*, he writes that it is correct for an outsider to make *jumu'ah* prayer behind an imām who is a prisoner. (Trans.)

38. The *fatwā* is with Imām Abū Ḥanīfah. See *Marāqi al-Falāḥ*. (Revs.)

39. The later scholars of *fiqh* are in agreement that *sajdah sahw* should not be made, for any reason, in '*Īd* prayer, as to do so would lead to great confusion. (Trans.)

40. *Sunnah mu'akkadah* is a classification of prayers which the Prophet, may the peace and blessings of Allāh be upon him, never failed to perform. Neglecting a *Sunnah mu'akkadah* is blameworthy. (Revs.)

41. The *fatwā* here is with Imām Abū Yūsuf. (Trans.)

42. *Sunnah ghayr mu'akkadah* is a category of prayers that the Prophet, may the peace and blessings of Allāh be upon him, performed on occasion. One may pray them or leave them, as one chooses to do so, but there is obvious merit in increasing one's worship. (Revs.)

43. Maulānā Ashraf 'Alī Thānwī pointed this out in a marginal note in his book, *Bahishtī Zewar* that praying even the two *nafl rak'ats* after *witr* prayer standing has greater reward except if one became tired. (Trans.)

44. *Tahajjud* is *Sunnah mu'akkadah* in the sense that the Prophet, may Allāh bless him and grant him peace, never failed to perform it, but the legal status for the Muslims is that it is voluntary or *nafl*. (Revs.)

45. It is narrated that Imām Abū Ḥanīfah used to recite the entire Qur'ān in one *rak'ah* of *tahajjud*. (Trans.)

46. An easier *masnūn* recitation, related by 'Abdullāh ibn 'Abbās, is as follows: *Sūrah Takāthur*, *Sūrah 'Aṣr*, *Sūrah Kāfirūn*, and *Sūrah Ikhlās*. (Trans.)

47. If it was folded over his shoulders from right to left, he should shift it to left to right, etc. (Trans.)

48. There is agreement among the Imāms of the *Ḥanafī* school on this point. Thus, a person who makes intention to perform two *rak'ats* of *nafl* prayer becomes responsible, in the same way that one is responsible for the performance of anything else which is *wājib*, for its completion. If one fails to complete the two *rak'ats* for any reason, it will then be *wājib* that one make *qaḍā'* of the prayer. There is a difference of opinion, however, in the event that one makes intention for four *rak'ats* of voluntary, *nafl*, prayer and then, for some reason, fails to perform them. In order to understand what follows, it will first be necessary for the student to acquaint him or herself with the basic principles underlying the opinions of each Imām:

    (1) according to Imām Abū Yūsuf, if owing to one's omission of recitation, the first two *rak'ats* are spoiled, the *taḥrīmah* or, in other words, the beginning will still hold good, and the second two *rak'ats* may properly be entered into;

    (2) according to Imām Muḥammad, one's omission of recitation in either of the first two *rak'ats* will render the *taḥrīmah* null and void; therefore the second two *rak'ats* may not be properly entered into;

    (3) according to Imām Abū Ḥanīfah, one's omission of recitation in both of the first two *rak'ats* will render the *taḥrīmah* null and void; therefore the second two *rak'ats* may not be properly entered into.

This means that if one were to make four *rak'ats* of voluntary, *nafl*, prayer without reciting in any of them, one would be responsible for *qaḍā'* of only two *rak'ats*, according to Imāms Abū Ḥanīfah and Muḥammad. This is because when the first two *rak'ats* went wrong, the *taḥrīmah* was nullified, and one's starting in on the second pair of *rak'ats* was improper, and thus not to be held against him or her. According to Imām Abū Yūsuf, however, one will have to make *qaḍā'* of all four *rak'ats* because the *taḥrīmah* will not have been nullified by neglecting to recite in the first pair of *rak'ats*. Thus, when one's starting in on the second pair was proper, one's failure to perform them properly makes one responsible for their *qaḍā'*. (Trans.)

49. According to Imām Abū Yūsuf, one will have to make four *rak'ats* of *qaḍā'*. According to Imāms Abū Ḥanīfah and Muḥammad, however, one will be responsible for only two *rak'ats* of *qaḍā'*. The *fatwā* in each case is with Imāms Abū Ḥanīfah and Muḥammad. See Ibn 'Ābidīn, *Radd al-Muḥtār*, Vol. V, pp. 465-466. (Trans.)

50. The *fatwā* here is with Imāms Abū Ḥanīfah and Abū Yūsuf. See Ibn 'Ābidīn, *Radd al-Muḥtār*, Vol. V, pp. 465-466. (Trans.)

51. The *fatwā* here is with Imāms Abū Ḥanīfah and Abū Yūsuf. See Ibn 'Ābidīn, *Radd al-Muḥtār*, Vol. I, p. 341. (Trans.)

52. It should be remembered that the afore-mentioned ruling deals with voluntary prayer only. The performance of *farḍ* prayer while mounted is permitted, according to Imām Abū Ḥanīfah and Imām Shāfi'ī, but only when one is being pursued and fears for one's life. In all other cases it is *ḥarām*.

With regard to prayer on board a ship while at sea, the *Ḥanafī* scholars have written, [and the later *Ḥanafī* scholars have determined that the same holds for prayer performed on board moving trains] that *farḍ* prayer must be performed standing. If it is performed sitting it will be *makrūh*, according to Imām Abū Ḥanīfah, and *ḥarām*, according to his two companions, Imāms Abū Yūsuf and Muḥammad.

Secondly, at the outset of prayer it is necessary to face the direction of the *qiblah*. Then, if the ship should alter its course, the one praying will have to alter position accordingly so that one faces the *qiblah* throughout the prayer. If one fears that by standing one will become dizzy or otherwise injure oneself, one may perform the prayer from a sitting position on the deck, making *rukū'* and *sajdah*. If the place is so crowded that one is unable to make *sajdah*, one must ask those around to make way while one prays. Nor should one be lax in making such a request as most people, regardless of their own religious beliefs, are willing to accommodate others in the performance of their religious duties.

If, finally, the one praying is still unable to make *sajdah*, one may perform one's prayer in the sitting position, gesturing for *rukū'* and *sajdah*. To be on the safe side one should, however, in such a case, repeat the prayer at a more opportune time. The same rules are applicable to a bus, car, or aeroplane;

except that in an aeroplane it is not absolutely necessary to face the *qiblah.* One other difference is that if the air traveller knows that he/she will be on the ground before the time for a certain prayer expires, he/she must delay performing that prayer until he or she is on the ground. This note is based on what I have been able to gather from speaking with my teacher, Muftī Walī Ḥasan Taunkī, of the Legal Office at *Jāmiʿah al-Ulum al-Islāmiyah*, Karachi; and from what my teacher, the Shaikh of *Ḥadīth*, Muḥammad Yūsuf al-Bannurī, may Allāh illumine his resting place, has written in his *Maʿārif as-Sunan*, Vol. 3, pp. 37-39 (a commentary on the collection of *ḥadīth* by Imām Abū ʿIsā known as the *Jāmiʿ at-Tirmidhī*, one of the six major collections of *aḥādīth*). (Trans.)

53. In such a case one will have to make *sajdah* again, after completing the prayer. (Trans.)

54. Either the *sajdah* is made in prayer, or it is not made at all; in which case one becomes guilty of having committed a wrong and should immediately make repentance and seek forgiveness from Allāh. If the one praying forgets to make *sajdah* and then, before completing one's prayer, remembers that one must make a prostration of recitation, one may at that very moment make the *sajdah*, regardless of whether one be in *rukūʿ* or *qaʿdah*, or even *sajdah*, though one will then have to repeat one's *rukūʿ*, or *qaʿdah*, etc., after the prostration of recitation. See ʿĀlamgīrī and other books of *Ḥanafī fiqh* for details.

CHAPTER 4

Janāzah

4.1 Funeral

4.1.1 PREPARATION AND BURIAL OF THE DECEASED

To always remember death and to carry the essentials of a will is *mustaḥab*, and when it seems likely that death is near, to make a will of what one is obliged (like debts etc.) is *wājib*.

It is related in a *ḥadīth* that whoever remembers death twenty times each day will be granted the rank of a *shahīd*.

On the Approach of Death

When death approaches a Muslim, *taqlīn* should be made to remember the *kalimah shahādah.*[1] *Sūrah Yāsīn* should also be read near his head. After someone expires, the mouth and eyes should be closed and, with all possible haste, the body should be prepared for burial.

Prerequisites to Washing the Dead Body

Before washing the body [the table should first be washed and then] burning incense should be passed over it three times. [After placing the body on the table, all jewellery, wigs, false teeth, etc., should be removed.] When the clothes have been removed from the body [facing the *qiblah*] on the table, only the *ʿawrah* remain covered. All actual impurity, *ḥaqīqī najāsah*, should be washed away. Then [if the deceased had reached the age of puberty, or was one on whom prayer was *farḍ* during one's life] the deceased must be given *wuḍū'*, though it is not necessary to rinse the mouth and nostrils.[2] The hair of the beard and head should [without combing] then be washed in water scented with hollyhock or the like. Soap will do if nothing else is available.[3] Thereafter, the body of the deceased should be washed with water in which the leaves of the lote or jujube tree have been boiled [or which has been otherwise organically scented].

Washing the Dead Body

The washing is performed by first turning the body over on its left side and washing the right [from head to toe], and then by turning it onto its right side and washing the left, allowing the water to flow freely over its entirety. Then, after the body has been stroked slowly [downward] and if anything comes out, it is to be washed away. It will not, however, be necessary to repeat the whole process of washing.[4] After towelling the body dry, scent should be applied to the beard and hair, and camphor to those parts of the body which used to come in contact with the ground when making *sajdah*. The body will then be ready to be dressed in *kafan*.

Shrouding the Body

For men, *kafan* in three pieces of [white cloth] is *Sunnah*, according to Imām Abū Ḥanīfah; one, [the shirt, *qamīṣ*] which reaches to halfway down the calf, and two, the *izār* which is wrapped round the waist, and three, the *lifāfah*, which stretch from head to toe. In an authentic *ḥadīth*, it is recorded that the Messenger, may the peace and blessings of Allāh be upon him, was buried in three shrouds and that there was no *qamīṣ*.[5]

If three shrouds are not available it will be enough to use only two for the burial. Ḥamzah, may Allāh be pleased with him, was buried in only one *kafan* which, when it was pulled over his feet, exposed his head. Finally, in accordance with the orders of the Prophet of Allāh, may the peace and blessings of Allāh be upon him, the *kafan* was pulled over his head and grass was used to cover his feet.

The Proper Method of Dressing the Male Deceased

The *masnūn* method of dressing the deceased male in a *kafan* is as follows:

1. spread the three *kafans* on the floor, on top of each other. First the *lifāfah*, then the *izār*, and then the *qamīṣ*;
2. lower the body onto them;
3. fold the *qamīṣ* over the body and remove the cloth used to cover the *ʿawrah* during washing;
4. fold the left flap of the *izār* over the *qamīṣ* and then the right;
5. fold the *lifāfah* in the same way over the *izār*;
6. and finally, close the ends of the *lifāfah* head and foot, by fastening them with strips of cloth. A strip may also be fastened around the middle to keep the *kafan* in place. It is *bidʿah* to dress the deceased in a turban or to write anything on the body or *kafan*.

The Proper Method of Dressing the Female Deceased

For a woman, two more shrouds are required. One, the *khimār* or veil, a scarf-like cloth in which her hair is to be folded and then placed on her breasts; and the other, *sīna-band* or *khirqah* [a piece of cloth] to hold the breasts and cover the torso to the thighs.

If five shrouds are not available, it will be enough to bury her in only three or less.

The *masnūn* method of dressing the deceased female in the *kafan* is as follows:

1. spread the four *kafans*, one on top of the other – first the *lifāfah*, then the *sīna-band*, then the *izār*, then the *qamīṣ* – on the ground, and lower the body onto them;
2. fold the *qamīṣ* over the body, and remove the cloth used to cover the *ʿawrah*;
3. part the hair into two folds, place them over the breasts, then cover the head and hair with the *khimār*, without fastening or folding it;
4. fold the left flap of the *izār* over the *qamīṣ* and *khimār*, and then the right flap;
5. close the *sīna-band* over the *izār* by folding the left flap of the *izār* over the *qamīṣ* and then the right;
6. close the *lifāfah* over the *sīna-band* in the same way as for men;
7. and lastly, close the ends of the *lifāfah*, head and foot, by fastening them with strips of cloth. A strip may also be fastened around the middle to keep the *kafan* in place.

4.1.2 Those responsible for the burial, *ghusl*, and funeral prayer

The *ghusl*, dressing for burial, performance of *janāzah* prayer, and burial, *dafan*, of the Muslim dead are *farḍ kifāyah*.[6]

4.1.3 *Ṣalāt al-Janāzah* – The funeral prayer

Janāzah prayer may not be performed until the body has been properly bathed and prepared for burial as outlined above.

4.1.4 The most suitable *imām*

The sulṭān [or any other kind of Muslim ruler] is the person most entitled to lead the *janāzah* prayer, then a *qāḍī*, then the imām of the local Masjid, then the closest of the deceased's relatives, then the next closest relative. The father of the deceased is more entitled to be the imām than the son.

4.1.5 How the funeral prayer is performed

The funeral prayer is performed while standing and contains no *rukū'*, *sajdah*, or *qa'dah,* and has four *takbīrs.*[7] It is *makrūh* to perform the funeral prayer in a Masjid. The funeral prayer is performed as follows:

1. after the first *takbīr*, the *thanā* (opening praise) should be recited;
   According to Imām Abū Ḥanīfah, it is not prescribed to recite the *Fātiḥah*[8] in the funeral prayer. Most other Imāms, however, prefer that the *Fātiḥah* be recited after the *thanā.*
2. after the second *takbīr* by the imām, *aṣ-Ṣalāt-'alan-Nabī, darūd* is to be recited;
3. after the third *takbīr, du'a'* is to be read by both the Imām and the followers for the deceased and for all Muslims, [one of the *masnūn du'a'* is related in *aḥādīth*] as follows:

اللَّهُمَّ اغْفِرْ لِحَيِّنَا وَمَيِّتِنَا، وَشَاهِدِنَا وَغَائِبِنَا، وَصَغِيْرِنَا وَكَبِيْرِنَا، وَذَكَرِنَا وَأُنْثَانَا، اللَّهُمَّ مَنْ أَحْيَيْتَهُ مِنَّا فَأَحْيِهِ عَلَى الْإِسْلَامِ، وَمَنْ تَوَفَّيْتَهُ مِنَّا فَتَوَفَّهُ عَلَى الْإِيمَانِ.

Allāhumma'ghfir li ḥayyinā wa mayyitinā wa shāhidinā wa ghā'ibinā wa ṣaghīrinā wa kabīrinā wa dhakarinā wa unthānā. Allāhumma! Man aḥyaytahū minnā fa aḥyihī 'ala'l islam, wa man tawaffaytahū minnā fa tawaffahū 'alal 'īmān. (O Allāh, forgive us, our living and our dead, our present and our absent, our young and our old, our men and our women. O Allāh! Whomsoever of us You keep alive, let him live in Islam; and whomsoever You cause to die, let him die with faith, *imān.*)[9]

At the funeral of a child, the following *du'a'* may be read after the third *takbīr:*

اللَّهُمَّ اجْعَلْهُ لَنَا فَرَطًا، وَاجْعَلْهُ لَنَا أَجْرًا وَذُخْرًا، وَاجْعَلْهُ لَنَا شَافِعًا وَمُشَفَّعًا.

Allāhumma: (I)j'alhu lanā faraṭa(n)w waj'alhu lanā ajra(n)w wa dhukhra(n)w waj'alhu lanā shāfi'a(n)w wa mushaffa'ā. (O Allāh, make him or her a source of our salvation, and make him or her a reward and treasure for us, and make him or her an intercessor for us, and one whose intercession is accepted.)

4. after the fourth *takbīr*, the imām and the followers in the congregation will [twice; once to the right, and once to the left] say, "*Asalāmu 'Alaikum Wa Raḥmatullāh.*"

The followers in the congregation will make their *salāms* silently. [It is improper to continue standing for the purpose of making *du'a'* after the funeral prayer].

It is not permitted to perform the funeral prayer while mounted on the back of a horse.[10]

It is not permitted to make the funeral prayer for someone not present, or for someone who has been dismembered to the extent that only less than half of their body is present.[11]

If the deceased is buried without having had the funeral prayer performed, the *janāzah* prayer may be performed at his grave at any time until three days from the time of burial. After three days the performance of *janāzah* prayer is forbidden, according to Imām Abū Ḥanīfah, may Allāh have mercy on him. As to the narration that the Prophet, may the peace and blessings of Allāh be upon him, before his death performed the *Janāzah* prayer for the martyrs of the Uḥud battle seven years after the event; this may be a special rule for martyrs because their bodies do not rot.

4.1.6 Latecomers to the funeral prayer

Anyone arriving after the imām has begun [the funeral prayer by] reciting [one or more] *takbīrs* should wait until the imām next recites a *takbīr*, and then join in the prayer behind him. After the imām makes the *salām*, the latecomer may make up whatever *takbīrs* he missed [by saying, "*Allāhu Akbar,*" for each one missed]. According to Imām Abū Yūsuf, the latecomer need not wait for the imām's *takbīr* before joining in, but may, like the person who misses the imām's *taḥrīmah* in one of the five daily *farḍ* prayers, join in whenever he arrives.[12]

4.1.7 The funeral prayer of a child

Janāzah prayer may be performed for a child who, at his or her birth, cries out loud [or shows any sign of life and then dies]; but not for a child who makes no sound at birth.[13]

A child taken prisoner in non-Muslim enemy territory without its mother or father, or whose mother or father [either of them] has become Muslim, or who himself, being of sound mind, accepts Islam; if this child should die, he or she will be eligible to have *janāzah* prayer performed for him.

4.1.8 The burial

It is *Sunnah* that four persons carry the coffin, and that they do so at a moderate pace [neither running nor lag behind], and that those accompanying the coffin to the graveyard walk behind it [making *dhikr* all the while], and that they do not sit until the coffin has been placed in the ground.

In the grave [dug to a depth roughly equal to the height of the deceased] a *laḥd* should be made.[14] The deceased should be lowered into the grave from the *qiblah* side. At that time the words, "*Bismillāhi Wa ʿAlā Millati Rasūlillāh,*" should be recited aloud. The body should be placed [on its right side] facing the *qiblah.*

When a woman is being lowered into her grave, she [and those burying her] should be covered [or screened from the sight of others].[15] Then, after covering the *laḥd*, with either unbaked bricks or bamboo [or the *shiq* with cut planks of wood or bamboo], the grave should be filled with earth and covered over by a mound the shape of a camel's hump [no more than 25-30 cm].[16]

It is *makrūh* to use baked bricks, sticks, or lime in the grave.

Graves

The lofty domes constructed over the graves of pious Muslims, and the lamps kept burning over their graves, and the many other abuses of this nature which are prevalent among Muslims are all *makrūh*, or *ḥarām*.[17]

4.2 *Shahīd – The Martyr*

Anyone killed at the hands of the disbelieving enemies of Islam in *jihād*, or at the hands of those in revolt against the *Khalīfah*, or by highway robbers, or who was the victim of another Muslim's injustice, or was otherwise found dead on the battlefield of *jihād*, will be a *shahīd* if the following conditions are met:

1. one's death must not have been the result of a case in which blood money was sufficient as punishment for the murder according to Islamic law;[18]
2. one must not have been a minor, insane, in the state of impurity, or a woman in her period;
3. one must not have consumed any food or drink, slept or talked excessively, received any medication, engaged in buying and selling, or bequeathed anything, from the time one was wounded to the time one expired;
4. and from the time one was wounded until the time one died, another prayer must not become *farḍ* upon that individual.[19] [One's performance or non-performance of the prayer in this case will be of no consequence whatsoever.]

If these conditions are not met, and the person was killed unjustly [martyred], in spite of the fact that he will receive the reward of a *shahīd* in the next world, the body must be given *ghusl* and prepared for burial in the usual manner.

The *shahīd*, however, must not be given a *ghusl* [nor even have the blood washed from the wounds], and must be buried in the clothes in which the *shahīd* died. Then the *janāzah* prayer may be performed over the body [before the burial, and in spite of the fact that the body has not been prepared for burial in the usual way].

A person killed in *qiṣāṣ* or *ḥadd* [legally executed by order of the *qaḍī* for crimes committed] is not a *shahīd.* Such a person will be given a *ghusl*, however, and have *janāzah* prayer read over the body.

A highway robber or rebel who is executed for their crimes is to be given a *ghusl* [and prepared for burial in the usual way], but is not to have *janāzah* prayer read over the body.[20]

4.3 Period of Mourning

4.3.1 Period of mourning for the widow

When a woman is widowed it becomes necessary that she observe a mourning period, *ma'tam*, of four months and ten days.

During this period she may not beautify herself by wearing bright colours like saffron or yellow. She may not use scents, oils, eye makeup, *koḥl*, or *ḥennā* unless she has an excuse for doing so. Nor may she leave the house of her husband, except when necessary [to do her daily shopping, or earn her daily bread]. She must spend the nights in her husband's house as well, unless she is evicted, or the house burns down, or she fears for her life or wealth.[21]

4.3.2 Period of mourning for all other relations

If a relative or person other than a woman's husband should die, it is *ḥarām* to observe *ma'tam* for more than three days.

4.3.3 How one may show grief

It is permitted to show grief in one's heart, and to shed tears over the deceased. However, the [deliberate] raising of one's voice when crying, wailing, *nawḥah*, over the dead, tearing one's clothes, and the beating of oneself about the face and head, are all *ḥarām.*

There are a good number of authentic, *ṣaḥīh aḥādīth* which indicate clearly that the deceased is made to suffer [in the grave] as a result of his family's excesses in mourning for him.[22] Concerning this matter, the *'ulamā'* hold various opinions. In the opinion of this humble author, the most tenable of those opinions is the one which holds that a person who in his lifetime made a habit of such excesses, or who left instructions in his will that he be mourned in such a way, or who would have been pleased by his family doing so, or who knew before passing away that his family would go to excesses in their mourning for him but who [in spite of this knowledge] refused to [do or say anything to] prevent them; in all of these cases the deceased will be punished in the grave if his family goes to excesses in mourning for him. Otherwise, a Muslim is not punished for the deeds of others.

4.4 *Easing the Family of the Deceased's Hardship*

It is *Sunnah* to send food to the family of the deceased on the day of their affliction [as they, in their grief, and their engagement in the matters of preparing the body, and *janāzah*, will probably not have had time to prepare food for themselves].

It is *Sunnah*, when afflicted by calamity, to first read the following verse from the Qur'ān: "*Innā lillāhi Wa innā ilaihi rāji'ūn,* إِنَّا لِلَّهِ وَإِنَّا إِلَيْهِ رَاجِعُونَ," (Surely we belong to Allāh, and unto Him we return [*al-Baqarah* 2: 106]), and then practise patience.

4.5 *Visiting the Graveyard*

It is lawful for men, not for women, to visit graveyards.[23]

It is *Sunnah* when visiting the graveyard to read the following *du'a'*:

السَّلَامُ عَلَيْكُمْ أَهْلَ الدِّيَارِ مِنَ الْمُؤْمِنِينَ وَالْمُسْلِمِينَ ، أَنْتُمْ لَنَا سَلَفٌ، وَنَحْنُ لَكُمْ تَبَعٌ، وَإِنَّا إِنْ شَاءَ اللَّهُ بِكُمْ لَاحِقُونَ. يَرْحَمُ اللَّهُ الْمُسْتَقْدِمِينَ مِنَّا وَالْمُسْتَأْخِرِينَ. أَسْأَلُ اللَّهَ لَنَا وَلَكُمُ الْعَافِيَةَ، يَغْفِرُ اللّٰهُ لَنَا وَلَكُمْ.

"As-salāmu ʿalaikum ahlaʾd-diyāri minal-muʾminīna wal-muslimīn. Antum lanā salafun wa naḥnu lakūm tabaʿun. Wa innā inshāʾ ʾallāhu bikum lāḥiqūn. Yarḥamullāhuʾl mustaqdimīna minnā waʾl mustaʾkhirīn. Asʾalullāha lanā wa lakumul ʿāfiyah. Yaghfiruʾllāhu lanā wa lakum." (Peace be upon you, O people of this dwelling from among the believers and Muslims. You are our predecessors and we are your followers. If Allāh wills, we shall join you. May Allāh have mercy on both earlier and latecomers. I pray to Allāh, for our sake and for yours, that He may protect us from His torture and wrath and that He may forgive us and have mercy on us.)

4.6 Acquiring Blessings for the Deceased

Most scholars have agreed that if a person performs an act of devotion, *ʿibādah*, be it monetary like *ṣadaqah* or bodily [like *nafl* prayer or fast], with the intention of having the blessings of that act go to the deceased, then the blessings will indeed reach the deceased.

It has been related on the authority of ʿAlī, may Allāh be pleased with him, that the Messenger of Allāh, may the peace and blessings of Allāh be upon him, said that whoever passes by a graveyard of Muslims and reads *Sūrah Ikhlāṣ* eleven times as a prayer of blessings for the deceased therein, will receive the blessings equal to those received by those who are buried there.

It has been related on the authority of Abū Hurayrah, may Allāh be pleased with him, that the Messenger of Allāh, may the peace and blessings of Allāh be upon him, said that whoever recites *Sūrahs Fātiḥah*, *Ikhlāṣ*, and *Takāthur* for the benefit of the deceased, will in turn receive the intercession [on the Day of Judgement] of those buried there.

Anas, may Allāh be pleased with him, related a *ḥadīth* of the Messenger of Allāh, may the peace and blessings of Allāh be upon him, in which it is stated that whenever anyone recites *Sūrah Yā Sīn* at the graveyard for those buried there, Allāh will cause their torment to be lessened; and the one who recites it will be given a reward proportionate to the number of the dead who are buried there.

4.7 It is Forbidden to Worship at Graves

It is *ḥarām* to make *sajdah* to the graves of prophets and saints, to make *ṭawāf* [circumambulation] around a grave, to make *du'a'* to someone in the grave [thinking him directly responsible for the answer to one's prayers], or to make offerings to the inhabitants of graves [for their supposed 'help' in answering one's prayers]. In fact, these are things which lead straight to *kufr*. The Messenger of Allāh, may the peace and blessings of Allāh be upon him, cursed the people who do such things and forbade the *Ummah* from doing them, and ordered us not to make his grave an idol.

Notes

1. The *kalimah* should be chanted aloud before him by those present in such a manner that the dying Muslim will automatically take up the same chant, and thus leave this world with the *kalimah* on his lips. No attempt, however, should be made to force the person to recite the *kalimah*. One's response at such a moment might be irrational or, Allāh forbid, even contrary. A tactful

and unhurried chanting of the *kalimah*, called *talqīn*, is more likely to produce the desired result. (Trans.)

2. A moist cloth may be used to clean these organs. However, if a person died in a state of *janābah*, *ḥayḍ*, or *nifās*, the mouth and nostrils should be rinsed out with water. (Trans.)
3. The fingernails or hair of the deceased must not be trimmed. (Trans.)
4. At this point it is recommended that camphor water be poured over the body three times. (Trans.)
5. This *ḥadīth* was related by 'Ā'ishah, may Allāh be pleased with her, and was adduced by Imām Shāfi'ī as evidence for the use of three shrouds of equal size. Another *ḥadīth* was related by Ibn 'Abbās in which he states that the Messenger, may the peace and blessings of Allāh be upon him, was buried in three shrouds, one of which was a *qamīṣ*. For a number of reasons, among them the fact that Ibn 'Abbās, as a male relative, had access to the burial preparations whereas 'Ā'ishah did not, the *Ḥanafī 'ulamā'* have preferred the *ḥadīth* of Ibn 'Abbās, and thus considered the *qamīṣ* to be *Sunnah*. (Trans.)
6. In other words, while it is not essential that every Muslim perform these services for the dead, it is essential that some of them do so. If no one does, then everyone will be held responsible for the non-performance of a *farḍ*.
7. According to the *Ḥanafī 'ulamā'*, when making *takbīr* for the funeral prayer, one only raises the hands up for the first *takbīr* [which is the opening *takbīr*] and not for the remaining three. According to Imām Shāfi'ī, one raises the hands at each *takbīr*. (Revs.)
8. One may read *Sūrah al-Fātiḥah* by the intention of *du'a'*, but not as a prescribed recitation as in other regular prayers.
9. The person who has not learned this *du'a'*, or any of the other *masnūn du'a'* which may be read on this occasion, may instead read the *Fātiḥah* with the intention of *du'a'*.
10. Nor on any other animal (or carriage), unless there is a good reason for it. The same applies to performing it in a sitting position. (Trans.)
11. And, for that matter, all of the body but not the head. (Trans.)
12. The latecomer will then have to make up whatever *takbīrs* one missed. The *fatwā* here is with Imām Abū Yūsuf. (Trans.)
13. The child, however, should be given a *ghusl*, wrapped in cloth, and buried. (Trans.)
14. A *laḥd* is a wedge-shaped recess at the floor of the grave in the *qiblah* side which runs the entire length of the grave and which is not visible from directly above. In cross-section it looks like a boot. Where the ground is not firm enough to allow the construction of a *laḥd*, a *shiq* may be dug instead.

A *shiq* is no more than a shallow trench running length-wise along the floor of the grave. (Trans.)

15. Close relatives, for example, may stand at the periphery and hold up sheets. (Trans.)

16. It is *Sunnah* to toss three handfuls of earth onto the grave when beginning to fill it, saying with the first toss, "*Min hā Khalaqnā kum*," [from it We created you]. With the second toss one says, "*Wa Fīhā Nuʿīdu Kum*," [unto it We return you]. And with the third toss, "*Wa Min hā Nukhriju Kum Tāratan Ukhrā*," [and from it We shall bring you out again]. (Trans.)

17. If anyone has any doubts about abuses of this nature, one should discuss the matter with the *ʿulamāʾ* of one's community. (Trans.)

18. For example, he was killed by mistake or by such a means which does not usually result in death. In this case the person will be rewarded as a *shahīd* but will not be considered among those martyrs who are exempt from *ghusl* before burial. (Trans.)

19. For example, a man who is wounded at 11 a.m. and then dies at 4 p.m. from his wounds would not legally be a *shahīd* even if all the other requirements have been satisfied, because while he was wounded another prayer, *ẓuhr*, became *farḍ* upon him. (Trans.)

20. As crimes of which such people are guilty are crimes against society, the punishment meted out is accordingly severe and of an exemplary nature. For this reason they are deprived of the blessings of *janāzah* prayer even though, as Muslims, they are entitled to it. According to many *Ḥanafī* great scholars *ghusl* should also not be given to such people. The suicide victim is also deserving of *janāzah* prayer. It is recommended, however, that people of importance, learning, and piety do not attend, as a sign to others that suicide is a very serious wrong and one that is hateful both to Allāh and society. (Trans.)

21. In each of these cases she is allowed to take accommodation elsewhere. The practice of confining a widow to her room for the duration of her waiting period, *ʿiddah,* is inhuman and without foundation in the *Sharīʿah* of Islam. (Trans.)

22. Some of those excesses were mentioned above. (Trans.)

23. Near the beginning of his prophetic mission, the Messenger of Allāh, may the peace and blessings of Allāh be upon him, prohibited the Muslims from visiting their graveyards. This was done in order to ensure that the Muslims would no longer have anything to do with the pagan customs practised then with regard to burial and the dead. However, once the community had been educated in the ways of Islam, permission was given to visit the graveyards.

    The Imāms of *ḥadīth,* Ibn Mājah, Muslim, and Ḥākim have all related that the Prophet, may the peace and blessings of Allāh be upon him, said,

"I had prohibited you from visiting the graveyard. But now, listen, you may go and visit."

The use of the masculine pronoun, you, in the last sentence of this *ḥadīth* prompted certain scholars to conclude that the prohibition was lifted for men only, and that women have never been given permission to visit the graveyard. This, however, is most unlikely as the use of the second person plural masculine pronoun to include both men and women is quite common in the classical Arabic language. Indeed, the best example of this particular grammatical usage is the Qur'ān itself.

Furthermore, the evidence of the *ḥadīth* does not support this claim. 'Ā'ishah, may Allāh be pleased with her, is mentioned in a number of authentic *aḥādīth* as asking the Prophet, may the peace and blessings of Allāh be upon him, about the proper *du'a'* to be read when visiting the graveyard. Obviously, if the prohibition had still been in effect, she would have had no need to ask about that particular *du'a'*.

In the *Iṣābah* by Ḥāfiz ibn Ḥajar it is related that when 'Ā'ishah's brother 'Abd ar-Raḥmān died, she went and visited his grave. Had there not been permission to do so, she clearly would not have gone there.

A *ḥadīth* related by Imām Ḥākim has it that Fāṭimah used to visit the grave of Ḥamzah, her father's uncle, may Allāh be pleased with them, every *Jumu'ah*.

Based on the evidence of these and other *ḥadīth*, most scholars are of the opinion that women may visit the graveyard as long as they are able to retain their composure, are properly covered, and are accompanied by one or more of their menfolk. And Allāh knows best. (Trans.)

CHAPTER 5

Zakāh

5.1 Purification of One's Wealth

5.1.1 PAYMENT OF *ZAKĀH*

The second of Islām's five Pillars [after *īmān*] is *zakāh*. After the passing away of the Messenger of Allāh, may the peace and blessings of Allāh be upon him, certain Arabian tribes revolted, deciding to withhold payment of *zakāh*. The *Khalīfah*, Abū Bakr, may Allāh be pleased with him, ordered, with the consensus of the Companions, a *jihād* against the withholders.[1]

A person who denies the necessity of paying *zakāh* is a *kāfir*.[2] However, a person who [while acknowledging the necessity of doing so] does not pay his *zakāh*, [out of negligence or parsimony] is a *fāsiq* or wrongdoer [and must repent of his wrong].

5.1.2 WHO MUST PAY *ZAKĀH*

Zakāh becomes obligatory when the following conditions are met:

1. being in a state of Islam. [*Zakāh* is not obligatory on the wealth owned by non-Muslims living in a Muslim country. Rather, they will pay *jizyah*, a protection tax];

2. Maturity;
3. Sanity; *Zakāh* is not *wājib* on the *niṣāb* possessed by children or the insane, according to Imām Abū Ḥanīfah. According to the other Imāms, Mālik, Shāfiʿī, and Aḥmad, it is *wājib*, and must be paid for by their parents or guardians.
4. Possession of a *niṣāb* [a sum of wealth large enough to require the possessor to pay *zakāh* on it] from which all debts and essentials [like food, clothing, and shelter] have been deducted, which is capable of growth [either actual growth, as in cattle, merchandise or fiscal growth, as in capital investments or being in possession of gold or silver and he or his agent is able to invest it for growth];
5. And the *niṣāb's* having been in one's possession for a full [lunar] year.[3]

5.1.3 Conditions for the payment of *zakāh* to be valid*

The following conditions must exist for one's payment of *zakāh* to be considered valid:

1. To be in a state of Islam;
2. To give *zakāh* to the prescribed recipients;
3. Sanity;
4. Maturity;
5. To make the recipient the rightful owner of the *zakāh* money;
6. And the intention to give one's wealth as *zakāh*.

Making intention at either the time of giving *zakāh* or when separating that which is going to be used for *zakāh* from one's other wealth is a condition [essential to the proper performance of the act of giving *zakāh*].

If, without making intention for *zakāh*, one gives all his wealth in *ṣadaqah*, then the obligation for him to give *zakāh* [on that wealth]

* Conditions 1-5 have been added by the revisers from *Marāqi al-Falāḥ*.

will cease. If, however, one gives only a portion of his wealth in *ṣadaqah*, then, according to Imām Abū Yūsuf, the obligation will not cease. According to Imām Muḥammad, whatever percentage of one's wealth was given away in *ṣadaqah* will be deducted accordingly from the *zakāh* he had to pay.[4]

5.2 Wealth Capable of Growth

The wealth capable of increase on which *zakāh* is *wājib* is of three kinds:

1. *Naqd* (ready wealth), Gold and Silver;
2. *'Urūḍ tijārah* (Trading Property);
3. *Sawā'im* (Livestock).

Naqd

Gold and silver, regardless of whether it be stamped into coins, newly-mined nuggets, crafted into jewellery, or used in plating on vessels [or utensils].[5] The amount of *zakāh* due on these two types of wealth is a 1/40 part of the total [or 2.5%].

The *niṣāb* for gold is 20 *mithqāls*, [where each *mithqāl* equals about 4.5-5.0 grams; or in other words, around 90-100 grams of gold] and the *niṣāb* for silver is 200 *dirhams* or 140 *mithqāls* [which is about 630-700 grams of silver].

If there should be less gold than the amount of the *niṣāb*, or less silver then, according to Imām Abū Ḥanīfah, the two may be resolved into one *niṣāb* by a general valuation of both, while having regard for the welfare of the poor.[6]

As according to Imāms Abū Yūsuf and Muḥammad, the completion of a *niṣāb*, in this case, must be on the basis of amounts of gold and silver combined, and not their general valuation.

Therefore, it will be necessary to pay *zakāh* on [the combination of] 100 *dirhams* of silver and 10 *mithqāls* of gold according to all of them.[7] However, if there are 100 *dirhams* of silver and only 5 *mithqāls* of gold, *zakāh* will have to be paid only if the total value of the two exceeds the *niṣāb* of either according to Imām Abū Ḥanīfah while according to Imāms Abū Yūsuf and Muḥammad, *zakāh* will not be paid in this case as not even the total value of both reaches the price of *niṣāb* of either.

If gold or silver is alloyed [with another metal, or is plated over another metal], then when the gold or silver is dominant, the item will be accounted as gold or silver; and when the alloys prevail, the item will be accounted as *ʿurūḍ*, goods (general) property.

ʿUrūḍ Tijārah – Trading Property

All wealth purchased with the intention of using it in trade is subject to *zakāh* at a rate of 2.5%, which is *wājib*.

The *niṣāb* for trading goods is the value of the trading goods equal to or exceeding the *niṣāb* value for gold or silver.

If someone receives wealth as a gift, or through another's *waṣīyyah* (bequest), or if a woman should receive in *mahr*, a dowry, or if a man should receive for *khulaʿ*[8] or in lieu of *qiṣāṣ* (retaliation) and, in each of these cases if the recipient should intend at the moment of receipt to use the wealth in trade, then, according to Imām Abū Yūsuf, *zakāh* will be *wājib* on that wealth; while according to Imām Muḥammad, it will not be *wājib* until such a time as the recipient actually begins to trade with that property.[9]

If someone should receive property through *mirāth* (inheritance), it is agreed by all that even if the recipient should intend when receiving the money to use it in trade, it will not be considered trading property, and one will not have to pay *zakāh* on it [until the recipient actually begins to trade with that property].

ʿUrūḍ tijārah may be combined with gold or silver [to make one *niṣāb* from them all] while having regard [in the manner explained above] for the poor. When the value exceeds the *niṣāb* of one of the constituent items [gold or silver], 2.5% will be due in *zakāh*.

Sawā'im – Livestock

This includes camels, oxen, and goats, male and female, which spend most of the year grazing in pasture [and are fed, therefore, on forage for less than half the year].

The explanation of what constitutes a *niṣāb* in the case of each species of livestock and of how much is to be levied on each is a lengthy matter, and in this region this kind of wealth is generally not of such a quantity as to require that *zakāh* be paid on it. Therefore, the various legal questions dealing with livestock need not be mentioned here.[10]

'Ushr on Farm Produce

Similarly, the laws dealing with the *zakāh* (*'ushr*) on farm produce,[11] details of these need not be mentioned in this little book.[12]

5.3 *Those Eligible for Zakāh*

The following categories are of those who are eligible to receive *zakāh*:

5.3.1 *Faqīr* – Needy person

Any person possessing less than a *niṣāb*, [in other words, a person who himself does not have to pay *zakāh* is a poor person].

5.3.2 *Miskīn* – The destitute and helpless

Any person who possesses nothing aside from a few basic necessities of his own is destitute and helpless.

5.3.3 *Madyūn* – The one in debt

A person who, though in possession of a *niṣāb*, has debts in excess of the amount of the *niṣāb*.

5.3.4 *Ghāzī* – Soldier of Islam in whatever capacity

One who has not the means to purchase equipment with which to do battle for the sake of Allāh.

5.3.5 *Musāfir* – Traveller

Any person who possesses wealth in his or her own country, but who is on a journey and finds oneself far from home without any means of support.

5.4 Division of Zakāh

Zakāh money may be spent entirely on only one of these categories, or distributed among them all equally. [It is permissible not to inform a recipient that they are being given *zakāh*]. The intention, however, to give the money as *zakāh* must exist.

5.4.1 To whom *zakāh* must not be given

One paying the *zakāh* may not give it to one's [near relatives]; neither one's elders, nor offspring.[13] This includes husbands and wives. Nor may one give it to a *kāfir* or a member of the family of the Banī Hāshim, [the family of 'Alī, 'Abbās, Ja'far, 'Aqīl, and Ḥārith ibn 'Abdul Muṭṭalib]. One may, however, give them charity, *ṣadaqah*. Furthermore, one may not spend it on the construction of a Masjid [or of a bridge, well, road, or canal], or on the burial of a dead person, or on repayment of the debts of a dead person, or on the [dependent] son of a rich man.

5.4.2 Giving *zakāh* to an undeserving recipient unknowingly

If a person gives *zakāh* to someone, thinking they are eligible to receive it, and then comes to find out that one is [not eligible, being] a *kāfir* a rich man, Ḥāshimī, or one's immediate relative [as explained above], then according to Imām Abū Ḥanīfah [and Imām Muḥammad], it will not be necessary to pay *zakāh* again. According to Imām Abū Yūsuf he must pay *zakāh* again.

5.5 *Proper Amounts to Give to Recipients of Zakāh*

It is *mustaḥab* to give the needy, *faqīr*, only that amount of money which [being enough to provide for one's essentials] will relieve one from begging for at least a day.

It is *makrūh* to give [in payment of *zakāh*] the amount of a *niṣāb* or more to only one *faqīr* who is not in debt[14] [or to only one of any of the other above-mentioned eligible], and for the inhabitants of one city to send *zakāh* to an inhabitant of another city, unless they be a relative or more deserving than the local eligible.

5.5.1 Paying *zakāh* early

If, after becoming the possessor of a *niṣāb*, someone wants to pay one's *zakāh* [on it], even though the *niṣāb* has not been in one's possession for a year, [then one may pay it, and] one's *zakāh* will be considered to have been paid in full for that year. Likewise if one paid *zakāh* in advance for more than one year his payment is correct.

5.5.2 Paying *zakāh* before possessing a *niṣāb*

If a person possessing one *niṣāb* should pay *zakāh* for a number of *niṣābs* and then come into possession of that same number of *niṣābs*, then his *zakāh* will be considered to have been paid in full.

5.5.3 FLUCTUATING *NIṢĀB*

If at the beginning and the end of the year one is in possession of a full *niṣāb*, even though at times during the year the amount possessed falls short of the *niṣāb*, *zakāh* will have to be given [as if] for a complete year; the mid-year shortage notwithstanding.

5.6 Finding Mines of Precious Metals

If a Muslim or a non-Muslim subject finds, in the desert [or on any remote tract of land], a mine of gold, silver, iron, copper, or the like, then 1/5 of one's find will be taken as *zakāh* and the remaining 4/5 will become the property of the finder, if the land is ownerless. If there is an owner, however, the remaining 4/5 will go to the owner. If it is discovered in the finder's own home, then, according to Imām Abū Ḥanīfah, one will not have to pay [in *zakāh*] a 1/5 [part of one's find]. According to Imāms Abū Yūsuf and Muḥammad, however, it is *wājib* that one pays 1/5.[15] The position, when one finds a mine in one's own farmland, there are two contrary rulings given.[16]

5.6.1 *ZAKĀH* ON FOUND TREASURE

If a treasure is found bearing the markings of Islām, like currency marked with the *kalimah*, etc., it will be given the ruling of *luqṭah*, a lost property which is picked up, and its owner should be sought out.[17] If, however, the treasure bears the mark of *kufr* [like currency marked with a pyramid with an eye in it, etc.] then 1/5 will be taken and the remaining 4/5 will become the possession of the finder.

5.7 Zakāh on an Outstanding Claim

The *zakāh* on an outstanding claim is to be paid as soon as it is collected.[18]

When payment of a claim in exchange for merchandise is received, *zakāh* must be given if the payment exceeds forty *dirhams* [at the rate of one for every forty]. If the claim be for wealth other than merchandise, like the price of something which was usurped, then its *zakāh* will be paid only if the amount received exceeds the *niṣāb*. If the claim is in exchange for something other than wealth, like dowry, *mahr*, or *khulaʿ* then *zakāh* will have to be paid after the passing of a year if the amount received exceeds the *niṣāb*, according to Imām Abū Ḥanīfah.

According to Imāms Abū Yūsuf and Muḥammad, however, *zakāh* must be paid on whatever is collected [regardless of whether or not it exceeds the *niṣāb* or has been in one's possession for a year].[19]

5.8 Situations Where Zakāh is not Necessary

There is no *zakāh* to be paid on:

Ḍimār [i.e., property from which it is highly unlikely that any benefit will ever be realised] as, for example:

- property that has become lost;
- property that has fallen into a river;
- property that was seized unlawfully without there being any witness to its usurpation;
- property that was buried in the desert and its whereabouts forgotten;
- an outstanding claim denied by the debtor and for which there was no evidence;
- and property that was seized by the sulṭān or the like [nationalised by the government].

If any such wealth should again come into one's possession, it will not be necessary to pay *zakāh* on it for the time gone by [when it was not in hand].

If, however, the outstanding claim is admitted by the debtor [from above], even though one is bankrupt [or legally declared by a *qāḍī* to be insolvent], or if there are witnesses to the claim, or if the *qāḍī* has knowledge of the claim, or if some wealth was buried in one's house and then lost [its whereabouts forgotten], on such property *zakāh* is *wājib*, and likewise [it will be necessary to pay *zakāh* on it for] the time gone by.

5.9 Begging

Whoever possesses the means to obtain food enough to last one day is prohibited by the *Sharī'ah* from begging.

5.10 Ṣadaqah al-Fiṭr

Ṣadaqah al-fiṭr is *wājib* on every Muslim who possesses a *niṣāb*, when the amount of the *niṣāb* exceeds [the amount needed to cover both] one's debts and basic needs. That the *niṣāb* be capable of increase is not a condition. Furthermore, it is *ḥarām* for one possessing such a *niṣāb* to take *ṣadaqah al-fiṭr* [from others for himself].

The possessor of such a *niṣāb* is responsible for giving *ṣadaqah al-fiṭr* for oneself and one's own small children; provided that the children are not themselves in possession of a *niṣāb*. If they are, then he may give of their money for them. A man is not responsible for giving *ṣadaqah al-fiṭr* for his wife or mature children.[20]

Ṣadaqah al-fiṭr becomes *wājib* from the dawning of the *'Īd* day [i.e. *'Īd al-Fiṭr*]. Therefore, if someone should die before dawn, or a child is born after dawn, or come into possession of a *niṣāb* only after the dawn, or thereafter become a Muslim, then *ṣadaqah al-fiṭr* will not be *wājib* on that person.

One may pay his *ṣadaqah al-fiṭr* before the *'Īd* day, but the way of the *Sunnah* is to pay it [after *Fajr* prayer and] before leaving for the place where *'Īd* prayer is going to be performed.

If *ṣadaqah al-fiṭr* is not paid on the day of *'Īd*, then it can be paid [as *qaḍā*] at any [convenient] time.

The amount to be paid in *ṣadaqah al-fiṭr* is half of a *ṣā'*[21] from wheat or one *ṣā'* from dates or barley. Raisins are like wheat according to Imām Abū Ḥanīfah, hence like barley it will also be paid a *ṣā'* according to Imāms Abū Yūsuf and Muḥammad. *Ṣadaqah al-fiṭr* can be paid in money the equivalent to the price of food mentioned above.[22]

5.11 *Nafl Ṣadaqah – Voluntary Charity*

Nafl ṣadaqah may be given to parents, close relatives, orphans, the poor, neighbours, beggars, and so on. It is recommended that one gives only of that money which is in excess of his basic needs, debts, customary expenditures and financial responsibilities. Charity may not be given in the way of wrongdoing.[23]

Nafl ṣadaqah should be given first of all to members of Banī Ḥāshim, as it is *ḥarām* to give them *zakāh.* Owing to their relationship with the Messenger of Allāh, may the peace and blessings of Allāh be upon him, they should be approached [by the donor] with humility and respect.

Nafl ṣadaqah may be given to members of other faiths, the *dhimmī's* who have agreed to live peacefully in Muslim lands as subjects of Muslim government, but not to (other) disbelievers the subjects of non-Muslim government.[24]

After the conquest at Khaybar, the Messenger of Allāh, may peace and blessings of Allāh be upon him, presented his wives with provision enough to cover their expenses for a full year. Nor did he, upon whom be peace, ever save anything [for luxuries] for himself, or hoard up great stores. Rather, whenever it became possible for him to do so, he would spend in the way of Allāh. The Messenger of Allāh, may the peace and blessings of Allāh be upon him, said to Bilāl, "Spend, O Bilal! And fear not poverty from the Monarch of the Heavenly Throne."

Yet a Muslim is not to spend indiscriminately. Allāh, the Most High has called such squanderers "the brothers of Satan" [*Banī Isrā'īl* 17: 27]. Indiscriminate spending may be defined as that in which there are neither blessings in the next world, *thawāb*, nor benefit [in this world]. Furthermore, selfish pleasures are not more important than the responsibilities one has to oneself.

The hospitality of a guest is *sunnah mu'akkadah* for three days after that it is *mustaḥab*.

Notes

1. Their withholding *zakāh*, as it was based on their conviction that the Qur'ānic verses of *zakāh* had no validity after the death of the Messenger of Allāh, may the peace and blessings of Allāh be upon him, was in fact an outright denial of the Qur'ān, which is *kufr*. Thus their crime, and the one for which the *Khalīfah* declared *jihād* against them, was no less than apostasy. (Trans.)
2. This is because, in doing so one denies the Qur'ān, which clearly states that *zakāh* is necessary. (Trans.)
3. *Zakāh* is not due on an amount of money reserved for legitimate needs likely to occur during the year, but if the need is to occur some time in the future beyond a year, *zakāh* will have to be paid on the amount. (Revs.)
4. The *fatwā* here is with Imām Abū Yūsuf. (Trans.)
5. This would also include the equivalent in currency. (Revs.)
6. The way to have regard is as follows. If the price of gold is high at the time of the general valuation, then, after valuing the two as one, the *zakāh* should be paid as if on silver alone; and if the price of silver is high then *zakāh* should be paid as if on gold alone. Thus, a greater amount will be ensured for those receiving *zakāh*. (Trans.)
7. Because as according to Imām Abū Ḥanīfah, in this is more regard to the needy and also the total value of the two exceeds the *niṣāb* of at least one of the two and according to them the amount of gold and silver required for *niṣāb* is completed. (Trans.)
8. An amount of money agreed upon in exchange for his giving his wife a divorce. (Trans.)
9. The *fatwā* here is with Imām Muḥammad. (Trans.)
10. The *niṣāb* for cows and buffaloes is 30 in quantity. The rate of *zakāh* is 1 animal (1 year old) for every 30, and 1 animal (2 years old) for every 40. The *niṣāb* for goats and sheep is 40 in quantity. The rate of *zakāh* is 1 animal for every 40. 2 animals for every 120. 3 animals for every 300. One adds 1 more animal for every 100 more animals above 300. (Revs.)

11. Farm produce is regarded as a fourth kind of wealth on which *zakāh* (*ʿushr*) becomes due provided the fulfilling of its conditions. In this context, there are two kinds of lands. One: on which *kharāj* (land tax) is levied, the second is a land on which *zakāh* (*ʿushr*) is obliged.

12. According to Imām Abū Ḥanīfah, in *Ushrī* land, however, *zakāh* is paid on the farm produce regardless of its quantity, while according to Imāms Abū Yūsuf and Muḥammad, the *niṣāb* for farm produce is five *wasaq* which is equal to about 950 kg. The rate of *zakāh* is 5% for produce grown with irrigated water; and 10% for produce grown with natural rain. (Revs.)

13. Near relatives to whom *zakāh* should not be given are those family members who are direct parents or progeny such as one's parents, grandparents, great-grandparents and on up, as well as one's children, grandchildren, and great-grandchildren and on down. Therefore, *zakāh* may be given to eligible and deserving relatives such as one's brothers, sisters, uncles, aunts, nieces, nephews, father-in-laws, mother-in-laws, son-in-laws, daughter-in-laws, etc. (Revs.)

14. If a poor person has debts he may be paid from *zakāh* the amount to pay his debts off, even if the amount is more than a *niṣāb*. This is because the one who has debts, will be regarded as a poor person. (Azami.)

15. The *fatwā* here is with Imāms Abū Yūsuf and Muḥammad. In the *Jāmiʿ Ṣaghīr* the same opinion is attributed to Imām Abū Ḥanīfah as well. (Trans.)

16. One is that 1/5 is not due, and this is preferred by the author of *Kanz-ul-Daqā'iq*. According to the narration of *Jāmiʿ Ṣaghīr*, 1/5 is due in this finding also.

17. The discovery is to be advertised for a period of upwards of three months after which, if the owner does not come forward to claim the treasure, the finder will take legal possession. (Trans.)

18. To understand what follows it should be mentioned that claims are of three basic kinds: weak, middling, and strong. The laws of *zakāh* with regard to each kind will be found to differ somewhat, and it was the purpose of *Qāḍī* Thanā'ullāh, in what follows of this ruling, to illustrate these differences. First, however, it should facilitate matters somewhat if we define the three kinds of claims.

    (a) **A Weak Claim** is that which,

    (i) comes into one's possession without one doing or exchanging anything for it, like inheritance, *mirāth*;

    (ii) or which comes to one through someone's deed, but not in exchange for anything, like bequest, *waṣīyah*;

    (iii) or which comes to one through someone's deeds and in exchange for something as well, but for something which is not real wealth, like dowry, *mahr*, which is given in exchange for a woman's honour.

When this type of claim is collected, *zakāh* will become *wājib* if the amount of the claim exceeds the *niṣāb* and if it remains in one's possession for a year's time.

(b) **The Middling Claim** is that which establishes one's right to possession in exchange for some kind of wealth other than wealth intended for trade, like the price of one's own clothes if they were taken by someone else. When this type of claim is collected, *zakāh* will have to be paid if the amount of the claim exceeds the *niṣāb*; though it is not necessary in this case that it should have remained in one's possession for a year.

(c) **The Strong Claim** is that which establishes one's right to possession in exchange for some kind of wealth intended for trade merchandise. *Zakāh* on this type of claim is to be given over immediately upon receiving payment, at the rate of one *dirham* for every forty. (Trans.)

19. The *fatwā* on this question is with Imām Abū Ḥanīfah. For a more detailed explanation see Maulānā Ashraf 'Alī Thānwī's *Bahishtī Zewar*, Part 3, p. 26. (Trans.)

20. Of course, the reverse is also true. In the extended family system where all the family members, including one's wife and mature children live together, and their wealth is not divided, the leader of the family has to pay *ṣadaqah al-fiṭr*.

21. A *Ṣā'* is equal to 3.17 kg.

22. *Ṣadaqah al-fiṭr* depends more or less on the kind of food consumed in each locality. It is, therefore, advisable to consult *'ulāmā'* and imāms of the mosques in one's locality.

23. Thus it is not proper to present, as charity, someone with tickets to a gambling casino, etc. (Trans.)

24. Here, the author, it seems, does not allow giving *nafl ṣadaqah* to disbelievers except *dhimmīs*. However, *'ulamā'* generally allow to give charity to non-Muslims who are not at war and have a peace agreement with Muslims.

CHAPTER 6

Ṣawm

6.1 The Fast of Ramaḍān

Fasting, *ṣawm*, during the sacred month of *Ramaḍān* is also a Pillar of Islam. This fast is a confirmed *farḍ* upon every [legally] competent Muslim. To deny this is to commit *kufr*. To neglect to fast, without excuse, is to commit wrongdoing, *fisq*. However, if this neglect is due to denial of the need to fast, then this is *kufr* [and not merely *fisq*].

Imāms Bukhārī and Muslim have related on the authority of Abū Hurayrah, may Allāh be pleased with him, that the Messenger of Allāh, may the peace and blessings of Allāh be upon him, said, Allāh, Most High said: "The children of Ādam will find increase for their good deeds, from ten to seven hundred times over, except for a fast which is undertaken solely for Me, and I am its reward."[1]

6.2 *The Injunctions of Fasting*

The Farḍ Elements of Fasting[*]

Fasting is to abstain from eating, drinking and sexual relations with one's spouse, during the time period from just before true dawn until sunset, with the intention of seeking the pleasure of Allāh, the Most High. These above-mentioned aspects form the *farḍ* elements of fasting.

The Sunnah Elements of Fasting

Some of the *Sunnah* elements which ought to be observed are as follows.

It is best to observe the following during one's fast:

- before beginning the day's fast, one is encouraged to have a meal before dawn (*suḥūr*);
- it is *Sunnah* to delay the early morning meal to as close to the time of commencement of the fast [i.e. the beginning of *fajr*] as possible;
- the fast should be broken, *ifṭār*, immediately after the time of *maghrib* (sunset);
- and to have the intention to fast the next day before going to sleep.

6.2.1 The types of fasts

The types of fasting are divided into six categories:

- the fast of *Ramaḍān*;
- the make up fast, *qaḍā*;
- the fast of a specific vow, *nadhr*;
- the fast of a non-specific vow;

---

[*] This paragraph has been added by the revisers for clarification and is not part of *Mālā Budda Minhu*.

- the fast of expiation, *kaffārah*;
- and the voluntary, *nafl*, fast.

6.2.2 The conditions of fasting

The conditions which must be satisfied before the correct performance of the fast are as follows:

- having the intention, *niyah*, to fast; and
- freedom from menstrual bleeding, *ḥayḍ*, and post-childbirth bleeding, *nifās*.[2]

Intention

According to Imām Abū Ḥanīfah, performance of the fast of *Ramaḍān* will be proper if one makes a general [unspecified, but all-inclusive] intention, or a specific intention for the *farḍ* at hand, or an intention for a *nafl* fast.[3]

If a person makes an intention to make up a fast or to observe a fast of expiation, he is a resident and is a healthy individual, then it will serve for the proper performance of the *farḍ* fast at hand, and no other.[4] If a person is sick, however, or a traveller, then whatever one intends to perform in *Ramaḍān* with the intention of a make-up fast or fast of expiation will be correct. According to Imāms Abū Yūsuf and Muḥammad, however, only the *farḍ* at hand [a fast of *Ramaḍān*] will be correct.[5]

According to Imāms Mālik, Shāfiʿī, and Aḥmad, it is necessary even for the fast of *Ramaḍān* to make a specific intention for the *farḍ* at hand.

The fast of a specific vow, according to Imām Abū Ḥanīfah, may be properly observed by making an intention for a vow only, making a general intention, or by making an intention for a *nafl* fast. If an intention is made for some other *wājib* fast specifically, then only that fast [and not the fast of a specific vow] may be performed thereafter. Most of the other Imāms, however, opine that a fast of a specific vow will not be correct unless it is preceded by an intention for a fast of a specific vow [and nothing else].

There is general agreement on the propriety of a *nafl* fast when preceded by a general intention. Similarly, there is agreement on the need for specifying the intention when setting out to perform a make up fast or a fast of expiation, *kaffārah*.

The Proper Time for Making Intention

The time for making intention is from sunset [of the preceding day] to the true dawn [of the day the fast is to be observed]. After the rising of the dawn, the intention will be improper, except in the case of a *nafl* fast, as long as the intention is made before noon, according to Imāms Shāfiʿī and Aḥmad. According to Imām Mālik, however, after the rising of the dawn, not even the intention for a *nafl* fast will be correct. According to Imām Abū Ḥanīfah, the intention for a fast of *Ramaḍān*, for a specific vow, and for the *nafl* fast will be correct if it is made before midday [of the day on which the fast is being performed].

There is general agreement that the intention for a make up fast, a fast of expiation, or a fast of a non-specific vow will not be correct if it is made after the rising of the dawn.

According to the three Imāms (Abū Ḥanīfah, Shāfiʿī, and Aḥmad ibn Ḥanbal) it is necessary to make a new intention for every day of fasting observed during the month of *Ramaḍān*. Imām Mālik, however, holds that the intention made from the first day of the fast for the whole month will suffice.

If, on the first night of the month of *Ramaḍān*, a person makes intention to observe the fast for the whole month and then, in mid-*Ramaḍān*, becomes temporarily insane without doing anything to break one's fast, then, according to Imām Mālik, [since he opines one *ni'yah* suffices for the whole month], all of his fasts will have been correct. According to the other Imāms, [since they opine it necessary to have intention for every fast individually], the fasts observed during the period of insanity will have to be made up owing to his not having made intention for them.

If a person has an attack of insanity which lasts the whole month [beginning before the new moon of *Ramaḍān* is sighted], he will be excused from making the fast, and he will not have to make up any of the fasts. If however, that same person should regain his or her sanity at any time during the month [even if only for a few moments], then he will be responsible for making up all the fasts missed, up to the time of regaining his sanity [and, of course, for all those which follow].

6.2.3 Sighting the new moon of *Ramaḍān*

The fast becomes *wājib* either by:

- the sighting of the new moon of *Ramaḍān*;
- or the passing of thirty days from the first of Shaʿbān.

For witnessing the new moon of *Ramaḍān* when the sky is overcast, the testimony of one honest man or woman will suffice. For witnessing the Shawwāl moon under similar conditions the testimony, of at least two honest men, or of one honest man and two honest women is required. If the sky is clear, for both the sighting of the *Ramaḍān* and Shawwāl moons, there should be testimony from a great number of people [though it is enough, according to a narration of Imām Abū Ḥanīfah, to have the testimony of two honest men in this situation as well].

If, after beginning the fast of *Ramaḍān* on the basis of testimony given by only one man, the moon should not appear on the 30th, then the fast will have to be kept on the following day as well.[6] If the fast was begun on the basis of testimony given by two men, and thirty days go by, the fast may be declared over, regardless of whether or not the Shawwāl moon is sighted.

If one witnessed the Shawwāl or *Ramaḍān* moon with one's own eyes, and if his testimony was rejected by the *qāḍī*, then in both cases, it will be necessary for that person to observe the fast [on his own]; if he does not, he will only have to make up the fast as *qaḍā'*, not as a fast of expiation, *kaffārah*.

6.3 *Qaḍā' and Kaffārah – Things which Necessitate a Make Up Fast or a Fast of Expiation*[7]

If someone, during the fast of *Ramaḍān*:

- has sexual intercourse intentionally, or is a willing partner in it;[8]
- or drinks or eats food or takes medicine intentionally,

his fast will be spoiled and he will have to redo the fast to make up for the spoiled one, *qaḍā'*, and observe a fast of expiation, *kaffārah*, as atonement of his sin.

The fast of expiation is a day after day fast [without break] for a period of two months, during which *Ramaḍān*, the two *'Īd* days, or the Days of *Tashrīq* [11th, 12th, and 13th of Dhu al-Ḥijjah] do not occur. If, at any time during this period, a fast should be missed with or without an excuse, except in case of menstruation or post-childbirth bleeding, then the whole two months of fasting will have to be observed all over again from the beginning. If a person is not fit to observe a fast of expiation, *kaffārah*, one will have to feed sixty poor people instead, where each person receives a portion equal to that value given as *ṣadaqah al-fiṭr* [or to one poor person for sixty days].

According to Imāms Shāfi'ī and Aḥmad, there can be no fast of expiation, *kaffārah*, except as a consequence of sexual intercourse.

There is general agreement that there is no fast of expiation for the deliberate spoiling of a make up fast, fast of expiation, or vow.

If, during one *Ramaḍān*, two or more fasts are spoiled in such a way as to necessitate a fast of expiation, *kaffārah*, then, if after spoiling the first fast, *kaffārah* is given immediately [in food or money to feed sixty poor people or one poor person for sixty days instead of fasting two months], a separate *kaffārah* will have to be given for the second spoiled fast; and so on and so forth with the third and fourth. But if the fast of expiation, *kaffārah*, is withheld after the first fast is spoiled until the end of the month, then one complete fast of expiation, *kaffārah*, will suffice for all fasts spoiled during the month.[9]

According to Imāms Mālik and Shāfi'ī, a number of spoiled fasts require an equal number of fasts of expiation. There is general agreement, however, on the need for observing two separate fasts of expiations, *kaffārahs*, for two fasts spoiled in two different *Ramaḍāns*, even though the fast of expiation for the first remains undischarged when the second is spoiled.

6.3.1 Cases where the fast of expiation is not necessary

In each of the following cases the fast will break and a make up fast will have to be made, but no fast of expiation is necessary if:

- by mistake, someone breaks their fast;[10]
- or is forced to break it against their will [with food or sexual intercourse, for example]; or
- puts drops of medicine into their eyes, ears, wound of stomach or head, which then penetrate to the inside of the body, brain, or stomach; or
- if pebbles, iron, or something else other than food or medicine should go down the throat; or
- if one intentionally vomits a mouthful; or
- if one eats, thinking it is still night time, and then finds out the day had already dawned; or
- if one eats, thinking that the sun had set, when in reality it had not; or
- if one should eat out of forgetfulness and then, thinking one's fast to be spoiled anyway, eats intentionally; or
- if water should go down the throat while sleeping; or
- if sexual intercourse was done, with a sleeping woman, or while she was temporarily insane, or while otherwise unconscious.

6.4 Errors in Making Intention

During *Ramaḍān*, if one neglects to make intention for either the fast, or for breaking it, and abstains from everything which could break the fast, then the fast will be considered invalid and one will have to make up the fast. One will not, however, be required to observe a fast of expiation, *kaffārah*.

If, during *Ramaḍān*, one does not have the intention to observe the fast [inspite of one's being competent to do so], and then eats, according to Imām Abū Ḥanīfah, one will not have to make a fast of expiation, *kaffārah*, and only has to make it up as *qaḍā'*. According to Imāms Abū Yūsuf and Muḥammad, however, the fast of expiation, *kaffārah*, is *wājib* in such a case.[11]

6.5 Things that do not Break the Fast

The fast is not broken by the following:

- Forgetfulness; if someone forgets altogether that one is observing the fast and then, while in the state of forgetfulness, eats, drinks, or has sexual intercourse, the fast will not be spoiled, and it will not have to be made up.
- Involuntary seminal discharge during sleep or otherwise;
- Rubbing of oil or lotion onto the skin;
- The application of antimony (*kuḥl – surmah*) to the eyes;
- Backbiting;
- Putting water into the ears, eyes, or nostrils as one commonly would when making *wuḍū'*;
- Vomiting unintentionally; [vomiting unintentionally, even though it be a large quantity, will not spoil the fast. Furthermore, the intentional vomiting of a small amount [i.e. less than a mouthful], will not spoil the fast, but if a mouthful is vomited, the fast will be spoiled and must be made up, but no fast of expiation, *kaffārah*, will be needed].

  If a person should vomit [unintentionally], filling one's mouth, and then intentionally swallow whatever had come up, one's fast will break. If, however, one vomits only a small amount and then unintentionally swallows it, one's fast will not break. If one re-swallows a whole mouthful unintentionally then, according to Imām Abū Yūsuf, one's fast will break and, according to Imām Muḥammad, it will not. If one re-swallows a small amount intentionally then, according to Imām Muḥammad, one's fast will break, while according to Imām Abū Yūsuf, it will not.[12]

- Kissing and caressing during the fast; if someone should kiss or caress another with lust, and an emission results, the fast will break; and if there is no emission, the fast will not break.
- Eating food lodged in one's mouth amounting to less than a chickpea [a gram];

  If a person should eat a particle of food that has become lodged between the teeth, which was dislodged with one's hand, the fast will be spoiled and must be made up, though one will not have to make a fast of expiation, *kaffārah.* If, however, one dislodged it with the tip of one's tongue, one will have to make up the fast, only if the particle was greater than a chickpea, otherwise the fast will not be spoiled.
- Sucking or chewing something while fasting when a need exists; It is *makrūh* while observing the fast to either suck or chew anything without an excuse. It is, however, permitted, if there is a need for it. For example, to chew a small child's food for him or her when feeding; to test the seasoning of food while cooking, etc.
- Using water to lessen the effects of heat; snuffing water into the nostrils or mouth to lessen the effects of heat during fasting, or taking a bath for the same reason, or dressing in wet clothes, according to Imām Abū Ḥanīfah, are *makrūh tanzīhi* and do not invalidate the fast. However, according to Imām Abū Yūsuf [and his is the more widely accepted of the two views], these things are not *makrūh.*
- Beginning the fast in the state of major ritual impurity; if during the night a person should become impure, *janābah*, due to sexual relations or seminal emission, and then begins one's fast in the morning in that state [before taking a *ghusl*], one's fast will be correct. It is, however, *mustaḥab* to take a *ghusl* before dawn.
- Or to use *miswak*, toothsticks, for cleaning the teeth, even if one tastes it;

- Swallowing of saliva or phlegm, cupping, acupuncture [or taking injection].

6.6 *What is Makrūh During Fasting*

The *ʿulamāʾ* are agreed that telling lies, backbiting, and name calling [abusing or cursing] are not things which break the fast. These are, none the less, very much *makrūh*. Imām Awzāʿī held the opinion that these were things which would actually spoil the fast. The Messenger of Allāh, may the peace and blessings of Allāh be upon him, said that the Almighty is in no need of the fast of a person who does not leave off speaking falsely and doing wrong.[13]

6.7 *Valid Reasons for Missing the Fast of Ramaḍān*

In each of the cases below, one may leave the days of fasting at hand and make up the fast at a later, more convenient date. A very old man or one with a severe, long illness, who is not able to fast, is allowed to leave the fast. Such a person, if he regains the strength for fasting, must make up the days he missed. A fast of *Ramaḍān* may be missed in the following circumstances:

- setting out on a journey as a traveller;
- temporary sickness;

  A sick person who fears [with good reason] an increase in their sickness [or a person who is well but fears that he or she may fall sick], or a traveller, all have permission to choose not to observe fasting, [opting, instead, to make it up at a more convenient time]. Thus, if one thinks it will not cause one any trouble, the best thing for a person travelling to do would be to observe the fast. If, however, one has undertaken one's journey for the purpose of *jihād*, or thinks that one's fasting may cause inconvenience to himself, or some kind of harm, then it is far better that one does not observe the fast. If it should seem likely that one's observing the fast will cause one's demise, it is essential (*wājib*) that one not keep the fast. If one does, he will have committed a great wrong.

A sick person or a person travelling who elects not to keep the fast and then dies, during either the illness or the journey, will not be responsible for making up the fasts that were missed. However, if one dies after regaining health or reaching his destination, one will be responsible only for making up as many fasts as there were days between the time of death and the end of his illness or journey [assuming that the number of days during this period are fewer than the number of fasts missed]. In the event that one does not make up those fasts during this period, it becomes binding, *wājib*, on that person's *walī* (close relative) to pay *fidyah* from the third part of the deceased's estate, if the deceased has done *waṣiyyah* (a will) for it. For each fast for which the deceased was responsible; giving food to one poor person in portions equal to *ṣadaqah al-fiṭr*. If the deceased left no instructions for *fidyah* to be taken from one's estate, then it is not necessary that it, *fidyah*, be given. If, however, someone would like to volunteer [to give it out of the goodness of their heart], then it will be accepted [and the responsibility of the deceased will come to an end].

- setting out on a campaign for *jihād*;
- pregnancy;
- breastfeeding a child;

A pregnant or nursing woman, if she fears for either her own health or her child's health, has permission not to keep the fast. Later she will have to make up the missed fasts, but she will not have to give *fidyah*.

- not being able to endure the fast due to unbearable hunger and thirst;
- old age or weakness;

- if one feels that he will be risking his life if the fast is observed;

  A person who is so weak and aged as to be unable to keep the fast has permission, should he or she choose, not to keep the fast; giving instead, for each fast one misses, food to the value of *ṣadaqah al-fiṭr*. Later, if one regains enough strength to perform the fast, he will become responsible for making up the fasts missed.

6.7.1 Making up a missed fast of *Ramaḍān*

Making up *qaḍā'* fasts of *Ramaḍān* may be done continuously or intermittently but not observed concurrently with the present *Ramaḍān's* fast.

If a whole year goes by without a person observing the missed fasts of *Ramaḍān* until another *Ramaḍān* comes along, then he will have to observe the fast for the current *Ramaḍān* and thereafter make up the fasts of the previous *Ramaḍān*. It is not necessary to pay *fidyah* when this happens.[14]

6.8 Voluntary Fasting

A voluntary, *nafl*, fast, once begun, becomes *wājib*.[15] However, a *nafl* fast begun on a day in which fasting is prohibited does not become *wājib*.[16]

A voluntary fast may not be broken without an excuse. In the event that an excuse should present itself, the fast may be broken [and should be made up at a later date]. The arrival of a guest, for instance, is considered a valid excuse.[17]

A woman should not keep a voluntary fast without first taking permission from her husband.[18]

If, during the daytime in the month of *Ramaḍān*, a child should pass into maturity, or a *kāfir* become a Muslim, or a traveller reach one's residence, or a woman finish her period of menstruation, *ḥayḍ*, or post-childbirth bleeding, *nifās*, then it is essential that the remainder of the day abstaining from eating, drinking, etc. be observed. Yet, regardless of whether or not the remainder of the fast is observed, there will be no need to make up the fast, except in the case of the traveller and the woman.

6.8.1 Days of voluntary fasting

i. *Six days during the month of Shawwāl*

It is in a *ḥadīth* of the Prophet, may Allāh bless him and grant him peace, that whoever keeps six fasts after *Ramaḍān*, in the month of Shawwāl, will receive a reward similar to that of keeping fast all the year long.

Certain *ʿulamāʾ* have said that the six fasts in Shawwāl should be observed a few days after, and not directly following *ʿĪd al-Fiṭr* to avoid imitation with Christians.[19] The *fatwā* however, is that it is not *makrūh* to fast immediately after *ʿĪd*.[20]

ii. *Fasting in the month of Shaʿbān*

The Messenger of Allāh, may the peace and blessings of Allāh be upon him, used to observe many fasts during the month of Shaʿbān. In some *aḥādīth*, however, fasting in the second half of Shaʿbān has been prohibited so as not to weaken the individual unduly before the fast of *Ramaḍān*.

iii. *To keep three fasts every month*

It is *sunnah* to observe three voluntary fasts in every month. It was the practice of the Messenger of Allāh, may the peace and blessings of Allāh be upon him, to keep fast sometimes on the 'white days' of the month, i.e. the 13th, 14th and 15th, and sometimes the first or last three days of the month, or after every tenth day during the month, or Thursday, Monday, and Thursday, or Monday, Thursday, and Monday, on Saturday, Sunday, and Monday of one month, and on Tuesday, Wednesday, and Thursday of another month.

iv. ***The Day of ʿArafah [the 9th of Dhu al-Ḥijjah]***

Whoever fasts this day will be forgiven the sins of two years, the past and the coming years.

v. ***The Day of ʿĀshurā' [the 10th of Muḥarram, the day Banī Isrā'īl were delivered from the hands of Pharaoh]***

Whoever fasts on this day will be forgiven all the sins one committed during the year. It is *mustahab* to add another day's fast to that of the day of ʿĀshurā', on either the day before or the day after.

vi. ***Fasting every Monday and Thursday***

vii. ***Fasting eight days during the first ten days of Dhu al-Ḥijjah***

6.9 When Fasting is Ḥarām

It is *ḥarām* to fast on *ʿĪd al-Fiṭr*, *ʿĪd al-Aḍḥā*, and the Days of *Tashrīq* [11th, 12th, and 13th of Dhu al-Ḥijjah]. A fast begun on those days does not become *wājib*. However, if someone makes a vow to observe the fast on those days, or on every day of the year then, in both cases, one will have to break one's fast and [later] make it up on a different day. If one continues with the fast, one will be doing wrong; but the vow will be fulfilled and one will not have to make up the fast.

6.10 Fasts Which are Makrūh

According to some *ʿulamā'*, it is *makrūh* to fast only on the day of *jumuʿah* [when it is not, for example, a part of a three-day fast]. According to Imāms Abū Ḥanīfah and Muḥammad, this is not *makrūh*.[21]

Both the *ṣawm ad-dahr* [the lifelong day-after-day fast] and the *ṣawm al-wiṣāl* [the unbroken day and night] are *makrūh*. The best of all fasts is what is known as the fast of Prophet Dāwūd, upon whom be peace, which is observed on every other day, with a day of rest in between; on the condition that the one doing so is physically able to continue with it indefinitely. The best worship is that which one can do regularly with continuity.

6.11 I'tikāf – Religious Retreat

I'tikāf in a *Masjid* [in which the five daily prayers are performed in congregation] is an act of worship, *'ibādah*. It consists of one's secluding oneself within the *Masjid* with the intention of making *i'tikāf*.

It is best to perform *i'tikāf* in a *Jāmi' Masjid*. *I'tikāf* becomes *wājib* when undertaken as a vow. [There are three kinds of *i'tikāf*]:

1. *wājib* by vow;
2. *Sunnah mu'akkadah*, in the last ten days of *Ramaḍān*;
3. and *mustaḥab*, any other time of the year.

The shortest period for making *i'tikāf* is one day, according to Imām Abū Ḥanīfah; the greater part of a day, according to Imām Abū Yūsuf; and any duration of time, according to Imām Muḥammad.[22] *I'tikāf* during the last ten days of *Ramaḍān* is *Sunnah mu'akkadah*.

A condition of the *wājib i'tikāf* is the concurrent observance of fasting. Similarly, according to one source, fasting is a condition for the proper performance of *nafl i'tikāf* as well.[23]

6.11.1 The *I'tikāf* of a Woman

A woman who intends to make *i'tikāf* should do so in that place in her home where she customarily makes her prayer.[24]

6.11.2 Things permitted and forbidden during *Iʿtikāf*

The one performing *iʿtikāf* may not leave the Masjid except to answer a call of nature. One may also leave it for purposes of purification, like *wuḍūʾ* or *ghusl*. Furthermore, if there is a real need for it, one may leave the Masjid as the need arises. For instance, a person who lives alone will have to go out for one's own food if one has no one else to bring it to him. One may also leave to perform *jumuʿah* prayer, giving himself enough time to make the prescribed number of *rakʿats* of *Sunnah* after *jumuʿah*, but not tarrying any longer than that. If one delays longer, his *iʿtikāf* will not be spoiled entirely [but it will surely decrease in merit].

If the person performing *iʿtikāf* leaves the Masjid [for any duration of time] without a valid excuse, one's *iʿtikāf* will be spoiled.

One performing *iʿtikāf* is permitted to eat, drink, sleep, and conduct business in the Masjid. He may not, however, have the goods to buy and sell to one in the Masjid. These things [i.e. their taking place inside the Masjid] are permitted to no one other than one in *iʿtikāf*.

It is *ḥarām* for one in *iʿtikāf* to either have sexual intercourse or do anything which might lead to intercourse.

Iʿtikāf is spoiled by kissing and caressing if they lead to an emission, otherwise [if there is no emission], *iʿtikāf* will not be spoiled.

In *iʿtikāf* it is *makrūh* to observe complete silence. It is even more *makrūh* to engage in vain or frivolous conversation. Instead, the ones in *iʿtikāf* should engage themselves in good discussion, learning and teaching *dīn*, *dhikr*, *tilāwah* of the Qurʾān, reading books of *Ḥadīth*, *tafsīr*, *sīrah*, or biographies of the righteous heroes of Islam.

If a person makes a vow to sit in *iʿtikāf* for a certain number of days, then one will have to stay in *iʿtikāf* during the nights of those days as well. Thus a vow for a stay of two days in *iʿtikāf* requires a stay of two nights also.

Notes

1. Thus, the author, may Allāh have mercy on him, has interpreted the *ḥadīth.* Most of the commentators of the *ḥadīth* have interpreted it as follows: Allāh, Most High, says: The fast is for Me, and I will [countlessly] reward for it. (Azami.)
2. A woman does not observe the fast when she is in her menses and must make up the missed days at a more convenient time. (Trans.)
3. Someone's thinking, "Tomorrow I will fast," for example, is a general intention. (Trans.)
4. In other words, once the intention for making up a fast or expiation, *kaffārah*, has been made, the performance of a fast of *Ramaḍān* will be correct; though the performance of any other kind of fast, including a make up fast or fast of expiation, will be improper. (Trans.)
5. The *fatwā* here is with Imāms Abū Yūsuf and Muḥammad. (Trans.)
6. This is in the event that the Shawwāl moon does not appear in spite of the sky's being clear. If the sky is overcast, the fast should be declared over. (Trans.)
7. The fast of expiation only pertains to spoiling the fast of the month of *Ramaḍān* and no other type of fast. (Trans.)
8. If one were to engage in a sexually pleasing act, *other* than intercourse, which results in orgasm or emission, the fast will be invalidated and must be made up, but there is no fast of expiation. (Revs.)
9. In other words, if *kaffārah* is not given immediately after the first fast is spoiled, and then two or more fasts are also spoiled, only one *kaffārah* will have to be given for all the spoiled fasts. However, if after one fast of *Ramaḍān* is spoiled, *kaffārah* is given immediately thereafter as food or money to feed sixty poor people, and then another fast of *Ramaḍān* is spoiled, then another *kaffārah* will have to be given. (Trans.)
10. That is to say, if one did something which one thought breaks the fast, when in reality it does not, and because of that wrong assumption one thinks they broke the fast and resumes eating, etc. For example, suppose one were to swallow their phlegm while fasting [which doesn't break the fast in the *Ḥanafī* school] and they think the fast has become invalid and then resume eating; they would be responsible for making up the "spoiled" fast and would not have to perform a fast of expiation. (Revs.)
11. The *fatwā* here is with Imām Abū Ḥanīfah. (Trans.)
12. The *fatwā* in the last two cases is with Imām Muḥammad. (Trans.)
13. In other words, one's fast will not be accepted. (Trans.)

14. According to Imāms Mālik and Shāfiʿī, *fidyah* must be paid for every fast for which a make-up fast was not made during the year. (Trans.)

15. Thus failure to complete it is failure to complete a *wājib*, not just a *nafl*, and is therefore a serious matter. (Trans.)

16. Fasting is prohibited on the two *ʿĪds* and on the Days of *Tashrīq*. (Trans.)

17. The fast, however, should not be broken after midday except under the most pressing circumstances. (Trans.)

18. The Messenger of Allāh, may the peace and blessings of Allāh be upon him, said, "No woman may fast when her husband is present except with his permission." (Trans.)

19. It is narrated that the fasting of *Ramaḍān* was obligatory on Christians. Once it came in summer, they shifted it to spring, and to compensate they added ten days extra to it. Then one of their kings fell ill, and he vowed that if he recovered he and his ward would fast seven days more for Allāh. Then after that his son added three more fasts on to that so that eventually it became fifty. See *Maʿalim at-Tanzīl.*

20. See Ibn ʿĀbidīn, *Radd al-Muḥtār*, Vol. II, p.125. (Trans.)

21. The *fatwā* of the school is that fasting Friday alone is *makrūh*. See *Marāqi al-Falāḥ*. (Revs.)

22. The *fatwā* here is with Imām Muḥammad. See Ibn ʿĀbidīn, op. cit., Vol. II, p. 131. (Trans.)

23. The most reliable *Ḥanafī* sources indicate that the Imām and his two companions did not consider fasting an essential condition to the proper performance of *iʿtikāf*. (Trans.)

24. It is permitted, though *makrūh*, for a woman to make *iʿtikāf* in a Masjid. (*Fatāwā ʿĀlamgīrī*)

Chapter 7

*Pilgrimage to Makkah – Ḥajj and ʿUmrah**

7.1 Ḥajj

Ḥajj is the fifth Pillar of Islam. Linguistically *ḥajj* means "to aim for", and in the *Sharīʿah,* it means to aim for the Sacred House in order to perform the actions of *ḥajj-ṭawāf, saʿy*, standing at ʿArafāt and the rest of the rites in response to the command of Allāh and to seek His pleasure. It is *farḍ* according to the Qurʾān and the *Sunnah* and the consensus of the *Ummah.* Allāh the Almighty says,

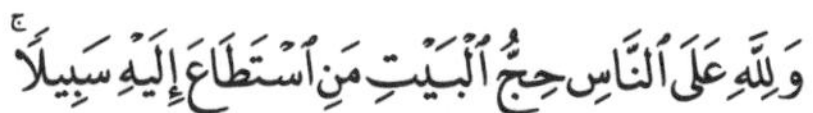

"*Pilgrimage to the House is a duty men owe to Allāh, those who can afford the journey,*" [*Āl ʿImrān* 3: 97]

* As this book was written 300 years ago in Delhi, and at that time travelling and expenses were not affordable for the common people, therefore the chapter on *ḥajj* was omitted by the author. However, nowadays this is not the case and by the Grace of Allāh, the Glorified and Exalted, many people from all over the world can afford to go to *ḥajj*. We have added this chapter on *ḥajj*. We do not claim to be able to imitate the author's lucid style but we hope that it will be useful for the students of *fiqh* for whom this book was originally written and will also give the general reader a relatively comprehensive knowledge on this fifth pillar of Islam.

The Prophet, may the peace and blessings of Allāh be upon him, said, "Islam is based on five," and one of them is *ḥajj*. He, may the peace and blessings of Allāh be upon him, said, "Perform *ḥajj* before you cannot make *ḥajj*." (Bayhaqī in the *Sunan*) It is a postulate of the *dīn* that whoever rejects it is an unbeliever. The *Ummah* agrees on that. It is *farḍ* once in a lifetime. Al-Aqraʿ ibn Ḥabis, may Allāh be pleased with him, asked the Messenger of Allāh, may the peace and blessings of Allāh be upon him, "Is *ḥajj farḍ* every year or only once?" He said, "It is only once in a lifetime. Whoever does more, that is voluntary." (Aḥmad)

It is obligatory for the one who wants to go on *ḥajj* to learn its rules – what is obligatory, *farḍ*, what is forbidden, *ḥarām*, what is disliked, *makrūh*, and what is permitted, *jā'iz*, because Allāh does not want anyone to worship in ignorance. If an action is obligatory, then knowledge of it is obligatory. Allāh Almighty says,

... فَسْـَٔلُوٓاْ أَهْلَ ٱلذِّكْرِ إِن كُنتُمْ لَا تَعْلَمُونَ ﴿٤٣﴾

"*Ask the people of remembrance if you do not know.*"
[*an-Naḥl* 16: 43]

The Prophet, may the peace and blessings of Allāh be upon him, said, "Seeking knowledge is an obligation for every Muslim." (Bayhaqī) One variant has, "and Muslim woman".

The first thing one is obliged to learn is recognition of the lawful and the unlawful because the lawful helps towards obedience and takes away disobedience. Allāh is good and only accepts the good. Allāh the Almighty commanded the believers to do what He commanded the Messengers to do. The Almighty says,

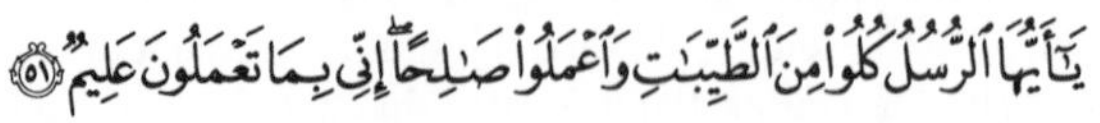

"*O you Messengers! enjoy (all) things good and pure,*"
[*al-Mu'minūn* 23: 51]

and the Almighty says,

يَٰٓأَيُّهَا ٱلَّذِينَ ءَامَنُواْ كُلُواْ مِن طَيِّبَٰتِ مَا رَزَقْنَٰكُمْ

"*O you who believe, eat of the good things that We have provided for you.*" [*al-Baqarah* 2: 172]

Whoever has good earnings purifies his actions. Whoever does not have good earnings it is feared that his actions are not accepted.

The Almighty says,

إِنَّمَا يَتَقَبَّلُ ٱللَّهُ مِنَ ٱلْمُتَّقِينَ

"*Allāh accepts from the godfearing.*" [*al-Mā'idah* 5: 27]

Ḥajj is the best of actions since the Messenger of Allāh, may the peace and blessings of Allāh be upon him, said, "The best of actions with Allāh is true *Īmān* in which there is no doubt, *jihād* in which there is no misappropriation of funds, and an accepted *ḥajj*." (Ibn Ḥibbān in his *Ṣaḥīḥ*)

The Prophet, may the peace and blessings of Allāh be upon him, said, "Whoever goes on *ḥajj* and does not speak immodestly or acts wickedly will return as he was on the day his mother bore him." (Bukhārī, Muslim)

Ḥajj is an obligation and it is best to hasten to perform it since the Prophet, may the peace and blessings of Allāh be upon him, said, "If anyone possesses the provision and transport which will take him to the House of Allāh and does not make *ḥajj*, there is nothing to stop him dying a Jew or a Christian." (Tirmidhī)

He, may the peace and blessings of Allāh be upon him, also said, "If anyone is not restrained by illness or obvious need or a tyrannical ruler and fails to perform *ḥajj*, he might as well die a Jew or a Christian." (Aḥmad)

7.2 *ʿUmrah*

Imām Shāfiʿī, may Allāh have mercy on him, says that *ʿUmrah* is obligatory *farḍ*. Evidence for this is Allāh's words,

وَأَتِمُّوا۟ ٱلْحَجَّ وَٱلْعُمْرَةَ لِلَّهِ

"And complete the Ḥajj and ʿumrah in the service of Allāh," [*al-Baqarah* 2: 196]

which means perform both of them completely. ʿĀ'ishah, may Allāh be pleased with her, asked: "O Messenger of Allāh, do women owe *jihād*?" He said: "Yes, *jihād* with no fighting in it: as *ḥajj* and *ʿumrah*." (Ibn Mājah, Bayhaqī and others)

Ḥanafī fuqahā' differ about it. Some say it is a *Sunnah Mu'akkadah* and some say that it is *wājib*. They are close in meaning. Their evidence is the *ḥadīth* related by Abū Hurayrah, may Allāh be pleased with him, that when a Bedouin asked the Messenger of Allāh, may Allāh bless him and grant him peace, about belief and the laws of Islam, and he clarified them, saying: "That you perform the prescribed prayer, pay the prescribed *zakāh* and make *ḥajj* to the House." The Bedouin asked, "Do I owe anything more than this?" He said, "No, unless you do it voluntarily." He did not mention *ʿumrah*. As for the *āyah*, some read it as, *" and ʿumrah in the service of Allāh,"* stopping after *"complete the ḥajj."* Even without the difference in the reading, it is not truly an evidence because the *āyah* was revealed about the people at al-Ḥudaybiyyah when they had set out in *iḥrām* for *ʿumrah*. It becomes obligatory by setting out. Then they were stopped and so they had to complete the *ʿumrah* by way of making it up.

7.3 When Ḥajj Becomes Obligatory

7.3.1 The conditions for the obligation for *ḤAJJ*

i. *Islam*

This is because it is an act of worship like the prayer and *zakāh*, and by the *ḥadīth* of Mu'ādh, may Allāh be pleased with him, the Prophet, may the peace and blessings of Allāh be upon him, enjoined him when he sent him to Yemen, "Invite them to testify: that there is no god but Allāh. If they obey you, then inform them that they must do such-and-such," and he mentioned *ḥajj*. It is not obligatory for the unbeliever.

ii. *Maturity*

The child is not obliged to make *ḥajj* since the Prophet, may the peace and blessings of Allāh be upon him, said, "The pen has been lifted from three," and he mentioned the child among them, and also by making an analogy with other acts of worship.

iii. *Sanity*

It is not obligatory for a mad person by the *ḥadīth*, "the pen has been lifted from three," and he mentioned the insane among them.

iv. *The Ability*

This is because the Almighty says,

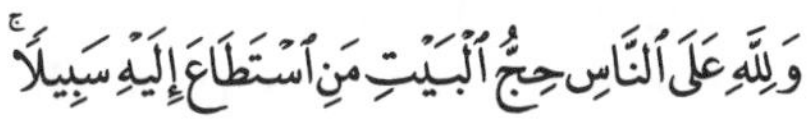

"*Pilgrimage to the House is a duty men owe to Allāh, those who can afford the journey,*" [*Āl 'Imrān* 3: 97]

There are two types of ability: the ability to do it oneself and the ability to perform it by delegation.

The ability to perform it personally entails the existence of the following:

- Someone who is far enough away from Makkah to be allowed to shorten prayers on the journey by ordinary travel must own or be able to hire transport. As for the one who is less than that distance from Makkah and he is capable of walking, *ḥajj* is obligatory on him and transport is not taken into consideration. If he is weak and not strong enough to walk or will incur clear harm then transport is a precondition.
- Provision which is enough for him to go and return. A precondition for provision and transport is that they are over and above what is required for his own maintenance and that of those he is obliged to maintain and clothe with all that they need for the time of his entire journey.
- The route is free. It means that his life, honour and property are safe.
- The possibility of arriving, which is that there is enough time to travel to *ḥajj* and arrive there in time to stand at ʿArafāt.
- The company of the husband or a *maḥram* for women performing the *ḥajj*.

A woman is obliged to make *ḥajj* if she fulfils the preconditions of the obligations which are being mentioned above. In addition she must be accompanied by her husband or *maḥram*. The rule of the *maḥram* is someone whom she is forever forbidden to marry because of lineage, affinity that is the relation by marriage, or suckling. Ibn ʿAbbās, may Allāh be pleased with him, said, "I heard the Messenger of Allāh, may the peace and blessings of Allāh be upon him, say, 'A man should not be alone with a woman unless she has a *maḥram* with her and a woman should only travel with a *maḥram*.' A man said, 'Messenger of Allāh, my wife has set out for *ḥajj* and I have been selected to go on a certain expedition (*jihād*).' He said, 'Go and make *ḥajj* with your wife.'" (Bukhārī, Muslim) Yaḥyā ibn

'Abbād said, "A woman wrote to the *Imām* Ibrāhīm an-Nakh'ī, may Allāh have mercy on him, 'I have not made the *ḥajj* of Islam. I have wealth, but I do not have any *maḥram* relative.' He wrote to her, 'You are one of those for whom Allāh has not made a way,'" referring to the *āyah*:

وَلِلَّهِ عَلَى ٱلنَّاسِ حِجُّ ٱلْبَيْتِ مَنِ ٱسْتَطَاعَ إِلَيْهِ سَبِيلًا

"*And pilgrimage to the House is a duty unto Allāh for mankind, for him who can find a way to it.*" [*Āl 'Imrān* 3: 97]

- and women who are not in their waiting period because of divorce or the death of their husband.

  Therefore, those in their waiting period are not obliged to perform the *ḥajj*.

The ability to perform it by delegation necessitates delegating someone to perform *ḥajj*. In case of someone who has died owing the *ḥajj*, it is paid from his legacy. If someone is unable to perform the practices because of his age or some other reason like serious illness, he either hires someone, if he is wealthy enough, or someone voluntarily takes on his obligation.

7.4 The Farḍ Elements of Ḥajj

7.4.1 *IḤRĀM*[1]

The *Iḥrām* is the intention to begin *ḥajj* (or *'umrah*) when one adopts the *iḥrām* clothes and recites the *talbiyah*. It is called *iḥrām* because the one in this state is forbidden certain things. The proof that it is obligatory is the words of the Prophet, may the peace and blessings of Allāh be upon him, "Actions are according to intentions."

It is recommended that one donning *Iḥrām* should wear a white waist-wrapper, *izār*, and cloak, *ridā'*, and sandals since Ibn al-

Mundhir said, "It is confirmed that the Messenger of Allāh, may the peace and blessings of Allāh be upon him, said, 'Let one of you go into *iḥrām* in a white waist-wrapper, *izār*, and cloak, *ridā'*, and sandals.'" In Bukhārī from Ibn 'Abbās, may Allāh be pleased with him, is that the Prophet, may the peace and blessings of Allāh be upon him, wore a waist-wrapper and cloak as did his Companions. Muslim also related this.

And he, may the peace and blessings of Allāh be upon him, also said, "Wear white clothes. It is the best of your clothes. Shroud your dead in it." (Abū Dāwūd and Tirmidhī who said it is *ḥasan ṣaḥīḥ*) Dyed clothes are disliked.

It is recommended to pray two *rak'ats* in which *Sūrah al-Kāfirūn* is recited in the first, and *al-Ikhlāṣ* in the second. If he has prayed the obligatory prayer, that satisfies the two *rak'ats* of *iḥrām*.

Know that the timing in relation to *ḥajj* is Shawwāl, Dhu al-Qa'dah, and the ten days of Dhu al-Ḥijjah, the last of which is the night of the Sacrifice since the Almighty says,

ٱلْحَجُّ أَشْهُرٌ مَّعْلُومَٰتٌ

"*For ḥajj are the months well known,*" [*al-Baqarah* 2: 197]

and He says,

﴿يَسْـَٔلُونَكَ عَنِ ٱلْأَهِلَّةِ قُلْ هِىَ مَوَٰقِيتُ لِلنَّاسِ وَٱلْحَجِّ

"*They ask you concerning the new moons. Say: They are but signs to mark fixed periods of time in the affairs of men and for pilgrimage.*" [*al-Baqarah* 2: 189]

In relation to *'umrah*, it is permitted during the entire year by the agreement of scholars, whether in the months of *ḥajj* or other months, except for five days: the Day of 'Arafah, the Day of Sacrifice, and the Days of *Tashrīq* because during that time the pilgrims are busy performing *ḥajj*.

Mīqāt

It is *wājib* to wear *Iḥrām* from *mīqāt*. For someone who is resident in Makkah, whether or not he is one of its people, his *mīqāt* for *ḥajj* is Makkah itself. It is said that it is Makkah and the rest of the *Ḥaram*. The *iḥrām* of the Makkan is from the door of his house. As for *'Umrah* his *mīqāt* is places like *at-Tan'īm*, or *al-Je'irrāmah*, etc. Someone who is not resident in Makkah whose house is between Makkah and the prescribed *mīqāts*, his *mīqāt* for *ḥajj* and *'Umrah* is the town where he lives or the camp where the Bedouin camps. If his house is beyond the *mīqāts*, his *mīqāt* is the one he passes. There are five *mīqāts*:

(a) Dhu al-Ḥulayfah

It is the *mīqāt* of someone coming from Madīnah.

(b) Al-Juḥfah near *Rābiqh*

It is the *mīqāt* for those coming from Syria, Egypt and the Maghrib (e.g. North West Africa).

(c) Yalamlam

It is the *mīqāt* of the people of the Yemen and countries like India, Pakistan, Malaysia, etc.

(d) Qarn al-Manāzil

It is the *mīqāt* of those coming from Najd.

(e) Dhāt 'Irq

It is the *mīqāt* of those coming from Iraq, Iran, Khurasan, etc.

If he passes the *mīqāt* without going into *iḥrām* for the rites, he must return to it before he begins the rites, even if he has adopted *iḥrām* subsequently. If he does not return or returns after beginning the rites, he must sacrifice, even if it is only due to forgetfulness or ignorance, but there is no sin incurred by someone who is ignorant or forgets. The required sacrifice is a one-year-old sheep or a two-year-old goat since the Prophet, may the peace and blessings of

Allāh be upon him, said, "Whoever abandons a practice owes a sacrifice." If he goes back to the *mīqāt* and goes into *iḥrām* from there, then he does not have to sacrifice, provided that he has not begun the rites. If he has begun the rites, the need to sacrifice is not removed from him whether those rites are obligatory or voluntary.

It is best to put on *iḥrām* from the beginning of the *mīqāt* and to cover the rest of the distance in *iḥrām* except in the case of *Dhu al-Ḥulayfah* where it is better to go into *iḥrām* from the mosque from which the Messenger of Allāh, may the peace and blessings of Allāh be upon him, went into *iḥrām*.

7.4.2 Standing at *'Arafāt*

The second *farḍ* element of *ḥajj* is standing at 'Arafāt. That is to say, to halt at the plain of 'Arafāt on the 9th of Dhu al-Ḥijjah.

This is because the Messenger of Allāh, may the peace and blessings of Allāh be upon him, commanded a caller to call, "*Ḥajj* is 'Arafah," i.e. the chief of the pillars of the *ḥajj*. Standing is achieved by being present at any part of 'Arafāt. If he passes through 'Arafāt while seeking a runaway servant, lost camel, or something else, or is asleep at 'Arafāt until the time passes, that fulfils his obligation, even if just for a few moments from the decline of the sun on the 9th of Dhu al-Ḥijjah until the coming of the dawn for the next day.

It is *wājib* to stay at 'Arafāt from after the time of the sun's zenith up to the time of sunset and one must not leave 'Arafāt before sunset. This is for the one who reached there during the daytime. As for the one who reached there after sunset he can leave for Muzdalifah even after a moment of stay at 'Arafāt.

7.4.3 *Ṭawāf az-Ziyārah*, which is also called *Ṭawāf al-Ifāḍah*

The third *farḍ* element of *ḥajj* is *Ṭawāf az-Ziyārah.* That is to say, to make *ṭawāf* of the Ka'bah after halting at 'Arafāt on the 10th of Dhu al-Ḥijjah. If this is missed on the 10th it must be performed by the 12th of Dhu al-Ḥijjah.

This is by consensus what is meant by the words of the Almighty,

...وَلْيَطَّوَّفُوا۟ بِٱلْبَيْتِ ٱلْعَتِيقِ ﴿٢٩﴾

"*Let them circumambulate the Ancient House,*" [*al-Ḥajj* 22: 29]

and by the *ḥadīth* of *Umm al-Mu'minīn* Ṣafiyyah, may Allāh be pleased with her. 'Ā'ishah, may Allāh be pleased with her, related that Ṣafiyyah bint Ḥuyay entered her period of menses after performing *Ṭawāf az-Ziyārah.* I mentioned of her menses to Allāh's Messenger, may the peace and blessings of Allāh be upon him, whereupon he remarked: Will she then detain us? I said, Messenger of Allāh! She has performed *Ṭawāf az-Ziyārah,* and it was after that she entered her period of menses. Thereupon the Messenger of Allāh, may the peace and blessings of Allāh be upon him, said (if it is so) then proceed forth. (Muslim)

It is *Sunnah* to do *dhikr* while doing *ṭawāf*, according to the *ḥadīth* of 'Abdullāh ibn as-Sā'ib, may Allāh be pleased with him, who said, "I heard the Messenger of Allāh, may the peace and blessings of Allāh be upon him, say between the Yemeni corner and the Black Stone,

رَبَّنَآ ءَاتِنَا فِى ٱلدُّنْيَا حَسَنَةً وَفِى ٱلْءَاخِرَةِ حَسَنَةً وَقِنَا عَذَابَ ٱلنَّارِ

Rabbanā ātinā fid-dunyā Ḥasanatan wa fil ākhirati Ḥasanatan wa qinā adhāban-nār. (Our Lord, give us good in this world and good in the Next world and protect us from the punishment of the Fire.)" (Aḥmad, Abū Dāwūd and an-Nasā'ī. Ibn Ḥibbān and Ḥākim say it is *ṣaḥiḥ*.)

Abū Hurayrah, may Allāh be pleased with him, said, "If anyone does *ṭawāf* of the House seven times in which he only says,

سُبْحَانَ اللّٰهِ وَالْحَمْدُ لِلّٰهِ وَلَا إِلَهَ إِلاَّ اللّٰهُ وَاللّٰهُ أَكْبَر
وَلَا حَوْلَ وَلَا قُوَّةَ إِلاَّ بِاللّٰه

Subḥānallāhi wal-ḥamdu lillāhi wa lā ilāha illallāhu wallāhu Akbar wa la ḥawla wa la quwwata illa billah, (Glory be to Allāh and praise belongs to Allāh. There is no god but Allāh and Allāh is most great. There is no power nor strength except by Allāh),

ten evil deeds will be erased from him and ten good deeds will be written for him and by them he will be elevated ten degrees." (Ibn Mājah) 'Ā'ishah, may Allāh be pleased with her, said, "The Messenger of Allāh, may the peace and blessings of Allāh be upon him, said, '*Ṭawāf* of the House and *Ṣafā* and *Marwah* are to establish the remembrance of Allāh.'" (Abū Dāwūd and Ḥākim)

It is *wājib* to make *ṭawāf az-Ziyārah* in the time period during the 10th, 11th, or 12th of Dhu al-Ḥijjah and to offer two *rak'ats* behind the Station of Ibrāhīm after the obligatory *ṭawāf* of *ḥajj*, *ṭawāf az-Ziyārah.*

The Wājib and Sunnah Elements of Ṭawāf

The performance of the following are *wājib* elements of *ṭawāf*:

1. being free from both the state of major and minor impurity, i.e. one should have *wuḍū'*, and should be free from *ḥayḍ* and *nifās* or *janābah*, that is anything that requires one to perform *ghusl* when performing *ṭawāf*;
2. covering the *'awrah*;
3. to begin the circuits of *ṭawāf* around the Ka'bah at the corner of the Black Stone;
4. to make circuits of the Ka'bah counter-clockwise, with the Ka'bah on one's left side;
5. to perform *ṭawāf* on foot, though one may perform it while mounted if an excuse exists. Voluntary *ṭawāf*, however, may be performed riding even if a need does not exist;
6. to make seven circuits of the Ka'bah; the first four being *farḍ*;
7. to offer two *rak'āts* of prayer behind the *maqām* Ibrāhīm, at the conclusion of the *ṭawāf*;

If it is too crowded at the *maqām* Ibrāhīm, then the two *rakʿāts* should be made anywhere in *Masjid al-Ḥarām* that is convenient. If someone did *ṭawāf* in a time when prayer is prohibited (for example after *Fajr* or *ʿAṣr*) whether he is travelling or staying in Makkah, then he should perform these two *rakʿāts* as soon as possible after the prohibited times.[2]

It is *makrūh* to observe two *ṭawāfs* without observing two *rakʿāts* of prayer in between; [except if someone does *ṭawāf* at a time when prayer is prohibited then he can do *ṭawāf* as much as he can and afterwards he should pray for each seven circuits, two *rakʿats*.[3]

8. to pass around, not within, the *Ḥaṭīm*, including it in each circuit of *ṭawāf*, as it is a part of the Kaʿbah;
9. and to perform the *ṭawāf* within the precincts of the *Masjid al-Ḥarām*.

The performance of the following are *sunnah* elements of *ṭawāf*:

1. to be free from actual filth, *najāsah*;
2. it is *Sunnah* during both the *ḥajj* and *ʿumrah* that males observe *ramal*[4] or making circuits at a swift pace if one intends to perform *saʿy* after completing the *ṭawāf* during the first three circuits of *ṭawāf*, and *iḍṭibāʿ* or throwing the upper garment of the *iḥrām* across the body in such manner as to leave the right arm and shoulder bare;
3. to kiss the Black Stone at the inception and completion of every circuit;

   If it is not possible to kiss the Black Stone due to the density of the crowd, one may touch it with a stick or some other object and then kiss the object. If one is so far away as to not even be able to touch it with an extended object, one may raise one's right hand and gesture as to touch the Black Stone, and then kiss the hand.
4. and to touch the Yemeni corner of the Kaʿbah when making *ṭawāf*, if one is not prevented from doing so.

7.5 The Wājib Elements of Ḥajj

The *farḍ* elements of *Ḥajj* have already been mentioned. We will now clarify the *wājib* elements. The difference between them is that the rites are dependent on the *farḍ* elements and their omission cannot be rectified by sacrifice. The rites' existence are not dependent on the *wājib* elements and therefore can be rectified by sacrifice.

These are the *wājibat* of *ḥajj*:

1. To make *sa'y* between Ṣafā and Marwah.

   Sa'y between Ṣafā and Marwah is one of the obligations of the *ḥajj* since the Messenger of Allāh, may the peace and blessings of Allāh be upon him, did it and said while he was doing it, "Do *sa'y*, Allāh the Almighty has prescribed it for you."

   It is obligatory that the *sa'y* is done after a sound *ṭawāf*. The order is also obligatory, so he begins with Ṣafā and ends with Marwah. When he reaches Marwah, it is counted as one. The second begins with Marwah, and when he reaches Ṣafā again, it is the second time. He must do *sa'y* seven times between Ṣafā and Marwah since the Prophet, may the peace and blessings of Allāh be upon him, did that.

   It is permitted to do *sa'y* mounted if an excuse exists, otherwise walking is obligatory.
2. To halt at the plain of Muzdalifah any time between (the true) dawn and sunrise on the 10th of Dhu al-Ḥijjah; and to combine the *maghrib* and *'ishā* prayers at the time of *'ishā* at Muzdalifah.
3. To stone the three *jamrahs* each day during the three Days of *Tashrīq* except for the *jamrah al-'aqabah* which is stoned alone on the 10th of Dhu al-Ḥijjah. Each *jamrah* is stoned with seven pebbles. If one wants to leave early, the stoning of the third day of the Days of *Tashrīq*, the 13th of Dhu al-Ḥijjah, can be omitted.

The number of pebbles used on each of these days is twenty-one, seven pebbles for each *jamrah.* A condition in stoning the *jamrah* is doing it in the proper order so that you first stone the first *jamrah,* which is next to the mosque of Khayf, and then the middle one and finally the *jamrah al-ʿaqabah,* which is the last.

The obligation of stoning implies that to which the name *ramy* – stoning, is usually applied. If one places the pebbles on what one is stoning, it is not acceptable because it is not called *ramy*. The aim of the person to stone the pillar of *jamrah* is a precondition. If he throws it in the air and it lands on the *jamrah,* that is not acceptable. It is a precondition that he throws with his hand. If he kicks it with his foot or shoots it with a bow, that is not allowed. It is a precondition that he throws seven pebbles seven times. If he throws two pebbles at once and they hit the object, that is only considered as one pebble. Even if he were to throw seven at once, it is still only considered one. If he is unable to throw due to illness or something else, he can delegate someone to throw for him provided that the delegate has already stoned for himself. Otherwise it is not valid.

4. To offer sacrifice; this is *wājib* for a person who performs the *qirān* and *tamattuʿ* types of *ḥajj* and must be done on the three days of sacrifice, 10th–12th of Dhu al-Ḥijjah, but is not obligatory for those who performed the *ifrād ḥajj.*
5. To shave or cut one's hair after the conclusion of throwing pebbles at the *jamrah* of *al-ʿaqabah* on the 10th of Dhu al-Ḥijjah, and it should take place within the boundaries of the *Ḥaram* of Makkah.

Shaving or cutting the hair short since the Almighty says,

"*with heads shaved, hair cut short,*" [*al-Fatḥ* 48: 27]

and the Prophet, may the peace and blessings of Allāh be upon him, said, "May Allāh have mercy on those who shave their heads." They said, "And those who cut their hair short, Messenger of Allāh?" He said, "And those who cut their hair short." In the *ḥadīth* of Jābir, may Allāh be pleased with him, is related that the Prophet, may the peace and blessings of Allāh be upon him, commanded his Companions to shave their head or shorten their hair. It is best for men to shave since the Prophet, may the peace and blessings of Allāh be upon him, did that in the Farewell *Ḥajj* (Muslim), and since he, may the peace and blessings of Allāh be upon him, said, "O Allāh, have mercy on those who shave their heads," and the third time he added, "And those who cut their hair short." It is recommended that someone with no hair, like a bald person, run the razor over his head.

6. It is also necessary to keep the sequence of casting pebbles at the pillar of *al-ʿaqabah*, offering of sacrifice, and then shaving or cutting the hair on the 10th of Dhu al-Ḥijjah, the Day of Sacrifice.
7. To observe the *ṭawāf* of the Kaʿbah when bidding farewell to the *Masjid al-Ḥaram*, known as *ṭawāf al-wadāʿ Ṭawāf of farewell*; this is to be observed by those coming from outside the appointed *miqāts*.

The *ṭawāf* of farewell is the last thing that a pilgrim does as related from ʿUmar, may Allāh be pleased with him, "The last of the practices of *ḥajj* is *ṭawāf* of the House." (Mālik in the *Muwaṭṭā*')

7.6 The Sunnah Elements of Ḥajj

Elements other than the above mentioned are considered *sunnah* and if omitted, do not effect the validity of the *ḥajj*; nor do they require one to offer *damm*, sacrifice or *fidyah*.

Among the *Sunnah* acts are the following:

- To make *ghusl* or *wuḍū* when the pilgrim enters *iḥrām*; *ghusl* is *Sunnah* even though the pilgrim is a woman during her *ḥayḍ* or *nifās*.

- To wear new, white seamless clothing used by men for *iḥrām*, to use scent, and to thereafter perform two *rakʿats* of *nafl* prayer, when a pilgrim intends to enter *iḥrām*.
- After taking *iḥrām*, to read *talbiyah* with a loud voice at every ritual prayer, when ascending a hill, descending a valley, meeting a group of pilgrims, and at dawn.

  The *Talbiyah* is,

  لَبَّيْكَ اللّٰهُمَّ لَبَّيْكَ، لَبَّيْكَ لَا شَرِيْكَ لَكَ لَبَّيْكَ، إِنَّ الْحَمْدَ وَالنِّعْمَةَ لَكَ وَالْمُلْكَ، لَا شَرِيْكَ لَكْ

  Labbayka, Allāhumma labbayka, Labbayka, lā sharīka laka labbayka, innal-ḥamda, wan-niʿmata, laka wal-mulk lā sharīka laka. (At Your service, O Allāh, at Your service. At Your service, none can be associated with You, at Your service. All praise and blessing belongs to You as does the Kingdom. None can be associated with You.)

The *Sunnah* is to recite it a lot in the state of *iḥrām*. It is recommended standing, sitting, riding, walking, and even in the state of *janābah* and while a woman is menstruating. It is particularly recommended during every ascent and descent, when mounting and dismounting, when companions meet, when the night comes or the day comes, and in the mosque of Khayf and the Sacred Ḥaram Mosque.

It is not recommended during the *ṭawāf* of arrival or the *saʿy* because they have *adhkār* particular to them. *Talbiyah* should definitely not be recited in the *ṭawāf az-Ziyārah* and *ṭawāf* of farewell since the time for *talbiyah* has then passed by stoning at the *jamrah al-ʿaqabah*. It is recommended for men rather than women to raise their voices with it. When he finishes it, it is recommended to send salutations on the Prophet, may the peace and blessings of Allāh be upon him, and to ask for Allāh's pleasure and Paradise, and to seek refuge from the Fire. Then he makes whatever supplication he wishes. He does not speak during the *talbiyah*. It is disliked to greet him, but if he is greeted, he returns the greeting.

- Repetition of the *talbiyah* whenever reciting it.
- After taking *iḥrām*, to invoke blessings on the Prophet, may the peace and blessings of Allāh be upon him, make *du'a'* for Paradise and companionship of the pious therein, and protection from the Hellfire.
- To make *ghusl* for entering the *Ḥaram* of Makkah.
- To say, "*Allāhu Akbar*", and "*Lā ilāha illallāh*", when the pilgrim arrives at the place opposite to the Ka'bah.
- *Du'a'* for anything the pilgrim desires when he or she sees the Ka'bah for the first time, which is accepted by Allāh.
- To perform *iḍṭibā'* in *ṭawāf al-qudūm.*
- To perform *ramal* in *ṭawāf al-qudūm* if *sa'y* is to be performed after this *ṭawāf.*
- To run when passing between the green pillars doing *sa'y* between Ṣafā and Marwah for men, but women will pass by with ease.
- To make voluntary *ṭawāf* as often as possible.
- To leave Makkah for Minā after sunrise on the 8th of Dhu al-Ḥijjah (*Yawm at-Tarwiyah*) and to pass the night there.
- To depart from Minā for 'Arafāt after sunrise on the 9th of Dhu al-Ḥijjah.
- The pilgrim's utmost effort to show humility, and submissiveness to Allāh in weeping and in prayer for the good of this world and good of the Hereafter for himself, his parents, and his Muslim brothers and sisters at Muzdalifah and 'Arafāt.
- To depart after sunset from 'Arafāt with ease of mind, to stop at Muzdalifah which is higher than the interior of the valley and which is near the Quzaḥ Hill (*Jabal Quzaḥ*), and to pass the night in Muzdalifah.

- To pass the nights in Minā in the days of Minā. It is *makrūh* to stay in Makkah while the pilgrims are in Minā.
- To stone the *jamrah al-ʿaqabah* on the 10th of Dhu al-Ḥijjah after sunrise until the sun reaches its zenith; however it is permissible to stone up to sunset.
- To stone the *jamrahs* during the time between the sun passing its meridian and sunset on the days of the 11th, 12th, and 13th of Dhu al-Ḥijjah.
- To offer sacrifice by the pilgrim who performs the *ifrād* type of *ḥajj*.
- To eat the meat of a sacrifice offered voluntarily or the sacrifice offered by the pilgrims who performed the *tamattuʿ* and *qirān* types of *ḥajj*.
- If a pilgrim has intended to leave Minā for Makkah on the 12th of Dhu al-Ḥijjah, it is *Sunnah* to leave before sunset. If however, he stays at Minā at sunset or after it, no atonement is necessary but he has committed an error. Should he prolong his stay at Minā until the appearance of the dawn of the 13th of Dhu al-Ḥijjah, it is *wājib* for him to stone the three *jamrahs* on that day also.
- After leaving Minā for Makkah, to stop at a place called Muḥassab for a while.
- To face towards the Kaʿbah and to look at it standing.
- To drink the water of the well of Zamzam; to drink it from the palm, and to pour it on the head and on other parts of the body.
- Taking hold of the Multazam, the wall of the Kaʿbah lying between the door and the Black Stone by putting one's chest and face on it and taking hold of the veil of the Kaʿbah for a while, praying to Allāh for whatever one wishes.
- Kissing the threshold of the door of the Kaʿbah in full reverence and honour and entering into it with full courtesy and respect.
- It is highly recommended to visit the mosque and noble grave of the Prophet, may the peace and blessings of Allāh be upon him.

7.7 *The Unlawful and Permissible Actions while in a State of Iḥrām*

7.7.1 What is unlawful for someone in *iḥrām*

The following things are forbidden for someone in *iḥrām:*

- to engage in sexual intercourse, amorous talk, or anything that may potentially lead to sex;
- to kill or hunt game, or to help, guide, or co-operate with others who are hunting;

Game consists of every animal or bird naturally wild which can only be caught by a contrived plan, whether it is domesticated or not. As killing is forbidden, so is hunting. The basis of that is the statement of the Almighty,

وَحُرِّمَ عَلَيْكُمْ صَيْدُ ٱلْبَرِّ مَا دُمْتُمْ حُرُمًا

"*Forbidden is the pursuit of land-game as long as you are in the Sacred Precincts or in pilgrim garb.*" [*al-Mā'idah* 5: 96]

There is a category which it is recommended for the one in *iḥrām* and others to kill. That is harmful creatures which include snakes, scorpions, mice, wild dogs, crows, wolves, lions, tigers, bears, leopards, eagles, fleas, bedbugs, and hornets.

- to hurt, abuse, or argue with other Muslims;
- for men to wear clothes with seams and stitching;

If a man goes into *iḥrām*, he is forbidden to wear something which covers all of his body and head, whether it is sewn, like shirt and trousers, or anything else like a turban, based on what is in the *Ṣaḥīḥain* (Bukhārī and Muslim); that a man asked the Prophet, may the peace and blessings of Allāh be upon him, "What clothes should a man in *iḥrām* wear?" He replied, "He should not wear a shirt, turban, trousers, burnoose (hooded cloak) or leather socks unless he cannot find sandals in which case he can wear leather socks, cutting off what is above the ankles. You should not wear any clothes which have been touched by saffron or *wirs* (a yellowish perfume)."

It is permitted to knot the waist-wrapper, *izār*, and to tie it with a string. It is permitted to give it something like a waist-band and put a string in it which is not the case with the cloak. It is not permitted to knot the cloak, *ridā*, or to tie it end to end with a string. Men can gird on a sword and tie the scabbard on their waist.

- to use perfume;

  Using perfume on clothes or body because it is considered a luxury and the pilgrim is dishevelled and dusty, as the tradition states and because the Prophet, may the peace and blessings of Allāh be upon him, said, "Wash off any perfume on you three times." (Bukhārī) Perfume is what clearly has the aim of scenting like rose, jasmine, and violet. Using it is to apply it to the body. If he carries musk or something else in a bag or tied rag, that it not unlawful whether he smells it or not.

- to cover the head or face; women however must cover their head at all times, as it is obligatory;

  As for his head, it is based on what the Prophet, may the peace and blessings of Allāh be upon him, said about the one in *iḥrām* who was killed in a fall from a camel, "Do not cover his head, and do not bring any perfume near to him as he will be raised up on the Day of Rising saying the *talbiyah*." (Bukhārī, Muslim)

  As for the woman, for her the face is like a man's head. She leaves her face uncovered. All of her head is concealed by sewn garments. She can cover her face with a cloth or rag provided that it does not touch her face, whether it is for a need or not, due to heat or cold or fear of temptation and the like.

- to wash the body or hair with soap or other abrasive chemicals;
- to remove hair from any part of the body by any means;

It is forbidden to comb the hair and to scratch it with the nails when one knows that combing or scratching will pull out hair because it is entangled or the like. It is forbidden to remove hair by shaving since the Almighty says,

وَلَا تَحْلِقُوا رُءُوسَكُمْ حَتَّىٰ يَبْلُغَ الْهَدْيُ مَحِلَّهُ

> "*Do not shave your heads until the offering reaches the place of sacrifice.*" [*al-Baqarah* 2: 196]

There is no difference between shaving, plucking, clipping, burning, and removing with tweezers and the like.

- or to clip one's nails.

  Cutting the nails is like hair. There is no difference between clipping, cutting with a knife, breaking and the like, because of the agreement of scholars that it is forbidden.

7.7.2 The performance of the following are permissible (*jā'iz*) in *iḥrām*

1. to seek rest in a shady place;
2. to wash one's body and hair with water alone;
3. to scratch the body, taking care not to pull out any hair;
4. to carry money, a weapon, etc., on one's person in a purse or bag;
5. to change or wash the *iḥrām* garment;
6. to wear glasses, a wristwatch, a ring; i.e. those things normally necessary for one's use;
7. to get married; the marriage of the person in *iḥrām* is considered valid, however the consummation of the marriage is forbidden. According to Imām Shāfi'ī and other Imāms, even a marriage contract while in the state of *iḥrām* is unlawful and the marriage is invalid.
8. to kill harmful animals such as rats, crows, kites, scorpions, snakes, and vicious dogs and wolves;
9. and to do business.

7.8 The Ḥajj of Women

Women are the same as men in respect of the *ḥajj* except with regard to certain matters which include the following:

- It is not unlawful for them to wear stitched garments.
- They must cover their heads, but not cover their faces.
- They do not raise their voices in the *talbiyah.*
- They do not observe *ramal* and *iḍṭibāʿ* in the *ṭawāf.*
- They do not run in the bottom of the valley between Ṣafā and Marwah but walk normally.
- They do not shave their heads but cut their hair, taking approximately a finger's length from it.
- They are excused the *ṭawāf* of farewell, *ṭawāf al-wadāʿ* in the *ḥajj* if they are menstruating or have post-childbirth bleeding.
- It is not prohibited for them to delay the *ṭawāf al-ziyārah* after the days of Sacrifice, 10th–12th Dhu al-Ḥijjah until their menstruation or post-childbirth bleeding has stopped.

7.9 Ḥajj on Behalf of Someone Else

When one is able to make *ḥajj* and then becomes unable to do so on account of an illness from which he does not hope to recover, or because of old age, they must delegate someone else to make *ḥajj* for them. The evidence for this is found in the *ḥadīth* of Ibn ʿAbbās, may Allāh be pleased with him, that a woman of Khathʿam said, "Messenger of Allāh, Allāh has obliged the *ḥajj* from His slaves. My father is very old and cannot remain firm on a mount. Can I make *ḥajj* for him?" He said, "Yes." (Mālik, Shāfiʿī, Bukhārī, Muslim, Abū Dāwūd and Nasāʾī) Tirmidhī said that more than one *ḥadīth* is sound from the Prophet, may the peace and blessings of Allāh be upon him, in this area.

Whoever dies owing *ḥajj* of Islam, it is obligatory for his *walī* to provide someone to make *ḥajj* for him based on what is related from a woman of Juhaynah who came to the Messenger of Allāh, may the peace and blessings of Allāh be upon him, and said, "My mother made a vow to go on *ḥajj* but did not go on *ḥajj* before she died. Shall I perform *ḥajj* for her?" He said, "Yes, go on *ḥajj* for her."

7.10 Important Rulings on Failure Upon Donning the Iḥrām to Perform Ḥajj, ʿUmrah and Violating the Restrictions of Iḥrām

- ***Al-Iḥṣār*** – prevention from *ḥajj* or *ʿumrah* after donning of *iḥrām*;
- ***Al-Fawāt*** – missing standing at ʿArafāt at its fixed time and thereby missing the *ḥajj;* and
- ***Al-Jināyāt ʿalal-iḥrām*** – violating the restrictions of *iḥrām* or sanctity of the *Ḥaram;* or
- not observing some of the *wājib* elements of *ḥajj.*

7.10.1 *Al-Iḥṣār* – Prevention from *Ḥajj* or *ʿUmrah*

When the pilgrim doing *ḥajj* or one doing *ʿumrah* is prevented from completing his rites, he comes out of *iḥrām* and makes a sacrifice wherever he is prevented. This is according to the three schools of *fiqh*, while according to Imām Abū Ḥanīfah, he should send a *hadiy*, a sacrificial animal or money so that a *hadiy* can be bought and sacrificed in *ḥaram.* He should fix a time with the person whom he has delegated for it. After that he can come out of *iḥrām.* Its minimum is a sheep which satisfies the *udḥiyyah*, sacrifices. There must be the intention to come out of *iḥrām.* The basis for that is the words of the Almighty,

فَإِنْ أُحْصِرْتُمْ فَمَا ٱسْتَيْسَرَ مِنَ ٱلْهَدْيِ

> "*If you are prevented, then such offering as may be feasible.*" [*al-Baqarah* 2: 196]

The *āyah* means: if you are prevented, then you come out of *iḥrām* and make whatever sacrifice is feasible. A *ḥadīth* quoted in the two *Ṣaḥiḥ* collections of Bukhārī and Muslim, "The Prophet, may the peace and blessings of Allāh be upon him, came out of *iḥrām* at al-Ḥudaybiyyah when the idol worshippers barred him. He was in *iḥrām* for *'umrah.*" Sacrifice must precede shaving since the Almighty says,

وَلَا تَحْلِقُوا رُءُوسَكُمْ حَتَّىٰ يَبْلُغَ الْهَدْيُ مَحِلَّهُ

"*Do not shave your heads until the offering reaches the place of sacrifice.*" [*al-Baqarah* 2: 196]

7.10.2 *Al-Fawāt* – Anyone who misses standing at 'Arafāt

If anyone misses standing at 'Arafāt so that the dawn rises on the Day of Sacrifice, he has missed *ḥajj* since the Prophet, may the peace and blessings of Allāh be upon him, said, "Whoever catches 'Arafah at night, has caught the *ḥajj*. Whoever misses 'Arafah at night has missed the *ḥajj* and should begin *'umrah* and he owes *ḥajj* the following year." (Dāraquṭnī) He should come out of *iḥrām* by doing *'umrah* and do *qaḍā'*, the next year. He is obliged to make up the missed *ḥajj* whether it was a *farḍ* or only a *nafl*, voluntary *ḥajj*. *Hadiy*, to sacrifice an animal is not *wājib* neither now nor while making it up for missing, though it is recommended to do so according to Imām Abū Ḥanīfah.

According to the other three Imāms, as making it up is *wājib*, so sacrifice is also *wājib*. It is narrated in Imām Mālik's *al-Muwaṭṭā*, with a sound *isnād* that Abū Ayyūb al-Anṣārī, may Allāh be pleased with him, left Madinah to perform *ḥajj*. When he was at An-Nāziah he lost his mount, so was delayed on the way and missed standing at 'Arafāt at its time. He came to Amīr al-Mumīnin 'Umar ibn al-Khaṭṭāb, may Allāh be pleased with him, on the 10th of Dhu al-Ḥijjah and mentioned what had happened to him. 'Umar, may Allāh be pleased with him, said, "Go to Makkah, do *ṭawāf* of the House, run between Ṣafā and Marwah, shave the hair and come out of *Iḥrām*. Then return next year, do *ḥajj* and sacrifice whatever you can."

7.10.3 *Al-Jināyāt ʿalal-Iḥrām* – Violations of the State of *Iḥrām*

If someone violates the restrictions of *iḥrām*, i.e. is involved in doing what is prohibited, either deliberately, by mistake or ignorance, it necessitates an expiation. Doing it deliberately is a sin and it is feared that the one responsible is deprived of his *ḥajj* being *mabrūr*, not accepted. The expiation differs according to the degree of violation.

Sexual relationship

A *muḥrim*'s involvement in sexual intercourse is the most grievous violation of *al-Iḥrām*. It nullifies *ʿumrah*; making it up is obligatory and offering a *damm*, sacrificing a sheep or a goat as expiation. In the *iḥrām* of *ḥajj*, if it occurs before standing at ʿArafāt:

1. It nullifies *ḥajj* and obliges one to carry on the defected *ḥajj* to the end;
2. To make it up in the following year, and
3. Offer a *damm*, sacrifice a sheep in expiation. This is according to Imām Abū Ḥanīfah, and a camel or a cow according to other Imāms. If it occurs after standing at ʿArafāt and before the shaving of the head it does not nullify the *ḥajj* according to Imām Abū Ḥanīfah but it necessitates a *damm*, sacrificing a camel as expiation; while it nullifies the *ḥajj* and necessitates a camel as expiation according to other Imāms. If this involvement occurred after shaving the head but before *ṭawāf al-ifāḍah*; it obliges a sheep according to Imām Abū Ḥanīfah and a camel according to others; and in this case *ḥajj* is not nullified.

To groom oneself

Shaving, clipping the nails, wearing sewn clothes, covering the head and face for men and covering the face for women, also necessitates expiation. It also differs according to its prerequisites, for example, if anyone shaves more than a fourth of his head, or does the like of that with his nails by cutting five or more nails in total from either the hand or feet or he covers his head or face for about as long as a day or night or applies perfume to a full limb of his body, he owes a *damm,* sacrifice a sheep, goat or a seventh share of a camel or a cow. If he is unable to do that then to give as *ṣadaqah* six *ṣāʿ* of barley or dates to six poor people of *ḥaram* or three *ṣāʿ* of wheat to six people, half a *ṣāʿ* of wheat to each person. According to Imām Abū Ḥanīfah, may Allāh have mercy on him, the expiation of offering a sheep is fixed in the case of one who did it deliberately or without excuse, but according to other Imāms the choice of three alternatives in expiation is general, though according to all *fuqahāʿ* if someone did it without excuse he is a sinner.

The basis for the choice are the words of the Almighty,

فَمَن كَانَ مِنكُم مَّرِيضًا أَوْ بِهِۦٓ أَذًى مِّن رَّأْسِهِۦ فَفِدْيَةٌ مِّن صِيَامٍ أَوْ صَدَقَةٍ أَوْ نُسُكٍ

> "*And if any of you is ill or has an ailment in his scalp, he should in compensation either fast, or feed the poor, or offer sacrifice.*" [*al-Baqarah* 2: 196].

The Messenger of Allāh, may the peace and blessings of Allāh be upon him, made that clear when he said to Kaʿb ibn ʿUjrah, may Allāh be pleased with him, "Are your head-lice troubling you?" He replied, "Yes." The Prophet, may the peace and blessings of Allāh be upon him, said, "Sacrifice a sheep or fast three days or feed three *saʿ* of food to six poor people." (Bukhārī and Muslim)

Hunting land game

Expiation is obliged for killing game. When someone in *iḥrām* kills game, and it has a "like", he can choose between sacrificing its like and giving it as *ṣadaqah* to the poor of the *Ḥaram* or estimating the cost of the "like" in money, and using them to buy food for them or fasting a day for every *mudd* since He, glory be to Him, said:

فَجَزَآءٌ مِّثْلُ مَا قَتَلَ مِنَ ٱلنَّعَمِ يَحْكُمُ بِهِۦ ذَوَا عَدْلٍ مِّنكُمْ هَدْيًۢا
بَٰلِغَ ٱلْكَعْبَةِ أَوْ كَفَّٰرَةٌ طَعَامُ مَسَٰكِينَ أَوْ عَدْلُ ذَٰلِكَ صِيَامًا

"*There shall be recompense – the like of what he has slain, in flocks, as shall be judged by two men of equity among you, an offering to reach the Ka'bah, or expiation – food for poor persons or the equivalent of that in fasting.*" [*al-Mā'idah* 5: 95]

If the game has no counterpart, he can choose between giving its value in food or fasting a day for every *mudd*. In estimating its value, one should consider the place it was killed. What is meant by the "like" is the animal closest in appearance to the game. It does not mean the like in species, so that an ostrich is obliged for an ostrich and a gazelle for a gazelle. When He, glory be to Him and may He be exalted! limited it to "flocks", He moved from the species to the form of livestock. A group of Companions, may Allāh be pleased with them all, judged more than once that there was a camel for an ostrich and a cow for an onager, and a ram for a hyena. Jābir, may Allāh be pleased with him, reported the decision of the Messenger of Allāh, may the peace and blessings of Allāh be upon him, and it was also the decision of a group of Companions. The Companions decided a goat was the equivalent of a gazelle, and a young goat of a rabbit. There is small for small, large for large, male for male and female for female, healthy for healthy and broken for broken to preserve the resemblance which the *āyah* demands.

Omitting wājib elements of ḥajj

The omission of a *wājib* element of *ḥajj* also necessitates an expiation by offering a *damm*, sacrificing a sheep, a goat or a seventh share of a camel or cow. Omission of a *wājib* element deliberately, by ignorance or mistake oblige a sacrifice, except:

1. the *wuqūf* at Muzdalifah, in which it is allowed for ill or feeble people to leave for Minā at night without staying at Muzdalifah until the morning. This is based on the *sunnah* of the Prophet, may the peace and blessings of Allāh be upon him, that he sent the feeble members of his family to Minā at night, instructing them not to do *ramy* of *jamrah al-ʿAqabah* before sunrise.
2. in the *ramy* of *jamrāt* one is allowed to delegate someone else to do *ramy* on his behalf if he is unable to do it himself.

For minor violations, expiation is necessary but not *damm*, such as the removal of a few strands of hair. In these cases a knowledgeable person should be consulted for clarification.

7.10.4 The Place of Sacrifice and Feeding

All sacrifices, either in case of *iḥṣār*, *fawāt* or for the expiation obliged by an unlawful action or omission of an obligatory part, should be offered in the vicinity of the *Ḥaram* because the Almighty says, *"An offering to reach the Kaʿbah."* Its meat must be given to the poor of the *Ḥaram*. There is no difference between the poor who are residents and visitors, although it is better to give it to residents. If one gives food as *ṣadaqah* instead of sacrificing, he is also obliged to single out the poor of the *Ḥaram* for it. However if one is fasting, he may do it wherever he wishes since there is nothing for the poor in fasting in the *Ḥaram*. The least that will satisfy is that the obligation be paid to three poor people. It is not obligatory to give equally to them. He is permitted to give more or less to one of them.

All the sacrifices offered either in case of *iḥṣār*, *fawāt* or as *fidyah* (expiation) for *jināyāt* is not lawful for the person offering to consume from it. It is necessary to distribute among the poor of the *Ḥaram* as *ṣadaqah*. This is according to all the *fuqahā'*.

7.10.5 *Jināyāt ʿAlal-Ḥaram*, VIOLATION OF THE RESTRICTIONS OF THE *ḤARAM* BOUNDARY – KILLING THE GAME OF THE *ḤARAM* AND CUTTING DOWN TREES

It is unlawful to hunt in the *Ḥaram* of Makkah whether one is in *iḥrām* or not. As it is forbidden to cut down its plants, it is also forbidden to cut down its trees when they are fresh and not harmful. As for dry or harmful plants, it is not unlawful to interfere with them or with animals since the Prophet, may the peace and blessings of Allāh be upon him, said on the day Makkah was conquered, "This land is sacred because Allāh has made it sacred. Its trees should not be cut down nor its game chased and something dropped in it should not be picked up except by someone who announces it and its plants are not to be pulled down." ʿAbbās, may Allāh be pleased with him, said, "Messenger of Allāh, apart from the *idhkhir* herb for their goldsmiths and houses." He said, "Yes, apart from the *idhkhir* herb." (Bukhāri and Muslim)

It is permitted to take the leaves of the trees, but not to hit them fearing that it might strike its bark. If one pulls a branch and it does not grow back, then he will be liable. If it grows back that year, he is not liable, as is the case with leaves. As it is forbidden to cut down trees, it is also forbidden to cut the plants of the *Ḥaram* which are not cultivated, since the Prophet, may the peace and blessings of Allāh be upon him, said, "its plants are not to be pulled down," and that refers to fresh plants. If it is unlawful to cut, it is more than likely to be unlawful to uproot. It is not permitted to release animals in it to graze.

It is lawful for a person in the state of *iḥram* to kill harmful animals, whether it be in the *ḥaram* or outside the *ḥaram* area. ʿĀʾishah, may Allāh be pleased with her, related the Prophet, may Allāh bless him and grant him peace, as saying: "Five kinds of animals are harmful and should be killed in the *ḥaram*." These are a crow, a kite, a scorpion, a mouse and a rabid dog. It is also related from ʿAbdullāh ibn Masʿūd, may Allāh be pleased with him, "While we were in the company of the Prophet, may Allāh bless him and grant him peace, in a cave in Minā, *Sūrah al-Mursalāt* was revealed and he recited it and I heard it (directly) from his mouth as soon as he recited it, then suddenly a snake sprang at us and the Prophet, may Allāh bless him and grant him peace, ordered us to kill it; we ran to kill it but it escaped quickly. The Prophet, may Allāh bless him and grant him peace, said: 'It has escaped from your evil and you too have escaped from its evil.' " (Bukhārī)

7.11 The Description of 'Umrah

'Umrah consists of three *farḍ* elements: *iḥrām, ṭawāf* and *sa'y* between Ṣafā and Marwah. Shaving or shortening the hair is a *wājib* of ending *'umrah.*

When someone from outside the precincts of Makkah reaches the *miqāt* intending to perform *'umrah*, he should have a *ghusl* or do *wuḍū. Ghusl* is better. Then he puts on two cloths: a waist-wrapper, *izār*, and upper covering, *rida*, either washed or new, and whatever perfume he wishes and oils his hair with whatever oil he wishes. In the opinion of Imām Abū Ḥanīfah and Imām Abū Yūsuf it does not matter if the traces of that remain on his body after assuming *iḥrām.* But in the opinion of Imām Muḥammad and Imām Zufar, it is disliked to put on perfume whose traces remain after *iḥrām* has been adopted.

Then he prays two *rak'ats* and makes the intention of performing *'umrah*, saying the *talbiyah* after his prayer, in the manner we have already mentioned. Then he raises his voice in the *talbiyah* based on what is related from the Prophet, may the peace and blessings of Allāh be upon him, who said, "The best of *ḥajj* (and *'Umrah* is a lesser *ḥajj*) is the one where the voice is raised in *talbiyah* and when sacrifice is made." After adopting *iḥrām* the *talbiyah* should be repeated after all obligatory and voluntary prayers, whenever going up a slope or down into a valley, upon meeting another group, upon awakening from sleep and in the night before dawn.

That is what has come in reports from the Messenger of Allāh, may the peace and blessings of Allāh be upon him.

7.11.1 Entering Makkah

Upon arriving in Makkah – it does not matter whether one enters it in the day or the night – one should go to the *Masjid al-Ḥarām* and start *ṭawāf* from the Black Stone. When you come face to face with it, you say the *takbīr,* and raise your hands as you raise them in the prayer and then let them down. Then you should touch it if you are able to do so without annoying anyone. If you cannot, you say the *Allāhu Akbar, lā ilāha illa'llāh, Al-Ḥamdu lillāh* and say the salutation on the Prophet, may the peace and blessings of Allāh be upon him, with your hands raised as you face it. It is best to kiss the stone if you can and touch it. It is related that ʿUmar, may Allāh be pleased with him, kissed it and touched it, saying, "I saw the Messenger of Allāh, may the peace and blessings of Allāh be upon him, greet you." The *talbiyah* is stopped when greeting the Black Stone and is not said after that during the *ʿumrah.*

7.11.2 *Ṭawāf*

Then you go to the right of the Black Stone next to the door, do *iḍṭibāʿ*, adjust your upper covering so that your right shoulder is exposed and begin the *ṭawāf* of the Kaʿbah. You do seven circuits of the Kaʿbah, doing *ramal* in the first three, and walking in a more leisurely way in the other four, each circuit starting from the Black Stone and returning to it, which should be greeted every time you pass by. It is good to touch the Yemeni corner. The *ṭawāf* should be done outside the *Ḥaṭīm*[5] in every circuit, the *Ḥaṭīm* being considered part of the Kaʿbah.

When you finish the *ṭawāf*, you pray two *rakʿats* at the *Maqām-i-Ibrāhīm*. We consider that obligatory, *wājib*, but ash-Shāfiʿī said that it is *Sunnah*. After finishing the two *rakʿats*, you return to the Black Stone and greet it if you can or at least face it and say the *takbīr*, *"lā ilāha illa'llāh,"* and praise Allāh as we mentioned before.

7.11.3 *Sa'y* Between Ṣafā and Marwah

Then you leave by the Ṣafā door, or whichever door is convenient and make first for Ṣafā, climbing up it and standing where you can see the Ka'bah. You turn to face the Ka'bah, say the *Allāhu Akbar*, *lā ilāha illa'llāh*, *Al-Ḥamdu lillāh*, and glorify Him and say the salutation on the Prophet, may the peace and blessings of Allāh be upon him, and then ask Allāh Almighty for whatever you want, raising your hands with the palms upwards.

Then you descend from Ṣafā heading towards Marwah. When you reach the green marker you should run until you pass the other green marker[6] and then proceed to Marwah, walking.

When you reach it you climb over it, face towards the Ka'bah and do the same as you did on Ṣafā. You go between them seven times, ending at Marwah and running between the green markers each time you come to them.

7.11.4 Cutting the hair

When you finish the *sa'y*, you shave your head or cut your hair short, although shaving is better. With this your *'umrah* is completed and all the things which were forbidden in *iḥrām* are then allowed.

'Umrah on its own does not necessitate having to do a *ṭawāf* of farewell.

7.12 The Description of Ḥajj

There are three types of *ḥajj: ifrād, qirān* and *tamattu'*. There is no disagreement that each of them is permitted, but there is disagreement about which is best. The *qirān* is best in our opinion and then *tamattu'*, and then *ifrād*. Ash-Shāfi'ī says that *ifrād* is better than both of them. Mālik says that *tamattu'* is best, then *qirān* and then *ifrād*.

7.12.1 *Ḥajj al-Ifrād*

Ḥajj al-Ifrād is when you intend to adopt *iḥrām* for *ḥajj* alone at the *mīqāt*. If you have made this intention when you arrive in Makkah, you do the seven circuits of the *ṭawāf al-qudūm*, *ṭawāf* of arrival to greet the House. It is best not to do *sa'y* between Ṣafā and Marwah now, though it is allowed, and if it is done it will suffice for the *wājib sa'y* of *ḥajj*. You should delay *sa'y* until the *ṭawāf az-Ziyārah*. When *sa'y* is postponed until later to do it after there is no *ramal* in the *ṭawāf* of arrival. *Ramal* is *Sunnah* in the *ṭawāf* only if is immediately followed by the *sa'y*. You may do as much *ṭawāf* as you wish until the Day of *Tarwiyah* (the 8th of Dhu al-Hijjah), praying two *rak'ats* after every seven circuits provided it is a time in which voluntary prayers are permitted.

Staying at Minā (8th of Dhu al-Ḥijjah)

On the Day of *Tarwiyah*, which is the eighth day of Dhu al-Ḥijjah, you pray *fajr* in Makkah and then go with the people to Minā, pray *Ẓuhr*, *'Aṣr*, *Maghrib*, and *'Ishā'* there at their times, spend the night there and the following morning, the Day of 'Arafah, pray *Fajr* at Minā at its normal time.

Halting at 'Arafāt (9th of Dhu al-Ḥijjah)

When the sun rises, you move from Minā to 'Arafāt with calmness and gravity and when you reach it, you may stop anywhere you like except the valley of 'Uranah.

When the sun has passed the meridian, the *mu'adhdhin* gives the *adhān* while the Imām is on the *minbar*. When he finishes the *adhān*, the Imām stands and gives two *khuṭbahs* standing, sitting for a short while between them, as on the day of *Jumu'ah*. When the Imām has given the *khuṭbah*, the *mu'adhdhin* gives the *iqāmah*, and the Imām leads the people in *ẓuhr* prayer. Then the *iqāmah* is given again and the Imām leads them in the *'aṣr* prayer at the time of *zuhr* with one *adhān* and two *iqāmahs*. Neither the Imām nor the people do any *Sunnah* prayers between them.

When he finishes the prayer, the Imām returns to the *Mauqif* as do the people with him. It is better for the Imām to stay on his mount. Otherwise, he stands up and the people stand with him. All who are standing nearest to the Imām are in a better position because the Imām instructs the people in the matters of practices and they can hear him.

The whole of 'Arafāt is a place of standing except for the valley of 'Uranah. People should not stand there. They stand until sunset and say the *Allāhu Akbar*, *lā ilāha illa'llāh*, *Alḥamdu lillāh* and *Subḥānallāh*, say the salutation on the Prophet, may the peace and blessings of Allāh be upon him, and ask Allāh to fulfil their needs. It is a time of hopeful expectation. The Prophet, may the peace and blessings of Allāh be upon him, said, "The best supplication is that of the people of 'Arafah and the best of what I and the Prophets before me said is:

لاَ إِلَهَ إِلاَّ اللَّهُ وَحْدَهُ لاَ شَرِيكَ لَهُ، لَهُ الْمُلْكُ وَلَهُ الْحَمْدُ يُحْيِي وَيُمِيتُ وَهُوَ عَلَى كُلِّ شَيْءٍ قَدِيرٌ

> *Lā ilāha illallāhu, waḥdahu, Lā sharīka lahū, lahul-Mulku, wa lahul-ḥamdu, yuḥyī wa yumītu, wa Huwa 'alā kulli shay'in Qadīr.* (There is no god but Allāh without any partner. He has the kingdom and He has the praise. He gives life and makes death. And He has power over everything.)" (Tirmidhī)

It is related that the Prophet, may the peace and blessings of Allāh be upon him, said, "Allāh Almighty boasts of the people of 'Arafāt on the Day of 'Arafah, saying, 'Look, My angels, at My slaves. They come dishevelled, dusty, arriving from every deep ravine. Bear witness that I have forgiven them. They will return like the day their mothers bore them.'" When the sun sets, the Imām moves with all the people behind him calmly and with gravity to Muzdalifah without praying *maghrib* at 'Arafāt.

The time of standing at 'Arafāt is from midday on the day of 'Arafah until the time of *fajr* on the Day of Sacrifice, 10th of Dhu al-Ḥijjah. Anyone who is at 'Arafāt during this time, whether they know it or are ignorant of it, even if they are asleep or unconscious, and stands there or passes through there without standing, has caught the *ḥajj* for the Prophet, may the peace and blessings of Allāh be upon him, said, "*Ḥajj* is 'Arafah." So whoever stands there has done his *ḥajj*. However, if you reach 'Arafāt during the day you should stand there until sunset. If you do not stay there and continue on [to Muzdalifah] after midday before sunset, you must sacrifice. If you reach it after sunset, you do not stand but continue on directly and do not have to sacrifice.

Spending the night at Muzdalifah

Then all the people go on to Muzdalifah, each one stopping wherever he likes at Muzdalifah except in the valley of Muḥassir. It is disliked to camp on the road, but one should go to the right or left of it, so that passers-by are not inconvenienced. When twilight disappears and the time of *'ishā'* comes, the Imām leads everyone in the *maghrib* prayer at the time of *'ishā'* and then prays *'ishā'* with them with one *adhān* and one *iqāmah* and with no voluntary prayers in between. If he does voluntary prayers, then the *iqāmah* must be repeated. Then the Imām and the people spend the night at Muzdalifah.

When *fajr* arrives, the Imām leads the people in prayer in the dark and then stands with the people in the place of standing. The best is that the people stand behind the Imām at the mountain which is called Quzaḥ. The time of the standing at Muzdalifah is from after the rising of *fajr* of the Day of Sacrifice (the 10th of Dhu al-Ḥijjah) until the day has grown considerably bright. Whoever reaches part of Muzdalifah during this time has done the standing and owes no sacrifice although the *Sunnah* is as we have described. If someone goes on to Minā from Muzdalifah before dawn he must sacrifice since it is obligatory unless he has weakness or an illness and moves on at night because he fears the crush of the crowd. Such a person has no need to sacrifice based on what is related from the Prophet, may the peace and blessings of Allāh be upon him, that it is an allowance for the weak to hasten from Muzdalifah at night.

Leaving for Minā for stoning the Jamrah al-ʿAqabah (10th of Dhu al-Ḥijjah)

The Imām then goes on with the people from Muzdalifah before sunrise and comes to Minā. All the pebbles needed for stoning the *jamrahs* should be collected from Muzdalifah or from the road and not from the *jamrahs* themselves which have been stoned since it is said that they are the pebbles of someone whose *ḥajj* is not accepted. If someone has his *ḥajj* accepted, his pebbles are removed. Then you proceed to the *jamrah al-ʿaqabah* before midday and stone it with seven pebbles, and you should say the *takbīr* with each pebble you throw. You do not stone any other of the *jamrahs* on that day and do not stop at them. Anything you throw from the earth is adequate, whether it is stones or mud.

Sacrifice and cutting the hair

Then you return to Minā and sacrifice. If you are doing an *ifrād ḥajj* no sacrifice is owed so there is no harm in not sacrificing. You must, however, shave your head or cut your hair short, but shaving is better. If you are doing *qirān* or *tamattuʿ*, you must sacrifice first and then shave your head or cut your hair after that. Once you have shaved or cut your hair short, everything becomes lawful for you except sexual relations with your wife.

Ṭawāf az-Ziyārah (ṭawāf al-Ifāḍah)

Then you return to Makkah and visit the Kaʿbah for the *ṭawāf az-Ziyārah*, either on that day or the next day or the following day, the time of the *ṭawāf* being the three Days of Sacrifice, but the first day is best. If you did the *saʿy* after the *ṭawāf* of arrival, you do not do *ramal* in the first three circuits of *ṭawāf az-Ziyārah*. But if you did not do *saʿy* after the *ṭawāf* of arrival, you do it now after the *ṭawāf az-Ziyārah* and you also do *ramal* in this *ṭawāf*. When you have done the *ṭawāf az-Ziyārah*, sexual relations with your wife become lawful to you.

Spending the night in Minā and stoning the Jamarāt (11th–13th of Dhu al-Ḥijjah)

Then you return to Minā and do not spend the night at Makkah or on the road. It is disliked to spend the night anywhere other than Minā during the days of Minā.

On the second day of the Sacrifice, you stone the three *jamrahs* after midday. You begin with the first *jamrah* by the Khayf mosque, throwing seven pebbles at it as you did at *jamrah al-ʿAqabah* the previous day, saying *Allāhu Akbar* with each pebble you throw. Then you stand there a short while and say the *takbīr*, praise Allāh Almighty, glorify Him, say the *ṣalāt ʿalan Nabiy, Darūd,* on the Prophet, may the peace and blessings of Allāh be upon him, and ask Allāh for whatever you want, lifting up your hands in supplication. You then go to the middle *jamrah* and do the same as you did at the first. Then you go to the *jamrah al-ʿAqabah* and do the same except that you do not stand there when you have finished throwing.

On the third day, the 12th of Dhu al-Ḥijjah, you stone the three *jamrahs* in the same way and then return to your camp. If after that you intend to depart from Minā to Makkah, you can do so but you must hasten because you must leave before the sun sets. If you have not left before the sun sets, it is then best not to depart until you have stoned the three *jamrahs* on the following day. If you do leave after sunset and before dawn on the fourth day, the day of the 13th of Dhu al-Ḥijjah, you do not have to sacrifice but you have definitely acted improperly. According to Imām Shāfiʿī, after the sun sets on the third day it is not lawful to depart until you have stoned the three *jamrahs* on the fourth day. Our opinion is that if you have not left before dawn on the fourth day, the last of the Days of *Tashrīq*, you must stay and it is not lawful to depart until you have stoned the three *jamrahs*, as on the previous two days. If you do depart before stoning, you owe a sacrifice.

Leaving for Makkah

Anyone who departs on either of these two days should carry his baggage with him and not send it ahead because that might constitute a reason for the distraction of his heart. You should stop for a time at al-Abṭaḥ which is called al-Muḥaṣṣab between Minā and Makkah because the Prophet, may the peace and blessings of Allāh be upon him, camped there.

Ṭawāf al-Wadāʿ (Ṭawāf of Farewell)

You then enter Makkah and do the *ṭawāf* of farewell, based on what is reported from the Prophet, may the peace and blessings of Allāh be upon him, who said, "If someone makes *ḥajj* to the House, the last of his business with the House is *ṭawāf*." After you finish the *ṭawāf* of farewell, you go to the *Maqām-i-Ibrāhīm* and pray two *rakʿats* there and then to Zamzam and drink some of its water while standing, pouring some of it over your face and head. Then you go to *al-Multazam*, which is between the Black Stone and the door, placing your chest and face against it, catch hold of the shroud of the Kaʿbah and ask Allāh Almighty for whatever you want. Then you kiss the Black Stone, say the *takbīr* and depart.

The people of Makkah when they perform *ḥajj* and the people performing *ʿumrah* do not have to do the *ṭawāf* of farewell.

If you do leave before the *ṭawāf* of farewell and remember before passing the *mīqāt*, you should go back and do *ṭawāf* because it is obligatory. If you do pass the *mīqāt*, you owe a sacrifice. If you go back, you must put on the *iḥrām* of *ʿumrah,* and go back and do *ʿumrah* and then do the *ṭawāf al-wadāʿ*, *ṭawāf* of farewell. Menstruating women and women with post-childbirth bleeding do not have to do the *ṭawāf* of farewell and they owe no sacrifice for omitting it because the Prophet, may the peace and blessings of Allāh be upon him, allowed menstruating women to omit it and then did not order them to do anything in its place.

7.12.2 *Ḥajj Qirān*

The *qirān ḥajj* is the same as the *ifrād ḥajj*, except that the person doing it assumes *iḥrām* for both the *ḥajj* and *ʿumrah* together. When he arrives in Makkah he does *ṭawāf* for his *ʿumrah* and also does *saʿy*. Then after that he does *ṭawāf* and *saʿy* for his *ḥajj* at the appropriate time.

7.12.3 *Ḥajj Tamattu'*

Someone doing *tamattu'* goes into *iḥrām* for *'umrah* first and he does it before the Day of *Tarwiyah* and then assumes *iḥrām* for the *ḥajj*. Doing *tamattu'* means doing the *'umrah* and *ḥajj* in the months of *ḥajj*, in the same journey without returning in between.

Tamattu' and *qirān* are only proper for people who come from outside the *Ḥaram*. It is disliked for people who live around the *Masjid al-Ḥaram*, the people of Makkah and the people inside the *mīqāts*, to do them. The basis for this is the words of the Almighty,

فَمَن تَمَتَّعَ بِٱلْعُمْرَةِ إِلَى ٱلْحَجِّ ... ذَٰلِكَ لِمَن لَّمْ يَكُنْ أَهْلُهُۥ حَاضِرِى ٱلْمَسْجِدِ ٱلْحَرَامِ

> "*If anyone wishes to continue the 'umrah on to the ḥajj … This is for those whose household is not in (the precincts of) the Sacred Mosque.*" [*al-Baqarah* 2: 196].

If someone resident within the *mīqāt* does *tamattu'* or *qirān* it is allowed but they are obliged to sacrifice because of their bad behaviour. In their case, the sacrifice is considered as reparation and is not lawful for their own consumption. They must give it as *ṣadaqah* to the poor.

For people from elsewhere *tamattu'* and *qirān* are recommended and prescribed and they owe a sacrifice out of thankfulness for the blessing of Allāh, in enabling them to combine two acts in one journey so that in their case, it is lawful for them both to consume it themselves and to feed whomever they wish, rich or poor. They are not obliged to give *ṣadaqah* but what is recommended is for them to eat a third, give away a third as *ṣadaqah* and give a third as gifts to relatives and neighbours, as in *'Id al-Aḍḥā* sacrifices.

7.12.4 *Damm at-Tamattu'* or *Damm al-Qirān* – Sacrifice for *Qirān* and *Tamattu'*

Sacrifices should be made on the Days of Sacrifice (10th–12th Dhu al-Ḥijjah) and should take place in the area of the *ḥaram*.

Someone who is poor and does not have any means of sacrificing, should fast for three days before the Day of ʿArafah. People who do that should come on the Day of Sacrifice, shave or cut their hair and then fast a further seven days after the Days of Sacrifice and *Tashrīq*, even if they have not yet returned to their families.

Imām Shāfiʿī said that such people should fast the seven days after they have returned to their families and that it is not permitted before it, since Allāh Almighty says,

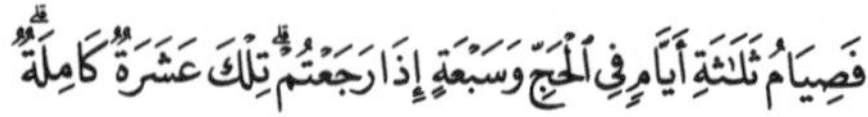

> "*He should fast three days during the Ḥajj and seven days on his return, making ten days in all.*" [*al-Baqarah* 2: 196]

We say that the meaning of 'return' in this context refers to completion of the actions of *Ḥajj*. That is what the people of *tafsīr* say.

The sacrifice which is offered for *Qirān* or *Tamattuʿ Ḥajj* is *damm ash-shukr*, sacrifice of thanksgiving to Allāh, the Glorified and Exalted, for enabling a person to perform '*Ḥajj* and '*Umrah* in one journey. It is lawful, rather *mustaḥab*, recommended for a person to eat from the sacrificial meat according to Imām Abū Ḥanīfah. According to Imām Shāfiʿī it is *damm al-Jubrān*, remedial sacrifice and it is not lawful to consume from this sacrifice but all of it must be given to the poor as *ṣadaqah*.

7.13 How the Prophet ﷺ Performed His Ḥajj*

When the command for *ḥajj* came, the Prophet, may the peace and blessings of Allāh be upon him, hastened towards it. After the announcement of his intention, people flocked to join him. The news spread quickly throughout Madīnah and people advanced from all directions to accompany the Prophet in their thousands for as far as the eye could see. The Prophet's wives also accompanied him.

He left for this virtuous act at noon after the *ẓuhr* prayer on the 25th of Dhu al-Qaʿdah on a Saturday.

At Madīnah, before setting off he prepared for the journey, and thus combed his hair, applied oil to it, dressed up, delivered a sermon and prayed four *rakʿats* of *ẓuhr*.

On his way to Dhu al-Ḥulayfah, the Angel Jibrīl, on whom be peace, appeared to the Prophet, may the peace and blessings of Allāh be upon him, at the Valley of *al-ʿAqīq*. At Dhu al-Ḥulayfah, the Prophet, may the peace and blessings of Allāh be upon him, prayed two *rakʿats* of *ʿaṣr* and spent the night there. The next day, at noon he took *ghusl* for *iḥrām*. ʿĀ'ishah, may Allāh be pleased with her, perfumed him with *Dharīr* (a fragrant powder) and other perfume, whose odour he did not remove. He put on his cloak and wrapper and prayed two *rakʿats* of *ẓuhr*, after which he proclaimed the *talbiyah* for *ʿumrah* and *ḥajj*.

Before wearing the *iḥrām* he girded a necklace around his camel and sliced a portion from its hump, after which blood came forth profusely. The sacrificial camel accompanied him throughout the journey.

---

* This section is a translation of the text prepared by our mentor *Shaikh-ul-Ḥadīth* Maulānā Muḥammad Zakariyyā, may Allāh have mercy on him. It is based on Ḥāfiẓ Ibn al-Qayyim's work for which *Shaikh-ul-Ḥadīth* wrote a comprehensive commentary, *Ḥajjat-ul-wadāʿ wa ʿumrāt-un-Nabiy* ﷺ. Since this book is regarded as the most comprehensive on this subject, we thought it would be useful to give the translation of the text done by Usama al-Aʿẓamī for students of *fiqh* to learn how the Prophet, may the peace and blessings of Allāh be upon him, performed his *ḥajj*. We believe that it would be more beneficial for the student to be taught this text with the help of the original commentary in Arabic.

With evidence of over twenty *aḥādīth* there is a consensus that the Prophet, may the peace and blessings of Allāh be upon him, did *ḥajj al-Qirān*, but he granted his companions the choice between the three types of *ḥajj*. It was at Dhu al-Hulayfah that Asmā' bint 'Umays, may Allāh be pleased with her, gave birth to Muḥammad ibn Abū Bakr. Once again the Angel Jibrīl, on whom be peace, appeared instructing the Prophet, may the peace and blessings of Allāh be upon him, to order the people to raise their voices in *talbiyah*.

At Malal, the top of the Prophet's foot, may the peace and blessings of Allāh be upon him, was treated by cupping, and further at Leḥyay Jamal his head.

On passing by al-Rawḥā', he saw a slaughtered onager whose owner al-Bahzī presented it to the Prophet, may the peace and blessings of Allāh be upon him, and the Prophet, may the peace and blessings of Allāh be upon him, asked Abū Bakr, may Allāh be pleased with him, to distribute it among the people. Further on, at Athāyah he saw a wounded deer lying curled in a heap of sand, with an arrow in it. The Prophet, may the peace and blessings of Allāh be upon him, ordered a man to guard it in case someone takes it.[7]

On the journey, descending towards 'Arj, the goods-camel which was shared between the Prophet, may the peace and blessings of Allāh be upon him, and Abū Bakr, may Allāh be pleased with him, was lost by his servant. At this Abū Bakr, may Allāh be pleased with him, reproached his slave, saying, "A single camel – how could you lose it?"

As the Prophet and his companions proceeded towards Abwā', Aṣ-Ṣa'b ibn Juthāmah presented him with a piece of meat from an onager, which the Prophet, may the peace and blessings of Allāh be upon him, did not accept.

On the way the camel of Umm al-Mu'minīn Ṣafiyyah bint Ḥuyay, may Allāh be pleased with her, fell sick, so he requested Zaynab bint Jaḥsh, may Allāh be pleased with her, to grant her, her spare camel. However, she refused, remarking, "Shall I grant your Jewess[8] a camel?" This angered the Prophet, may the peace and blessings of Allāh be upon him. Also, it was here that the Prophet, may the peace and blessings of Allāh be upon him, called the poet camel driver who was trying to race his camels, saying, "O Anjashah!, beware of the glass vessels." (referring to the women, mounted)

When the Prophet, may the peace and blessings of Allāh be upon him, passed the valley of ʿUsfān he asked Abū Bakr, may Allāh be pleased with him, "O Abū Bakr, which valley is this?" So he replied, "ʿUsfān", on which the Prophet, may the peace and blessings of Allāh be upon him, remarked that the Prophets Hūd and Ṣāleḥ passed by this valley on two red mounts, whose bridle was of date palm leaves, chanting the *talbiyah* and proceeding to do *ḥajj*. On this occasion Surāqah ibn Juʿsham, may Allāh be pleased with him, requested the Prophet, may the peace and blessings of Allāh be upon him, to clarify the rituals of *ḥajj* for him, so he did.

At Sarif, ʿĀʾishah, may Allāh be pleased with her, started to menstruate. Although there is sufficient evidence to support this fact, however, there are slight differences in opinions as to where she attained purity. It was at Sarif that the Prophet, may the peace and blessings of Allāh be upon him, granted those who did not have sacrificial animals to do *ʿumrah.*

He then proceeded towards Dhu Ṭuwā, spent the night and prayed *fajr*. That was Sunday night, 4th of Dhu al-Ḥijjah and then made *ghusl* and departed for Makkah passing via the valley Al-Azraq. While passing this valley the Prophet, may the peace and blessings of Allāh be upon him, said "as if I am looking at Prophet Mūsā raising his voice with *talbiyah* and supplicating to Allāh."

At forenoon he entered Makkah from its heights, and walked until he reached the Sacred mosque, where he faced towards the Kaʿbah and supplicated. There is difference of opinion on whether or not he raised his noble hands at the first glimpse of the Kaʿbah. However, what is certain is that he did not pray *taḥiyyat al-Masjid.* Rather he proceeded towards the Black Stone and on reaching it, kissed it. Then he did *ṭawāf* with *ramal.* Each time the Prophet, may the peace and blessings of Allāh be upon him, passed by the Black Stone, he pointed with his walking stick, said the *takbir*, and kissed the stick. During the *ṭawāf* the Prophet, may the peace and blessings of Allāh be upon him, did *iḍtibāʿ*. When he completed the *ṭawāf* he came to the *Maqām-i-Ibrāhīm* and recited:

وَٱتَّخِذُوا۟ مِن مَّقَامِ إِبْرَٰهِـۧمَ مُصَلًّى

"*And you take the station of Ibrāhīm as a place of prayer*" [*al-Baqarah* 2: 125]

and prayed two *rakʿats* behind it. He then kissed the Black Stone again and thereafter proceeded towards Mount Ṣafā. When he came close, he recited:

۞ إِنَّ ٱلصَّفَا وَٱلْمَرْوَةَ مِن شَعَآئِرِ ٱللَّهِ

"*Behold! Ṣafā and Marwah are among the symbols of Allāh*" [*al-Baqarah* 2: 158]

and said, "I begin with what Allāh began with" and climbed Safa, made supplication and then descended towards Marwah, walking and then running at the gorge of the valley. When he reached Marwah, he faced the Kaʿbah, and said the *Takbīr*. As soon as he completed the *saʿy* at Marwah, he ordered those companions who did not have a sacrificial camel with them to shave their head. There is an incorrect narration that the Prophet, may the peace and blessings of Allāh be upon him, also had his head shaved; in fact it was not on this occasion, but after the *ḥajj*.

The Prophet, may the peace and blessings of Allāh be upon him, halted for four days on the heights of Makkah at *al-Abtaḥ*, shortening his prayers. During this period, ʿAlī, may Allāh be pleased with him, arrived with his camels from Yemen. On Thursday forenoon he headed for Minā. Those companions who had shaven their heads were instructed to make a new intention for *ḥajj*.

The Prophet, may the peace and blessings of Allāh be upon him, spent the night at Minā and then after sunrise he set off towards ʿArafāt via Ḍabb. There he halted at the tent set up for him until the sun became pallid. When the sun had declined he delivered a sermon and on concluding it, he instructed Bilāl, may Allāh be pleased with him, to give the *adhān* and he led the prayers of *ẓuhr* and *ʿaṣr* together [two *rakʿats* each]. Thereafter he mounted and proceeded towards Mawqif. Here he faced the *qiblah* and supplicated. The supplication of forgiveness for all the *Ummah* was accepted, except injustices among themselves. During his stay at Mawqif, he also encountered a delegation from Najd and the last verses of the Qurʾān,

ٱلْيَوْمَ أَكْمَلْتُ لَكُمْ دِينَكُمْ وَأَتْمَمْتُ عَلَيْكُمْ نِعْمَتِي وَرَضِيتُ لَكُمُ ٱلْإِسْلَٰمَ دِينًا

> "*This day I have perfected your religion for you, completed My favour upon you and have chosen for you Islam as your religion.*" [*al-Maʾidah* 5: 3]

were revealed. It was here that a man fell from his mount and died. The Prophet, may Allāh bless him and grant him peace, instructed that he should be shrouded in his two (*iḥrām*) clothes and should not be perfumed and his head should not be covered as he will be raised on the Day of Judgement saying *Talbiyah*.

After sunset the Prophet, may the peace and blessings of Allāh be upon him, departed from ʿArafāt via Maʾzimīn and with him was Usāmah ibn Zaid, may Allāh be pleased with him, mounted behind him. On the way to Muzdalifah, he dismounted, urinated and did *wuḍū* and thereafter, he proceeded to Muzdalifah. Although the Prophet, may the peace and blessings of Allāh be upon him, did *wuḍū* on the way, he did not pray as Usāmah, may Allāh be pleased with him, asked him, "Prayer? O Messenger of Allāh," so he replied, "at Muzdalifah."

At Muzdalifah he renewed his *wuḍū* and prayed *maghrib* and *ʿishāʾ* together, and then he went to sleep until morning, whilst allowing the feeble amongst his family to advance towards Minā before dawn, whom he also told not to pelt the *jamrah* of al-ʿAqabah before sunrise.

At dawn, the Prophet, may the peace and blessings of Allāh be upon him, prayed *fajr* and renewed his supplication for the *Ummah*. Then he set off for Minā and this time Faḍl ibn ʿAbbās, may Allāh be pleased with him, was mounted behind him. On the way a woman from Khathʿam came and asked the Prophet, may the peace and blessings of Allāh be upon him, concerning the *ḥajj* due on her father. So he instructed her to do it on his behalf. Another man asked him concerning his mother's *ḥajj*. While passing the gorge al-Muḥassar, he spurred his camel and instructed his companions to do the same, [for it was here that Abrahah and his army was destroyed]. He remained chanting the *talbiyah*, until he reached the *jamrah* al-ʿAqabah. After sunrise he pelted the *jamrah*, reciting the *takbīr* before throwing each pebble. The *talbiyah* ceased with the first pebble he pelted. After pelting he returned to Minā and gave a sermon, in which he bade the people farewell, after which this *ḥajj* is named. Due to the vastness of the crowd, ʿAlī, may Allāh be pleased with him, relayed the sermon to those present to whom the Prophet's voice could not reach.

After the sermon, the Prophet, may the peace and blessings of Allāh be upon him, was asked about the order of performance of some of the rituals of *ḥajj*, such as someone shaving his head before throwing pebbles or some one sacrificing before *ramy*. "There's no harm in it," he replied. Then the people dispersed to their places of stay, and the Prophet, may the peace and blessings of Allāh be upon him, went to the sacrificial precinct and sacrificed sixty-three camels (one for each year of his age) and also a cow on behalf of his wives. After this he called upon the barber to shave his head. Then he put on his normal clothes and perfumed himself. His hair and nails were distributed amongst his close companions. Thereafter, he departed for Makkah before *ẓuhr* on his camel. At Makkah the Prophet, may the peace and blessings of Allāh be upon him, performed *ṭawāf al-ifaḍah*, while mounted. On completing the *ṭawāf* he came to Zamzam, and drank from its water while standing. He then returned to Minā and spent the night there. After the sun became pallid he walked to the *jamrah* and pelted the first, the second and the third. While supplicating after the first and the second he did not halt at the third, nor supplicate. There is a difference of opinion as to whether the Prophet, may the peace and blessings of Allāh be upon him, used to return to Makkah every night. However, he allowed ʿAbbās, may Allāh be pleased with him, to spend the night at Makkah due to his responsibility of providing water and being in charge of hosting the pilgrims. The camel herdsmen were also allowed to spend the night outside Minā. The Prophet, may the peace and blessings of Allāh be upon him, did not hasten to leave Minā the second day of *Tashrīq*, 12th of Dhu al-Ḥijjah, he completed the *ramy* of 13th of Dhu al-Ḥijjah. On Tuesday he departed for Makkah, briefly halting at Muḥaṣṣab (Muʿabadah). On reaching Makkah, he did the *ṭawāf* of Farewell, and *Umm-ul-Mu'mineen* Umm Salamah, may Allāh be pleased with her, did *ṭawāf* while mounted on her camel. On the way back from Minā, 'Āishah, may Allāh be pleased with her, desired to do *ʿumrah* and the Prophet, may the peace and blessings of Allāh be upon him, sent her with her brother ʿAbdur-Raḥmān to Tanʿīm and she completed her *ʿumrah* at night.

There is a difference of opinion as to whether the Prophet, may the peace and blessings of Allāh be upon him, entered inside the Kaʿbah during this *ḥajj* and also, whether he stood at Multazam and supplicated. Besides this, on the Morning of Farewell whether he prayed *fajr*, within or outside Makkah. Thereafter he departed for Madīnah via Kuday and he took with him some Zamzam water. On the way, at Gadīr-Khum, [a water reservoir named after its founder Khum], the Prophet, may the peace and blessings of Allāh be upon him, delivered a sermon, mentioning the virtues of 'Alī, may Allāh be pleased with him.

When he reached ar-Rowḥā', he encountered a caravan which he greeted. A woman came forward with a child from her mount and asked whether there is *ḥajj* for her child accompanying her. The Prophet, may the peace and blessings of Allāh be upon him, replied, "Yes, and for you is the reward."

At Baṭḥā' he spent the night and performed his prayers there.

The Prophet, may the peace and blessings of Allāh be upon him, entered Madīnah via Muʿarras. When he saw the first glimpse of Uḥud he remarked, "This mountain loves us and we love it," and entered while saying,

آيِبُونَ، تَائِبُونَ، عَابِدُونَ، سَاجِدُونَ، لِرَبِّنَا حَامِدُونَ صَدَقَ اللهُ وَعْدَهُ وَنَصَرَ عَبْدَهُ وَهَزَمَ الأَحْزَابَ وَحْدَهُ.

Āʾibūna, tāʾibūna, ʿābidūna, sājiduna, li Rabbinā ḥamidūn. Ṣadaqa(A) ullāhu waʿdahū wa naṣara ʿabdahu, wa ḥazamal-aḥzāba waḥdah. Allāhuma!(I)jʿal lī fīha qarāran wa rizqan ḥasanā. (Returning, repenting, worshipping, prostrating to our Lord and thanksgiving. Surely Allāh fulfilled His promise and consolidated His servants in humiliating the non-believers.)

Women besides Umm Sinān and Umm Maʿqal, may Allāh be pleased with them, came to him complaining that they had missed the opportunity to accompany him during the *ḥajj*. He consoled them by saying, "*ʿumrah* in *Ramaḍān* is equal to a *ḥajj* with me."

7.14 *Visiting the Mosque and Grave of the Prophet* ﷺ

When a pilgrim has performed his obligation and finished his practice for *ḥajj*, he should travel to Madīnah to visit the mosque of the noble Prophet, may the peace and blessings of Allāh be upon him, and to enjoy the visit to his noble grave and be near him. Imāms Bukhārī and Muslim related that Abū Hurayrah, may Allāh be pleased with him, said, "The Messenger of Allāh, may the peace and blessings of Allāh be upon him, said, 'One prayer in this mosque of mine is better than a thousand prayers in any other mosque except the Sacred Mosque, al-Masjid al-Ḥarām.' " He, may the peace and blessings of Allāh be upon him, said, "If anyone visits my grave, my intercession is mandatory for him." (Bazzār, Dāraquṭnī and Ibn 'Adī from Ibn 'Umar)

The Prophet, may the peace and blessings of Allāh be upon him, said, "If anyone comes to visit me for no other reason except visiting me, it is a duty for me to be his intercessor on the Day of Rising." (Dāraquṭnī, and Ṭabarānī in *al-Awsaṭ* from Ibn 'Umar) He, may the peace and blessings of Allāh be upon him, said, "If anyone makes *ḥajj* and visits my grave after my death, it is as if he visited me while I was alive." (Dāraquṭnī in the *Sunan*, Ṭabarānī in *al-Awsaṭ* and *al-Kabīr*, and Bayhaqī in *as-Sunan*) Qaḍī 'Iyāḍ, may Allāh have mercy on him, said, "Visiting the grave of the Prophet, may the peace and blessings of Allāh be upon him, is a *Sunnah* among the Muslims on which there is consensus. It is a virtue which is encouraged."

7.14.1 Proper behaviour in the visit

When a visitor heads for Madīnah, he sends salutations on the Prophet, may the peace and blessings of Allāh be upon him, in abundance on the way, and when his eyes alight on the trees and on the *Mosque* of Madīnah, he should ask Allāh Almighty to let him benefit from this visit and accept it from him.

It is recommended to bathe before entering Madīnah and to put on one's cleanest garments. When he enters it, he should say,

بِاسْمِ اللهِ ، رَبِّ أَدْخِلْنِي مُدْخَلَ صِدْقٍ وَأَخْرِجْنِي مُخْرَجَ صِدْقٍ وَاجْعَل لِّي مِن لَّدُنكَ سُلْطَانًا نَّصِيرًا .

Bismillāhi, Rabbī Adkhilnī mudkhala ṣidqin, wa akhrijnī mukhraja ṣidqin, waj'al lī min ladunka sulṭanan Naṣirā. (In the name of Allāh, 'O My Sustainer! Cause me to enter in a manner true and sincere, and cause me to leave [it] in a manner true and sincere and grant me out of Your grace, sustaining strength.')

اللَّهُمَّ افْتَحْ لِي أَبْوَابَ رَحْمَتِكَ، وَارْزُقْنِي زِيَارَةَ رَسُولِكَ صَلَّى اللهُ عَلَيْهِ وَسَلَّمَ مَا رَزَقْتَ أَوْلِيَاءَكَ وَأَهْلَ طَاعَتِكَ، وَاغْفِرْ لِي وَارْحَمْنِي يَا خَيْرَ مَسْؤُولٍ. اللَّهُمَّ إِنِّي أَسْأَلُكَ خَيْرَ هَذِهِ الْبَلْدَةِ وَخَيْرَ أَهْلِهَا وَخَيْرَ مَا فِيهَا، وَأَعُوذُ بِكَ مِنْ شَرِّهَا وَشَرِّ أَهْلِهَا وَشَرِّ مَا فِيهَا.

Allāhumma(I)ftaḥlī abwāba raḥmatika, warzuqnī ziyārata Rasūlilika, ṣallallāh alaihi wa sallama, mā razaqta awliyāaka wa ahla ṭā'atika. Wagfir lī, warḥamnī yā Khayra Mas'ūl. Allāhumma! Innī as'aluka khayra hādhihil baldati wa khayra ahlihā wa khayra mā fīhā, wa a'ūdhubika min sharrihā wa sharri ahlihā wa sharri mā fīhā. (O Allāh, open the gates of Your mercy for me and provide me with a visit to Your Messenger, may the peace and blessings of Allāh be upon him, as You have given it to Your friends and those who obey You. Forgive me and have mercy on me, O best of those who are asked! O Allāh, I ask You for the good of this land and the good of its people and the good of what is in it. I seek refuge with You from its evil, the evil of its people and the evil of what is in it.)

He should be humble, submissive and attentive. It is the land which Allāh Almighty chose as the abode of the *hijrah* of His Prophet, may the peace and blessings of Allāh be upon him, and the place where the revelation came down and the fount of the rulings of the *Sharīʿah*.

When he wants to enter the mosque, he should put his right foot first and say,

بِاسْمِ اللهِ، وَالصَّلَاةُ والسَّلَامُ عَلَى رَسُولِ اللهِ. رَبِّ اغْفِرْ لِي ذُنُوبِي وَافْتَحْ لِي أَبْوَابَ رَحْمَتِكَ، أَعُوذُ بِاللهِ الْعَظِيمِ، وَبِوَجْهِهِ الْكَرِيمِ، وَسُلْطَانِهِ الْقَدِيمِ، مِنَ الشَّيْطَانِ الرَّجِيمْ.

> *Bismillāhi waṣ-ṣalātu wassalāmu ʿalā Rasūlillāh. Rabbighfir lī dhunūbī waftaḥ lī abwāba rahmatika. Aʿūdhū billāhil-ʿAẓīmi, wa bi wajhihil-karīmi, wa sulṭanihil-qadīmi, minashayṭanir-rajīm.* (In the name of Allāh, and blessings be upon the Messenger of Allāh. O Lord, forgive me my sins and open for me the gates of Your mercy. I seek refuge with Allāh the Almighty and His noble countenance and ancient power from the accursed Shayṭān.)

Then he goes to the *Rawḍat-al-Jannah* between the noble grave and the *minbar* and prays two *rakʿats* in it. Abū Hurayrah, may Allāh be pleased with him, related that the Prophet, may the peace and blessings of Allāh be upon him, said, "What is between my house and my *minbar* is one of the Meadows of the Paradise. My *minbar* is on my Basin." (Mālik, Bukhārī, Muslim, and Tirmidhī who consider it *ṣaḥiḥ*)

7.14.2 How to visit

Then he goes to the noble grave. He should neither rush to it nor cling on to it nor stretch his hands out to it. He should face its wall with his back to the *qiblah* about two metres away since it is related that Ibn ʿUmar, may Allāh be pleased with him, said, "The best *Sunnah* to come to the grave of the Prophet, may the peace and blessings of Allāh be upon him, from the direction of the *qiblah* with the back to the *qiblah* and facing the grave. Then he should say,

السَّلَامُ عَلَيْكُمْ وَرَحْمَةُ اللَّهِ وَبَرَكَاتُهُ.

Assalāmu ʿalaykum wa raḥmatullāhi wa barakātuh (Peace be upon you and the mercy of Allāh and His blessings.)"

The visitor should add,

السَّلَامُ عَلَيْكَ يَا خَيْرَ خَلْقِ اللهِ، يَا إِمَامَ الْمُتَّقِينَ، يَا سَيِّدَ الْمُرْسَلِينَ، إِنِّي أَشْهَدُ أَن لَّا إِلَهَ إِلاَّ اللَّهُ، وَحْدَهُ لَا شَرِيكَ لَهُ، وَأَنَّكَ عَبْدُهُ وَرَسُولُهُ، قَدْ بَلَّغْتَ الرِّسَالَةَ، وَأَدَّيْتَ الأَمَانَةَ، وَنَصَحْتَ الْأُمَّةَ، فَجَزَاكَ اللهُ عَنَّا أَفْضَلَ مَا جَازَى نَبِيًّا عَنْ أُمَّتِهِ.

Assalāmu ʿalayka yā Khayra khalqillāhi, yā Imām-al-Muttāqīna, Yā Sayyid-al-Mursalīna. Innī ash-hadu a(n) lā ilāha illallāhu waḥdahū lā sharika lahū, wa annaka ʿabduhū wa rasūluhū. Qad ballaghtar-Risālata wa addaytal-amānata, wa naṣaḥtal-ʾUmmata. Fa jazākallāhu ʿannā afḍala mā jazā Nabiyyan ʿan Ummatihi. (Peace be upon you, O best of Allāh's creation, O Imām of the Godfearing, O Master of the Messengers. I testify that there is no god but Allāh alone with no partner and that you are His slave and Messenger. You conveyed the Message and carried out the trust and you were faithful to the community. May Allāh reward you for us with the best that a Prophet can be rewarded from his community.)

اللَّهُمَّ صَلِّ عَلَى مُحَمَّدٍ وَعَلَى آلِ مُحَمَّدٍ، كَمَا صَلَّيْتَ عَلَى إِبْرَاهِيمَ وَعَلَى آلِ إِبْرَاهِيمَ إِنَّكَ حَمِيدٌ مَّجِيدٌ. وَبَارِكْ عَلَى مُحَمَّدٍ وَعَلَى آلِ مُحَمَّدٍ كَمَا بَارَكْتَ عَلَى إِبْرَاهِيمَ وَعَلَى آلِ إِبرَاهِيمَ إِنَّكَ حَمِيدٌ مَّجِيدٌ. اللَّهُمَّ إِنَّكَ قُلْتَ: "وَلَوْ أَنَّهُمْ إِذ ظَّلَمُوٓاْ أَنفُسَهُمْ

جَآءُوكَ فَٱسْتَغْفَرُوا۟ ٱللَّهَ وَٱسْتَغْفَرَ لَهُمُ ٱلرَّسُولُ لَوَجَدُوا۟ ٱللَّهَ تَوَّابًا رَّحِيمًا". وَقَدْ أَتَيْتُكَ يَا رَسُولَ اللهِ مُسْتَشْفِعاً بِكَ إِلَى رَبِّي. فَأَسْأَلُكَ يَا رَبِّ أَنْ تُوجِبَ لِي الْمَغْفِرَةَ كَمَا أَوْجَبْتَهَا لِمَنْ أَتَاهُ فِي حَيَاتِهِ. اللَّهُمَّ اجْعَلْهُ أَوَّلَ الشَّافِعِينَ يَا أَرْحَمَ الرَّاحِمِينْ.

Allāhumma! Ṣalli ʿalā Muḥammadin wa ʿalā āli Muḥammadin, Kamā Ṣallayta ʿalā Ibrāhīma wa ʿalā āli Ibrāhīma innaka Ḥamīdum Majīd. Allāhumma Bārik ʿalā Muḥammadin wa ʿalā āli Muḥammadin, Kamā Bārakta ʿalā Ibrāhīma wa ʿalā āli Ibrāhīma innaka Ḥamīdum Majīd.

Allāhumma! Innaka qulta: [*Wa la-w annahum iẓ-ẓalamū anfusahum jāʾūka fastagfaru-(A)llāha wastaghfara lahum-ur-Rasūlu, la wajadu (A)llāha Tawwāb-ar-Raḥīmā*].

Wa qad ataytuka yā Rasūlallāhi mustashfiʿan bika ilā Rabbi. Fa as-aluka yā Rabbi an tūjiba li al-maghfirata kamā awjabtahā liman atāhu fī ḥayatihi. Allāhumma! (I)jʿalhu Awwala(a)Shshafiʿīna, Yā Arḥamar-Rāḥimīn.

(O Allāh, bless Muḥammad and the family of Muḥammad as You blessed Ibrāhīm. You are Praiseworthy, Glorious. Give blessings to Muḥammad and the family of Muḥammad as You gave blessings to Ibrāhīm and the family of Ibrāhīm. You are Praiseworthy, Glorious.

O Allāh, You said, "*If they had only, when they were unjust to themselves, come unto you and asked Allāh's forgiveness, and the Messenger had asked forgiveness for them, they would have found Allāh indeed Oft-Returning, Most Merciful.*" [*al-Nisa* 4: 64]

I have come to You, Messenger of Allāh, seeking your intercession with my Lord. I ask You, O Lord, to grant forgiveness for me as You granted it for the one who came to him when he was alive. O Allāh, make him the first of the intercessors, O Most Merciful of the Merciful!"

Then he makes supplication for his parents and the Muslims.

He conveys the greetings from those who told him to convey their greeting. He says,

السَّلَامُ عَلَيْكَ يَا رَسُولَ اللهِ مِنْ فُلَانِ ابْنِ فُلَانٍ

Assalāmu ʿalayka Yā Rasūlallāhi min – (mention the name) – "Peace be upon you, O Messenger of Allāh, from so-and-so," or,

فُلَانُ ابْنُ فُلَانٍ يُسَلِّمُ عَلَيْكَ يَا رَسُولَ اللهِ.

– (mention the name) – *Yusallimu ʿalayka Yā Rasūlallāh.* "So-and-so greets you, Messenger of Allāh."

Then he turns about half a metre to his right and says,

السَّلَامُ عَلَيْكَ يَا خَلِيفَةَ رَسُولِ اللهِ صَلَّى اللهُ عَلَيْهِ وَسَلَّمَ، السَّلَامُ عَلَيْكَ يَا صَاحِبَ رَسُولِ اللهِ صَلَّى اللهُ عَلَيْهِ وَسَلَّمَ وَأَنِيسَهُ فِي الْغَارِ، وَأَمِينَهُ عَلَى الأَسْرَارِ، جَزَاكَ اللهُ عَنْ أُمَّةِ مُحَمَّدٍ صَلَّى اللهُ عَلَيْهِ وَسَلَّمَ خَيْرًا.

Assalāmu ʿalayka yā Khalīfata Rasūlillahi (ﷺ), *Assalāmu ʿalayka yā Ṣāḥiba Rasūlillāhi wa Anīsahū fil-ghāri, wa Amīnahū fil-asrāri; Jazāka (A)llāhu ʿan 'Ummati Muḥammadin* (ﷺ) *khayrā.* (Peace be upon you, O Khalīfah of the Messenger of Allāh. Peace be upon you, O Companion of the Messenger of Allāh and his comrade in the cave and the one entrusted with his secrets! May Allāh reward you from the community of Muḥammad, may the peace and blessings of Allāh be upon him, with the best.)

Then he turns another half metre to his right and says,

السَّلَامُ عَلَيْكَ يَا أَمِيرَ الْمُؤْمِنِينَ، السَّلَامُ عَلَيْكَ يَا نَاصِرَ الْمُسْلِمِينَ،
السَّلَامُ عَلَيْكَ يَا مَنْ أَعَزَّ اللّٰهُ بِهِ الإِسْلَامَ، جَزَاكَ اللّٰهُ عَنْ أُمَّةِ مُحَمَّدٍ
صَلَّى اللّٰهُ عَلَيْهِ وَسَلَّمَ خَيْراً.

Assalāmu ʿalayka yā Amīr al-Muʾminīna. Assalamu ʿalayka yā Nāṣir al-Muslimīna. Assalāmu ʿalayka yā man aʿazza(A)llāhu bihiʾl-Islāma. Jazāka(A)llāhu ʿan ʾUmmatī Muḥammadi (ﷺ) *Khayrā.* (Peace be upon you, Amir al-Muʾminin. Peace be upon you, Helper of the Muslims. Peace be upon you, O you by whom Allāh made Islam mighty. May Allāh repay you for the community of Muḥammad, may the peace and blessings of Allāh be upon him, with the best.)

If someone wants to limit himself, it is enough for him to say, "*Peace be upon you, Messenger of Allāh,* السَّلَامُ عَلَيْكَ يَا رَسُولَ اللّٰه." Nāfiʿ related that when ʿAbdullāh Ibn ʿUmar, may Allāh be pleased with him, arrived from a journey, he used to enter the mosque and then go to the grave and say, "Peace be upon you, Messenger of Allāh. Peace be upon you, Abū Bakr. Peace be upon you, father." (Bayhaqī)

The visitor should remember that the Prophet, may the peace and blessings of Allāh be upon him, hears his greeting and returns the greeting to him by the *ḥadīth* of Abū Hurayrah, may Allāh be pleased with him, that the Prophet, may the peace and blessings of Allāh be upon him, said, "There is no one who greets me but that Allāh will return my spirit to me so that I can return the greeting to him." (Aḥmad, Abū Dāwūd and Bayhaqī with a *ṣaḥīḥ isnād*)

It is recommended for the visitor not to raise his voice in the mosque of the Messenger of Allāh, may the peace and blessings of Allāh be upon him, since as-Sāʾib ibn Yazīd said,

> "Once when I was lying down in the mosque, a man threw pebbles at me. I raised my head and it was ʿUmar, may Allāh be pleased with him. He said, 'Go and bring those two men to me.' I brought them and he said, 'Where are you from?'

They said, 'From the people of Ṭā'if.' He said, 'If you had been from the people of this city, I would have given you a painful flogging. You were raising your voices in the mosque of the Messenger of Allāh, may the peace and blessings of Allāh be upon him!'" (Bukhārī)

It is recommended after the visit for the visitor to say a lot of prayer and supplication in the noble Rawḍah and to intend *i'tikāf* whenever he enters the mosque, even if he is only passing.

7.14.3 Visiting al-Baqī' and the Martyrs

It is recommended to go out to al-Baqī' every day, especially on Friday and visit the graves. 'Ā'ishah, may Allāh be pleased with her, said, "The Messenger of Allāh, may the peace and blessings of Allāh be upon him, used to go out at the end of the night to al-Baqī' and say,

السَّلَامُ عَلَيْكُمْ دَارَ قَوْمٍ مُؤْمِنِينَ، وَأَتَاكُمْ مَا تُوعَدُونَ، غَدًا مُؤَجَّلُونَ، وَإِنَّا إِنْ شَاءَ اللَّهُ بِكُمْ لَاحِقُونَ. اللَّهُمَّ اغْفِرْ لِأَهْلِ الْبَقِيعِ الْغَرْقَدِ.

Assalāmu alaykum Dāra qawmin Mu'minīna. Wa atākum mā tū'adūna, ghadan mu'ajjalūna. Wa innā in shā'a(A)llāhu bikum lāḥiqūna. Allāhuma! (i)ghfir li ahlil-Baqī' il-gharqad. (Peace be upon you, abode of a believing people. What you were promised will come to you tomorrow as decreed. Allāh willing, we will join you. O Allāh, forgive the people of Baqi' al-Gharqad.) (Muslim and Bayhaqī)

Among the known graves one should especially visit are the grave of Ibrāhīm, the son of the Prophet, may the peace and blessings of Allāh be upon him, 'Uthmān ibn 'Affān, al-'Abbās, al-Ḥasan ibn 'Alī and others, and he should finish by visiting the grave of Ṣafiyyah, the aunt of the Messenger of Allāh, may the peace and blessings of Allāh be upon him, and may Allāh be pleased with all of them.

It is recommended to go to Uḥud early on Thursday and to visit its martyrs and to begin with the grave of Ḥamzah, may Allāh be pleased with him, the uncle of the Prophet, and leader of the martyrs.

During his visit, an intelligent person should be careful to avoid innovations in greetings, like touching and kissing the grave, walking in a circle around it, asking from the person buried there, and praying at it because what is prescribed is supplication and asking forgiveness for them. As for asking for something from them and taking oaths by them to Allāh Almighty; that is misguidance and innovation (by the agreement of the Imāms of the believers). None of the Companions did that. The Imāms agree that when one wants to make supplication, he should face the *qiblah* and not face the grave.

7.14.4 VISITING THE MOSQUES IN WHICH THE MESSENGER OF ALLĀH ﷺ PRAYED

The five most important of these mosques are:

i. *The Mosque of Qubā'*

It is recommended to visit it on a Saturday since Ibn 'Umar, may Allāh be pleased with him, said, "The Prophet, may the peace and blessings of Allāh be upon him, used to visit the mosque of Qubā' every Saturday riding or walking and prayed two *rak'ats* in it." (Bukhārī, Muslim, Abū Dāwūd, Nasā'ī and Bayhaqī)

ii. *The Mosque of al-Fatḥ*

It is *Sunnah* to visit it and pray in it and make supplication by the *ḥadīth* of Jābir ibn 'Abdullāh, may Allāh be pleased with him, that the Prophet, may peace and blessings of Allāh be upon him, made supplication, in the Mosque of al-Fatḥ three days: Monday, Tuesday and Wednesday. The Prophet, may the peace and blessings of Allāh be upon him, received an answer in it on Wednesday between the two prayers (*Ẓuhr* and *'Aṣr*), and joy was seen on his face. Jābir, may Allāh be pleased with him, said, "Nothing consequential happened to me but that I aimed for that time, went immediately and made supplication there and recognised the answer." (Aḥmad and Bazzār with an *isnād* of reliable narrators)

Ibn al-Ḥakam ibn Thawbān, may Allāh be pleased with him, said, "Someone who had prayed behind the Prophet, may the peace and blessings of Allāh be upon him, in the Mosque of al-Fatḥ informed me that he, may the peace and blessings of Allāh be upon him, then made supplication in which he said,

اللَّهُمَّ لَكَ الْحَمْدُ، هَدَيْتَنِي مِنَ الضَّلَالَةِ فَلَا مُكْرِمَ لِمَنْ أَهَنْتَ،
وَلَا مُعِزَّ لِمَنْ أَذْلَلْتَ، وَلَا مُذِلَّ لِمَنْ أَعْزَزْتَ، وَلَا نَاصِرَ لِمَنْ
خَذَلْتَ، وَلَا خَاذِلَ لِمَنْ نَصَرْتَ، وَلَا مُعْطِيَ لِمَنْ مَنَعْتَ، وَلَا
مَانِعَ لِمَا أَعْطَيْتَ، وَلَا رَازِقَ لِمَنْ حَرَمْتَ، وَلَا رَافِعَ لِمَنْ
خَفَضْتَ، وَلَا خَافِضَ لِمَنْ رَفَعْتَ، وَلَا خَارِقَ لِمَنْ سَتَرْتَ، وَلَا
سَاتِرَ لِمَنْ خَرَقْتَ، وَلَا مُقَرِّبَ لِمَا بَاعَدْتَ وَلَا مُبَاعِدَ لِمَا قَرَّبْتَ

Allāhumma! laka'l-ḥamdu, hadaytanī min aḍḍālati, falā mukrima li-man ahanta, wa lā muʿizza li-man adhlalta wa lā mudhilla li-man aʿzazta, wa lā nāṣira li-man khadhalta, wa lā khādhila li-man naṣarta, wa lā muʿṭiya li-man manaʿta, wa lā māniʿa li mā aʿṭayta, wa lā rāziqa li-man ḥaramta, wa lā rāfiʿa li-man khafaḍta, wa lā khāfida li-man rafaʿta, wa lā khāriqa li-man satarta wa lā sātira li-man kharaqta, wa lā muqarriba limā bāʿadta wa lā mubāʿida limā qarrabta. (O Allāh, praise belongs to You. You guided me from misguidance. None can honour the one You dishonour and none can exalt the one You debase and none can debase the one You exalt. None can help the one You disappoint nor disappoint the one You help, and none can give to the one You deny nor deny the one to whom You give. None can provide for the one You deprive nor elevate the one You lower nor lower the one You elevate. None can expose the one You conceal nor conceal the one You expose nor bring near the one You put far nor put far the one You bring near.)" (Aḥmad)

iii. *The Jumu'ah Mosque*

In *ḥadīth*, "The Messenger of Allāh, may the peace and blessings of Allāh be upon him, arrived (in his *Ḥijrah* journey), to the locality of the Banū Sālim ibn 'Awf and he prayed in the mosque at the bottom of the valley of Rānūnā'. It was the first *Jumu'ah* the Prophet, may Allāh bless him and grant him peace, prayed in Madīnah."

iv. *The Mosque of al-Fadīkh*

It is east of the Mosque of Qubā'. Ibn 'Umar, may Allāh be pleased with him, related that the Prophet, may the peace and blessings of Allāh be upon him, was brought some *fadīkh* (a type of *nabīdh* drink) in the mosque of al-Fadīkh and drank it. (Aḥmad) It is called that because when the Banū Naḍīr were besieged, the Prophet, may the peace and blessings of Allāh be upon him, pitched his tent at the site of this mosque and remained there. This is where the prohibition of wine was revealed.

v. *The Mosque of al-Aḥzāb, the Confederates*

It was built in the time of the Messenger of Allāh, may the peace and blessings of Allāh be upon him. Jābir ibn 'Abdullāh, may Allāh be pleased with him, related that the Prophet, may the peace and blessings of Allāh be upon him, went to the Mosque of *al-Aḥzāb*, placed his cloak and stood and raised his hands to supplicate against the confederates' unbelievers. He went out and supplicated, and went in again and supplicated against them. (Aḥmad)

7.14.5 Visiting the Wells from which the Prophet ﷺ Drank

They are numerous, and the five most important are:

i. *The well of Arīs south-west of the Mosque of Qubā'*

The Prophet's Signet-ring while in the possession of Khalīfah 'Uthmān, may Allāh be pleased with him, was lost in this well.

ii. *The well of Ihāb*

It was known as Zamzam because its water is like that of Zamzam and it was called that because of the great amount of blessing in its water. It was transported all over the world, as Zamzam water is.

iii. *Biruḥā'*

It is the well and garden north of the wall of Madīnah on the eastern side (now included in the new building of the Prophet's mosque). The Messenger of Allāh, may the peace and blessings of Allāh be upon him, used to enter it and enjoy its shade and drink its water.

iv. *The well of Buḍā'ah north-west of Biruḥā'*

Bathing in its waters for three days is done for healing. The Prophet, may the peace and blessings of Allāh be upon him, used to drink from it.

v. *The well of Rūmah*

It is known as the Well of 'Uthmān because he, may Allāh be pleased with him, purchased it and gave it as charity. Bishr ibn Bashīr al-Aslamī, may Allāh be pleased with him, related that his father said, "When the *Muhājirūn* came to Madīnah, they disliked the water, and a man of the Banū Ghifār had a spring called Rūmah. He used to sell a skin full of water for a *mudd* of grain. The Prophet, may the peace and blessings of Allāh be upon him, said to him, 'Will you sell it to me in exchange for a spring in the Paradise?' He said, 'Messenger of Allāh, it is all that I and my family have.' 'Uthmān, may Allāh be pleased with him, heard about it and bought it for 35,000 *dirhams*. Then he went to the Prophet, may the peace and blessings of Allāh be upon him, and said, 'Will you stipulate for me what you stipulated for him?' He said, 'Yes'. He said, 'I have given it to the Muslims.'" (Baghawī)

The person in Madīnah should visit all the blessed places, mosques and excellent shrines in Madīnah when he has a long visit. Otherwise, it is better to remain at the mosque of the Prophet, may the peace and blessings of Allāh be upon him.

It is recommended to fast in Madīnah as much as possible and to give *ṣadaqah* to its people and strangers who live there.

7.15 Proper Behaviour in Returning Home

It is recommended for anyone who wants to leave Madīnah to bid farewell to the noble mosque with two *rakʿats* by which he intends the *Sunnah* of saying farewell to the mosque. After the *Fātiḥah* he recites *Sūrahs al-Kāfirūn* in the first and *al-Ikhlāṣ* in the second. He makes whatever supplication he wishes for his *dīn* and this world, and he finishes with praise of Allāh and blessings and peace on the Messenger of Allāh, may the peace and blessings of Allāh be upon him. He renews repentance and then visits the grave of the Prophet, may the peace and blessings of Allāh be upon him, as he visited it the first time. Then he says,

اللّٰهُمَّ لاَ تَجْعَلْ هَذَا آخِرَ الْعَهْدِ بِنَبِيِّكَ وَمَسْجِدِهِ وَحَرَمِهِ، وَيَسِّرْ لَنَا الْعَوْدَةَ إِلَى زِيَارَتِهِ وَالْعُكُوفِ فِي حَضْرَتِهِ سَبِيلاً سَهْلاً وَارْزُقْنِي الْعَفْوَ وَالْعَافِيَةَ فِي الدُّنْيَا وَالآخِرَه.

Allāhumma! Lā tājʿal hādhā ākhira al-ʿahdi bi nabiyyika wa masjidihī wa ḥaramihī, Wa yassir lana al-ʿawdata ilā ziyāratihi wal-ʿukūfi fī ḥaḍratihī sabīlan sahlan. Warzuqnī al-ʿafwa wal-ʿāfiyata fiddunā wal-ākhirah. (O Allāh, do not make this the last visit to Your Prophet and his mosque and Ḥaram. Make it easy for me to return to visit him and remain in his presence. Grant me pardon and well-being in this world and the Next.)

Then he turns around and does not walk backwards. Then he says,

اللَّهُمَّ إِنَّا نَسْأَلُكَ فِي سَفَرِنَا هَذَا الْبِرَّ وَالتَّقْوَى وَمِنَ الْعَمَلِ مَا تَرْضَى

Allāhuma! Innā nas-aluka fī safarina hādhā al-birra wat-taqwā wa min al-ʿamali mā tarḍā. (O Allāh, I ask You in this journey of ours for uprightness, piety and such actions as are pleasing to You.)

It is recommended that he brings his family a present of Madīnan dates and the like, and that he says the *takbīr* at every high piece of ground and makes the previously mentioned supplication from Ibn ʿUmar, may Allāh be pleased with him. He said, "When the Prophet, may the peace and blessings of Allāh be upon him, travelled, he used to say the *takbir* three times on every hilltop and then say,

لاَ إِلَهَ إِلاَ اللَّهُ، وَحْدَهُ لاَ شَرِيْكَ لَهُ، لَهُ الْمُلْكُ وَلَهُ الْحَمْدُ، وَهُوَ عَلَى كُلِّ شَيءٍ قَدِيْرٌ. آيِبُونَ، تَائِبُونَ، عَابِدُونَ، سَاجِدُونَ، لِرَبِّنَا حَامِدُونْ. صَدَقَ اللَّهُ وَعْدَهُ، وَنَصَرَ عَبْدَهُ، وَهَزَمَ الْأَحْزَابَ وَحْدَهُ.

Lā ilāha illa(A)llāhu waḥdahū lā sharīka lahū, lahul-mulku wa lahu'l-ḥamdu, wa huwa ʿalā kulli shay'in Qadīr. Āʾibūna, tāʾibūna, ʿābidūna, sājiduna, li Rabbinā ḥamidūn. Ṣadaqa(A) llāhu waʿdahū wa naṣara ʿabdahu, wa ḥazamal-aḥzāba waḥdah. (There is no god but Allāh alone with no partner. His is the kingdom and His is the praise, and He has power over everything. We are returning, repenting, worshipping, prostrating to our Lord, in praise. Allāh has been true to His promise and helped His slave and alone defeated the parties.)" (Bayhaqī)

When he sees his own land, he should mention the name of Allāh and say,

آيِبُونَ، تَائِبُونَ، عَابِدُونَ، سَاجِدُونَ، لِرَبِّنَا حَامِدُونَ صَدَقَ اللهُ وَعْدَهُ وَنَصَرَ عَبْدَهُ وَهَزَمَ الأَحْزَابَ وَحْدَهُ. اللَّهُمَّ اجْعَلْ لِّي فِيهَا قَرَاراً وَرِزْقاً حَسَناً.

Āʾibūna, tāʾibūna, ʿābidūna, sājiduna, li Rabbinā ḥamidūn. Ṣadaqa(A) ullāhu waʿdahū wa naṣara ʿabdahu, wa ḥazamal-aḥzāba waḥdah. Allāhuma!(I)jʿal lī fīha qarāran wa rizqan ḥasanā. (We are returning, repenting, worshipping, prostrating to our Lord, praising. Allāh has been true to His promise and helped His slave and alone defeated the parties. O Allāh, appoint me residence in it and provide me with good.)

One should send someone to his family to inform them of his arrival. He should not arrive home unexpectedly. When he enters the town, he first goes to the mosque and prays two *rakʿats* in it. Based on the *ḥadīth* of Nāfiʿ from Ibn ʿUmar, may Allāh be pleased with him, that when the Messenger of Allāh, may the peace and blessings of Allāh be upon him, returned from his *ḥajj*, he entered Madīnah and made his camel kneel at the door of his mosque and then entered and prayed two *rakʿats* in it. Then he went to his house. Nāfiʿ said, "ʿAbdullāh ibn ʿUmar used to do the same." (Aḥmad and Abū Dāwūd with a good *isnād*)

7.16 Meeting The Ḥajī and Congratulating Him

It is recommended to meet the pilgrims before they enter their houses and to greet them and shake their hands and ask for supplication from them and congratulate them like saying, "May Allāh accept your *ḥajj* and increase your reward! May He replace your expense and forgive your sins." Ibn ʿUmar, may Allāh be pleased with him, related that the Prophet, may the peace and blessings of Allāh be upon him, said, “When a pilgrim returns, you should greet him, shake his hand and ask him to pray for forgiveness for you before he enters his house.” (Aḥmad and Ḥākim who said that it is *ṣaḥīḥ* with the conditions of Muslim)

7.17 Innovations in Ḥajj and the Visit

7.17.1 Innovations in *Ḥajj*

Pilgrims commit a number of innovations in the *ḥajj* and visit for which Allāh has not sent down any authority and which have been made to seem right to them by the accursed Shayṭān, in order to deprive them of its virtue and great reward, and put them far from the Straight Path.

These include:

- Entering ʿArafāt earlier than the prescribed time, which is between the decline of the sun on the Day of ʿArafah and the rising of dawn on the Day of Sacrifice. Ibn Isḥāq said that Nāfiʿ reported to him that Ibn ʿUmar, may Allāh be pleased with him, said, “The Messenger of Allāh, may the peace and blessings of Allāh be upon him, set out in the morning from Minā when he had prayed *fajr* in the morning of the Day of ʿArafah and went to ʿArafah and camped at Namirah until the *ẓuhr* prayer. The Messenger of Allāh, may the peace and blessings of Allāh be upon him, went out at midday and joined *ẓuhr* and *ʿaṣr.* Then he addressed the people and then went and stood at the standing place at ʿArafāt. (Aḥmad and Abū Dāwūd)
- There is the common belief that the Mount of Mercy is where one should stand at ʿArafāt rather than the rest of it. This is wrong. Rather, it is best to stand where the Prophet, may the peace and blessings of Allāh be upon him, stood: at the rocks at the left of the Mount, based on the *ḥadīth* of Sulaymān ibn

Mūsā from Jubayr ibn Muṭʿim, may Allāh be pleased with them, that the Prophet, may the peace and blessings of Allāh be upon him, said, "All of ʿArafāt is a place of standing. Come up above the bottom of ʿUranah." (Aḥmad, Bazzār and Ṭabarānī in *al-Kabīr* with an *isnād* of reliable narrators)

- There are the pilgrims who leave Makkah immediately for ʿArafāt at *ẓuhr* on the Day of ʿArafah, so that they miss some of the *sunan* – leaving Makkah for Minā after sunrise on the Day of *Tarwiyah*; and *Ẓuhr, ʿAṣr, Maghrib* and *ʿIshāʾ* prayers; spending the night there until praying *fajr* on the ninth; setting out after sunrise from Minā to ʿArafāt; camping at Namirah and then listening to the *khuṭbah* of the Imām of the *ḥajj* after the sun declines, and joining together *ẓuhr* and *ʿaṣr* at the Namirah mosque. Jābir, may Allāh be pleased with him, said in his description of the *ḥajj* of the Prophet, may the peace and blessings of Allāh be upon him, "On the Day of *Tarwiyah* (8th of Dhu al-Ḥijjah), they made for Minā with *iḥrām* for *ḥajj*. The Prophet, may the peace and blessings of Allāh be upon him, rode and he prayed *ẓuhr*, *ʿaṣr*, *maghrib*, *ʿishaʾ* and *fajr* at Minā. Then he waited until the sun rose."
- A lot of *Muṭawwifs*, the *ḥajj* guides, descend with the pilgrims from ʿArafāt before sunset and travel straight to Minā and do not spend the night at Muzdalifah nor do they stand there and so they miss this *Sunnah*. The Prophet, may the peace and blessings of Allāh be upon him, remained at Muzdalifah and prayed *fajr* there and did not give anyone permission to leave Muzdalifah at night for Minā except for women and the weak. Similarly the *ḥujjāj* rush to stone the *jamrahs* and they are impelled to stone them before the sun declines on the 11th–12th of Dhu al-Ḥijjah although its time only comes after the sun declines.
- There are also the people who sit around the Kaʿbah where the *ṭawāf* is done, a long time before the time for the *jamāʿah* prayer. They occupy the area where the *ṭawāf* is done, and it causes great annoyance and conflict between those sitting and those doing *ṭawāf*.

- When the prayer at the *Masjid al-Ḥarām* is being performed many of the pilgrims run between Ṣafā and Marwah and are not eager for the *jamāʿah* prayer. Worse and more unwise is when the *maghrib* prayer is performed while they are doing *saʿy*. They continue their *saʿy* until they miss the *maghrib* prayer. How can those people hope for good when they have deliberately abandoned the obligation of Allāh? The Prophet, may the peace and blessings of Allāh be upon him, said, "There is no portion in Islam for the one who abandons the prayer." (Aḥmad)

7.17.2 Innovations of the visit

The visit to the grave of the Prophet, may the peace and blessings of Allāh be upon him, is one of the most important and most excellent acts of nearness, which gives joy to the visitor in this world and the Hereafter. Obtaining it, is desired and hoped for. However, *Shayṭān* is always lying in wait for everyone who desires good, and he makes innovations in worship seem good to them in order to distance them from the pleasure of the Lord – glory be to Him and may He be exalted!

Part of that is touching and kissing the enclosure around the noble grave, stroking it, doing *ṭawāf* of it and praying to it, and bowing to the noble grave. Even worse is kissing the ground. All of that is agreed to be unlawful.

There is also what the people of Madīnah and others do when they stand on the eastern side of the enclosure, praying and greeting Jibrīl, Mika'īl and Isrāfīl, on whom be peace. It is an innovation without foundation.

There is the custom of the people of Madīnah when they go to visit Sayyidah Fāṭimah az-Zahrā' after greeting Abū Bakr and 'Umar, may Allāh be pleased with them, and returning to the noble grave. Then they return to the first place in front of the noble grave and stand a short time and then go to the side of the Ottoman *miḥrāb* and stand there facing the *qiblah* and making supplication. It is another innovation without foundation.

Part of that is when visitors form rows after each obligatory prayer and chant the *salām* on the Messenger of Allāh, may the peace and blessings of Allāh be upon him, and his two Companions with a single shout in a very unpleasant voice. This is objectionable and is forbidden by the Qur'ān, *Sunnah* and consensus of the *Ummah*. The Almighty says,

يَٰٓأَيُّهَا ٱلَّذِينَ ءَامَنُواْ لَا تَرْفَعُوٓاْ أَصْوَٰتَكُمْ فَوْقَ صَوْتِ ٱلنَّبِيِّ وَلَا تَجْهَرُواْ لَهُۥ بِٱلْقَوْلِ كَجَهْرِ بَعْضِكُمْ لِبَعْضٍ أَن تَحْبَطَ أَعْمَٰلُكُمْ وَأَنتُمْ لَا تَشْعُرُونَ ﴿٢﴾

"*O you who believe! Raise not your voices above the voice of the Prophet nor speak aloud to him in talk, as you may speak aloud to one another, lest your deeds become vain and you perceive not.*" [*al-Ḥujurat* 49: 2]

The *Ummah* agrees that the sanctity of the Messenger of Allāh, may the peace and blessings of Allāh be upon him, dead is like his sanctity when he was alive and that Allāh Almighty praised people for lowering their voices in the presence of the Messenger of Allāh, may the peace and blessings of Allāh be upon him, and gave them good news of an immense reward:

إِنَّ ٱلَّذِينَ يَغُضُّونَ أَصْوَٰتَهُمْ عِندَ رَسُولِ ٱللَّهِ أُوْلَٰٓئِكَ ٱلَّذِينَ ٱمْتَحَنَ ٱللَّهُ قُلُوبَهُمْ لِلتَّقْوَىٰ لَهُم مَّغْفِرَةٌ وَأَجْرٌ عَظِيمٌ ﴿٣﴾

"*Those that lower their voice in the presence of the Messenger of Allāh, their hearts has Allāh tested for piety. For them is forgiveness and a great reward.*" [*al-Ḥujurat* 49: 3]

He censured others for raising their voices in his presence, may the peace and blessings of Allāh be upon him, and denied their intelligence, saying,

إِنَّ ٱلَّذِينَ يُنَادُونَكَ مِن وَرَآءِ ٱلْحُجُرَٰتِ أَكْثَرُهُمْ لَا يَعْقِلُونَ ﴿٤﴾

"*Those who shout out to you from without the inner apartments, most of them lack understanding.*" [*al-Ḥujurat* 49: 4]

It is related that Caliph Abū Ja'far al-Manṣūr argued with Imām Mālik, may Allāh have mercy on him, in the mosque of the Prophet, may the peace and blessings of Allāh be upon him. Imām Mālik said, "Amīr al-Mu'minīn, do not raise your voice in this mosque. Allāh taught people, saying, '*Raise not your voices,*' and he censured others, saying, '*Those who shout out to you from behind the dwellings, most of them have no sense.*'" [*al-Ḥujurat* 49: 4]
So Abū Ja'far calmed down.

Part of it is rubbing the wall of the grave with the back and stomach and wiping it with the hand. It is disliked. The *adab*, proper behaviour is to be as far from it as he would be from the Prophet, may the peace and blessings of Allāh be upon him, if he had been present and alive.

Part of what is objectionable is what is commonly claimed that the Prophet, may the peace and blessings of Allāh be upon him, said, "Whoever visits me and visits my father Ibrāhīm in the same year has the Paradise guaranteed for him." This is false and fabricated and not recognised.

Miqāts of Iḥrām

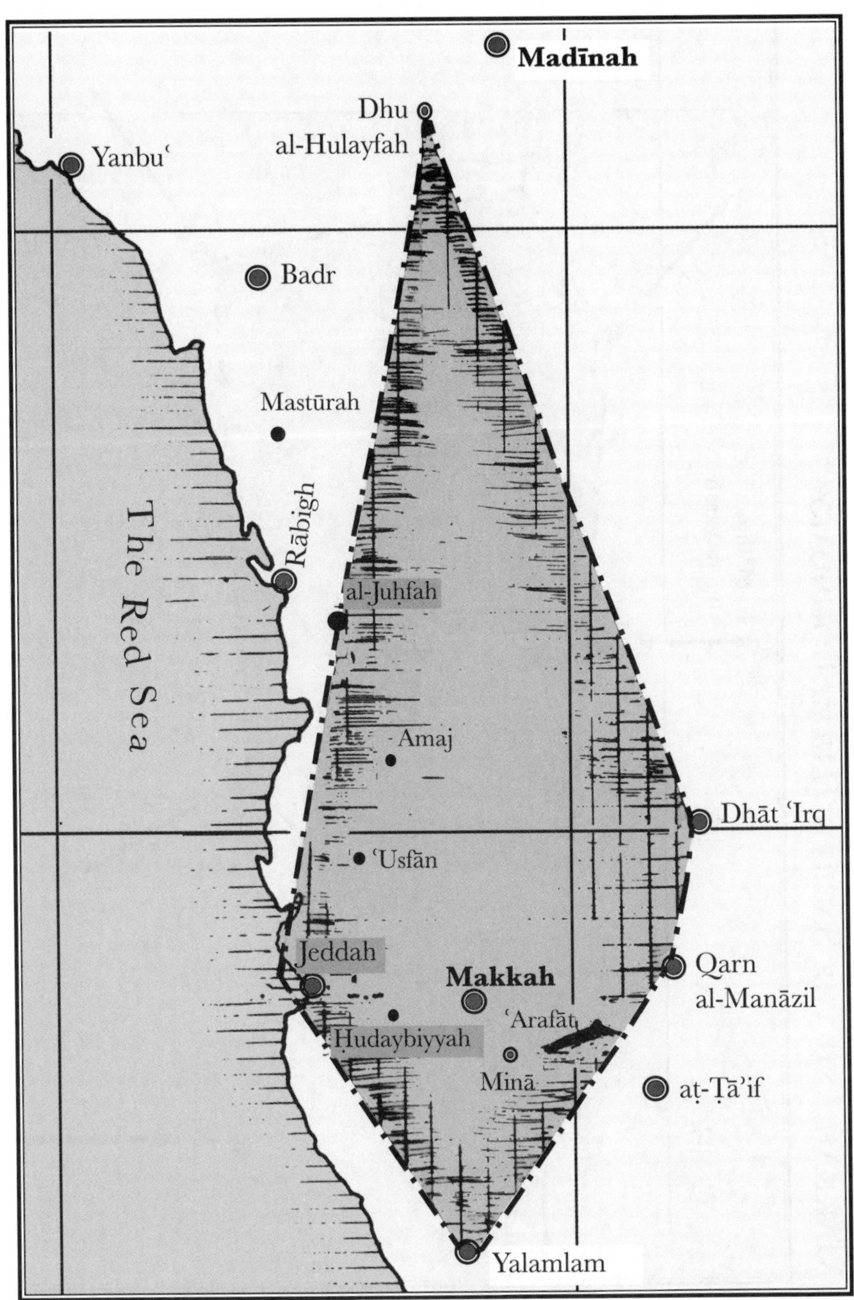

Makkah and the Sacred *Ḥaram* Boundary

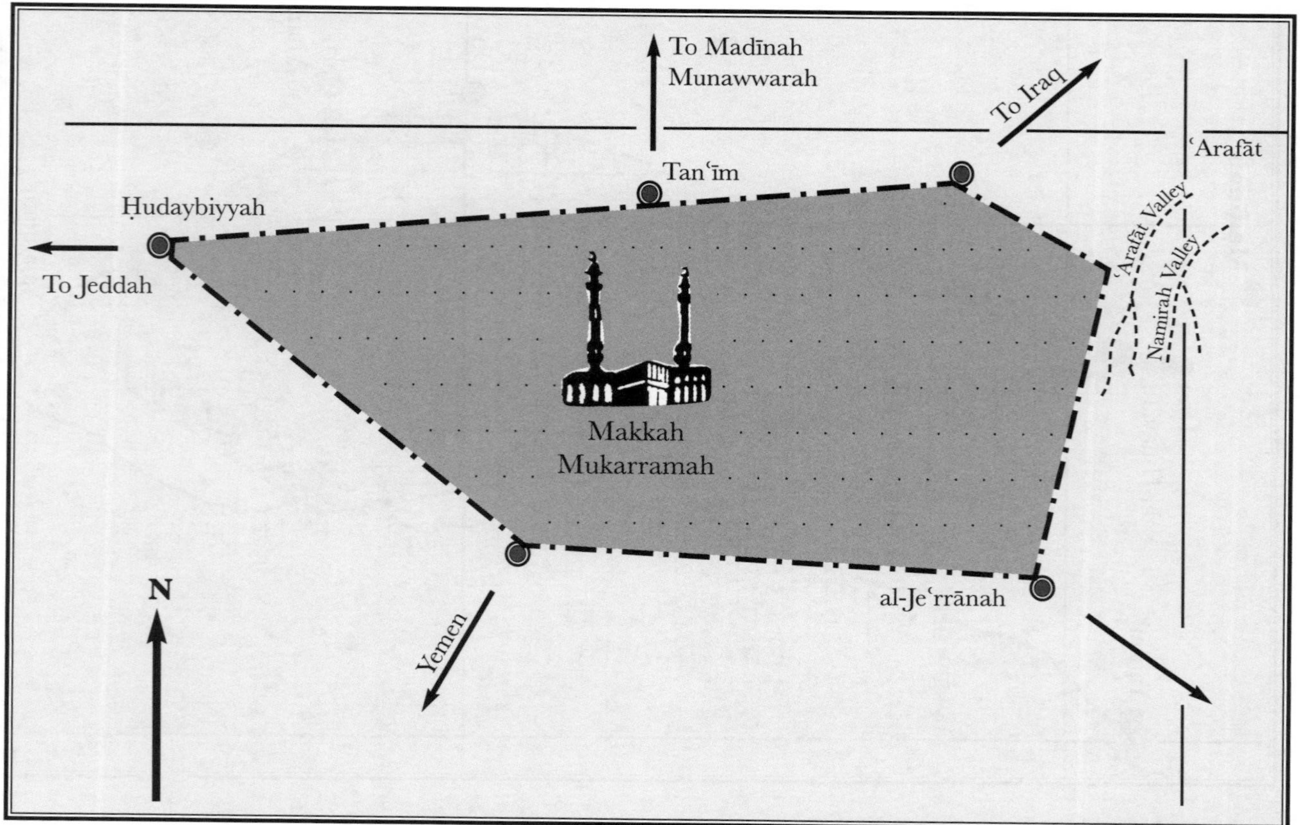

PLACES OF *ḤAJJ* RITUALS

The pilgrim performs the *ṭawāf* of arrival, and moves to Minā on the 8th of Dhu al-Ḥijjah. There he spends the night and the next day he proceeds to 'Arafāt where he resides until sunset and thereafter goes to Muzdalifah. The night is spent there; and on the morning of the 10th he returns to Minā. The roads leading to 'Arafāt have been widened, and the mountain which previously obstructed the two oldest routes (Ḍabb and al-Ma'zimīn) have been removed.

Madīnah Munawwarah

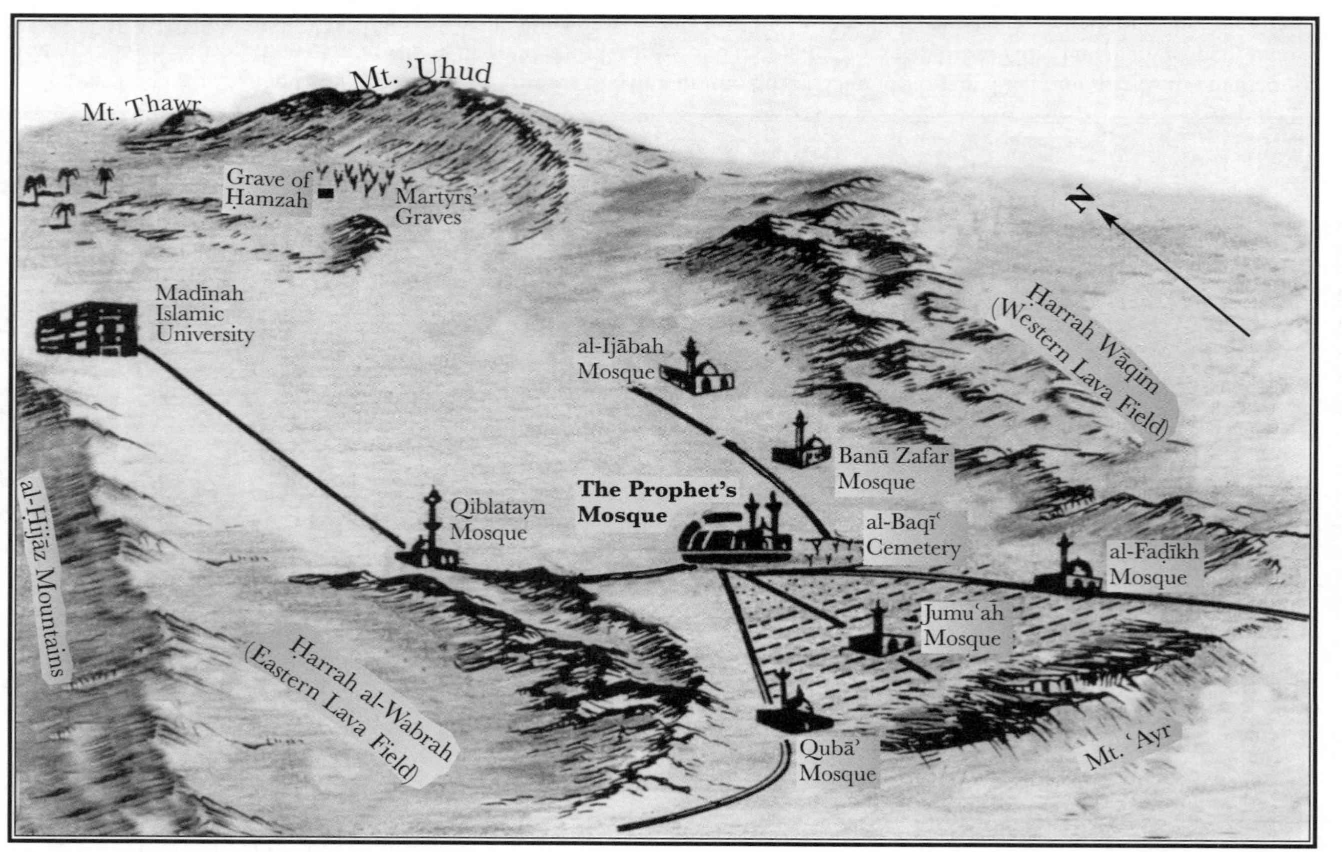

Notes

1. In the proper *fiqh* terminology, *Iḥrām* for *Ḥajj* is known as *sharṭ* (pre-condition), while the other two *farḍ* elements (i.e. standing at 'Arafāt and *Ṭawāf al-ifāḍah)*, are called *Rukn* (pillars). All three are *farḍ*, meaning that missing any of them will invalidate the *ḥajj* and cannot be remedied by atonement or sacrifice. To simplify this we have grouped these as *farḍ* elements. The same is the case with *'Umrah* where *iḥrām* is a *sharṭ* and *ṭawāf* and *sa'y* are *rukn*.

2. The praying of two *rak'ats* of *ṭawāf* after *'Aṣr* prayer before the sun sets completely and after *Fajr* prayer, before the sun rises, remained a matter of choice among the great imāms of this *ummah*. Imām Shāfi'ī and Imām Aḥmad, may Allāh have mercy on both of them, are of the opinion that the two *rak'ats* of *ṭawāf* done during these times is allowed, and that these two *rak'ats* are exempted from the general prohibition of performing *ṣalāt* in these times. Imām Abū Ḥanīfah, Imām Mālik and Imām Sufyān Thawrī and other great *fuqahā'*, may Allāh have mercy on them all, say that even the two *rak'ats* of *ṭawāf* are prohibited; so if someone does *ṭawāf* in these times he should defer praying these two *rak'ats* until the prohibited times have lapsed.

   To examine their evidence we can present some of these *aḥādīth* and practices of the *ṣaḥābah* to this effect.

   • The *aḥādīth* related by Bukhārī and Muslim, concerning prohibition of performing *ṣalāt* after *'Aṣr* before sunset and after *Fajr* before sunrise has no exemption of praying these *rak'ats* in Makkah. As for the *ḥadīth* in which the exemption of Makkah is mentioned it should be clarified that even the jurists who do not regard it as *makrūh* to pray after *'Aṣr* and *Fajr*, think that this *ḥadīth* is weak. Imām Bayhaqī mentions in his *Sunan Kubrā*, (Vol. 1, p. 461) that this *ḥadīth* is only narrated by 'Abdullāh ibn Mu'ammil and he is weak. Imām Aḥmad says that his *ḥadīth* is not acceptable.

   • On the other hand, it is narrated in Bukhārī (Vol. 1, p. 220) that 'Umar, may Allāh be pleased with him, performed *ṭawāf* after *Fajr* and after that he rode on his mount leaving for Madīnah. When he reached Dhū Ṭuwā he offered two *rak'āts* of *ṭawāf* there.

   • Imām Mālik narrates in *al-Muwaṭṭā* that 'Umar, may Allāh be pleased with him, did *ṭawāf* after *Fajr* and after that he rode and when he reached Dhū Ṭuwā, he stopped and prayed two *rak'ats*. This practice of 'Umar, may Allāh be pleased with him, is also mentioned in Bayhaqī (Vol. 1, p. 463).

   • It is also mentioned in *al-Muwaṭṭā* that 'Abdullāh ibn 'Abbās, may Allāh be pleased with him, used to do *ṭawāf* after *'Aṣr* and went home without praying two *rak'ats*.

   • Abū Zubair says, as mentioned in *al-Muwaṭṭā*, that, "I used to see the *Maṭāf* of Ka'bah becoming empty of people and no one used to do *ṭawāf* after *Fajr* and *'Aṣr* (because at that time two *rak'ats* of *ṭawāf* could not be prayed).

   • Ḥāfiẓ Ibn Ḥajar and Ḥāfiẓ Badruddīn 'Ainī have both mentioned it with reference to *Musnad Aḥmad* that Jābīr, may Allāh be pleased with him, said, "We were not doing *ṭawāf* after *Fajr* until sunrise and after *'Aṣr* until sunset," and he also said that I heard the Prophet, may Allāh bless him and grant him peace, saying that, "Sun is rising between two horns of *Shayṭān*".

- It is also mentioned in *Muṣannaf Ibn Abī Shaybah* (Vol. 1, p. 457), *Musnad Aḥmad* (Vol. 4, p. 219), *Musnad Ṭayālisī* (p. 117), *Sharḥ Maʿānī al-Āthār of Ṭaḥāwī* (Vol. 1, p.179) and Bayhaqī's *Sunnan Kubrā* (Vol. 2, p. 264) that Muʿadh Ibn ʿAfrāʾ, may Allāh be pleased with him, did *ṭawāf* after *Fajr* or *ʿAṣr* and he did not offer two *rakʿats* of *ṭawāf*. When he was asked about that he said that, "No prayer should be offered after *Fajr* until sunrise and after *ʿAṣr* until sunset."
- It is mentioned in Bayhaqī's *Sunan Kubrā* (Vol. 2, p. 464) that Abū Saʿīd Khudrī, may Allāh be pleased with him, came to Makkah and did *ṭawāf* after *Fajr*. Some people started discussing among themselves, "Let us see whether he prays two *rakʿats* of *ṭawāf* now or not." Abū Saʿīd Khudrī, may Allāh be pleased with him, remained sitting until the sun rose then offered two *rakʿāts*.
- Imām Bayhaqī also mentioned that it has been narrated from a group of *ṣaḥābah* and *tābiʿīn*, that they were delaying the offering of two *rakʿats* of *ṭawāf* until the rising of the sun.

3. It is related in *Muṣannaf* of Ibn Abī Shaybah from ʿAṭāʾ that ʿĀʾishah, may Allāh be pleased with her, said, "When you do *ṭawāf* after *Fajr* or *ʿAṣr* prayer delay the prayer until sun sets or sun rises then pray for every *ṭawāf* two *rakʿats*.

   The purpose of these details are that Imāms Abū Ḥanīfah, Mālik and Thawrī and others who are of the opinion that two *rakʿāts* of *ṭawāf* should not be offered in these times but offered later and those who act according to this are not without foundation, neither are they innovating in Islam, since this practice has been carried on from the days of the Companions. It is therefore not advisable to start arguments with the common people by confusing them especially in the *Ḥaram* when it is full of people from all over the world as this kind of behaviour will increase disparity among people and not unity which is one of the aims of this great international Muslim gathering. For further details refer to *Rahbar-e-Ḥujjāj* by Maulānā Ḥabīb-ur-Raḥmān Aʿẓamī, may Allāh have mercy on him. (Iqbal Ahmad Azami)

4. *Ramal* is *Sunnah* only in that *ṭawāf* which is to be followed by the *saʿy*. If a person forgets to observe *ramal* in the first three circuits, one need not observe it in the other remaining circuits; observance of *ramal* in all seven rounds is *makrūh*.

5. The *Ḥaṭīm* is a semi-circular wall of white marble opposite the north-west wall but not connected to it.

6. These are two green signs which indicate the old river bed.

7. The difference between the onager and the deer was that the person who hunted the onager was not in the state of *iḥrām* so his hunted animal was lawful for a person in *iḥrām* to consume it, while the hunter of the deer was not known (whether he was in the state of *iḥrām* or not), because any land animal or bird hunted by a person in the state of *iḥrām* is unlawful for anyone to eat.

8. Jewess refers to her origin, that she was of Jewish parents.

Chapter 8

Taqwā

8.1 Consciousness of Allāh

In addition to a Muslim's adherence to the pillars of Islam is his or her knowledge of what is forbidden, *ḥarām*, *makrūh*, and doubtful. Prudence in avoiding the doubtful things lest they lead one to *ḥarām* or *makrūh* is also among the obligations of Islam.

8.2 Food

8.2.1 Meat and slaughtering

It is *ḥarām* to eat the flesh of a carcass; that is, any animal which has died as a result of disease or other natural causes. Likewise, the flesh of an animal slaughtered by a disbeliever is *ḥarām*, except that he or she belongs to the People of the Book [Christian or Jew] on condition that the proper method of slaughter is employed, and Allāh's name is taken.[1]

Flesh of an animal slaughtered by a Muslim, Christian, or Jew who intentionally neglects to pronounce the name of Allāh[2] is also *ḥarām*. If, however, a Muslim neglects to say *bismillāh* out of forgetfulness then, according to Imām Abū Ḥanīfah and Imām Shāfiʿī, the meat will be *ḥalāl*. But according to Imām Mālik, it will be *ḥarām*.[3]

8.2.2 Flesh that is *ḥalāl* (lawful) for consumption

The following types of flesh are lawful for consumption:

- herbivorous animals [like cows, goats, deer, sheep, rabbits, camels, etc.];
- and fish.

8.2.3 Marine animals

All kinds of marine animals,[4] except fish, are *ḥarām*, according to Imām Abū Ḥanīfah. The flesh of a fish which has died in the water and is found floating on the surface of the water is *ḥarām*. It is not necessary to apply the proper Islamic method of slaughter to fish.[5]

8.2.4 Flesh that is *ḥarām* (unlawful) for consumption

The following types of flesh are unlawful for consumption:

- pig and all pork products;
- carnivorous quadrupeds [i.e. predators];
- birds of prey [i.e. raptors];
- hyenas [or any despoilers of the dead, i.e. scavengers];
- domesticated asses, mules, foxes, elephants;
- the creeping creatures of the earth [like mice, weasels, lizards, snakes, etc.];
- insects [like bees];

- tortoises [whether living on land or in the sea];
- and animals who derive strength from eating unclean things.

8.2.5 Flesh that is *makrūh* (disliked) for consumption

The following types of meat are disliked for consumption:

1. crows which live on seeds and *najāsah*;
2. and horseflesh is *ḥalāl* but according to Imām Abū Ḥanīfah it is *makrūh*.[6]

8.3 *Ḥarām Drinks*

Grape wine made from the untreated juice of grapes which have fermented and is intoxicating is absolutely *ḥarām*. A person who denies this [not out of ignorance] is a *kāfir*.[7]

Date wine, raisin [or currant] wine, fig wine, as well as intoxicants made of honey, wheat, mash, barley, hops, etc. are all *ḥarām*, according to Imām Muḥammad and a *fatwā* is given according to his opinion.

It is prohibited to make use of wine [or other intoxicants] in any way. It should not be used medicinally.[8]

The Messenger of Allāh, may the peace and blessings of Allāh be upon him, said that anything which in large quantities is intoxicating is *ḥarām* to consume even in small quantities [to even a drop]. Therefore, anything which intoxicates [liquid, solid, or gas] is like wine in that it is *ḥarām*.

8.4 *Eating Habits*

It is *farḍ* to take as much food as is necessary to maintain life. It is *mustaḥab* to take as much as will facilitate fasting and standing long in prayer. It is *Sunnah* to fill only half the stomach, though it is *mubāḥ* to fill the whole stomach. If the stomach is filled completely with the intention of preparing for *jihād* or seeking knowledge of Islam then that is *mustaḥab*. It is *ḥarām* to eat more when the stomach is full, except that it be with the intention of preparing for fasting, *ṣawm,* or out of regard for a guest.

8.4.1 In cases of extreme hunger

In a state of hunger or thirst so extreme as to make death appear inevitable (*makhmaṣah*), when no *ḥalāl* food or drink is available, one may resort to consuming *ḥarām* food or drink which, under the circumstances, becomes *ḥalāl.* A person in such a state may only take enough [of the ordinarily *ḥarām* food or drink] to save or preserve life, and no more. According to Imām Abū Ḥanīfah, it even becomes *farḍ* [for the preservation of life]. Hence, the person who [while in the state of *makhmaṣah*] chooses not to eat of the available, but ordinarily *ḥarām* food, and who then dies as a result of his or her decision not to eat, will die the death of a wrongdoer.

If someone in such a state [of *makhmaṣah*] should partake of someone else's wealth in order to save his or her own life, intending to pay the owner back, it will be permitted [even though the owner has no knowledge of it]. However, if he prefers to be prudent [and refrains from taking another's property] and then dies, his or her death will not be that of a wrongdoer.

8.4.2 Utensils for eating

The use of gold or silver utensils is *ḥarām.*[9]

8.4.3 The *Sunnah* of eating

It is *Sunnah* when eating or drinking to first say, "*Bismillāh,*" and upon completion [of the meal] to say, "*Al Ḥamdu Lillāh.*" It is *Sunnah* to wash the hands before and after a meal. When drinking, it is

Sunnah to finish the glass in three draughts; reciting "*Bismillāh*" at the beginning, and "*Al Ḥamdu Lillāh*" at the end of each draught.

8.5 Guests

It is *Sunnah mu'akkadah* to hospitably receive a guest for a period of three days. After that it is merely *mustaḥab.*

It is *ḥarām* to accept gifts or invitations from tyrants, dishonest politicians, or people who dance or sing in public for a living. However, if it is known that the major part of such a person's wealth came from *ḥalāl* means, then the invitation or gift may be accepted.

8.6 Medicine

The taking of medicines during illness is permitted, yet it is not *wājib*. If someone chooses not to take medicines and then dies, he or she will not die a wrongdoer.

8.7 Fruits and Vegetables

The consumption of various types of fruits, vegetables, and other delicacies is permitted. However, excess in exotic foods is not allowed.

8.8 Private Matters

The Messenger of Allāh, may the peace and blessings of Allāh be upon him, said, "The best among you are those of you who are the best in their treatment of their wives and families and I am good to them."

8.9 Covering ʿAwrah (Nakedness)

The male *ʿawrah* is from the navel to below the knee. The *ʿawrah* for women is the whole body except for the feet, hands, and face.[10]

A man may expose all but his *ʿawrah* to another man. A woman may not expose any of her body from the navel to the knees to another woman. She may, however, expose the other parts of her body to another woman. A woman, in the absence of lust, may look at a man who has exposed all but his *ʿawrah*. A man may not look at a non-*maḥram* woman except to see her hands and face [not her hair]. This is on condition that he looks without lust; otherwise he may not look at her at all.

The following verse was revealed in the Qur'ān:

قُل لِّلْمُؤْمِنِينَ يَغُضُّوا مِنْ أَبْصَٰرِهِمْ وَيَحْفَظُوا فُرُوجَهُمْ ۚ ذَٰلِكَ أَزْكَىٰ لَهُمْ ۗ
إِنَّ ٱللَّهَ خَبِيرٌۢ بِمَا يَصْنَعُونَ ﴿٣٠﴾ وَقُل لِّلْمُؤْمِنَٰتِ يَغْضُضْنَ مِنْ أَبْصَٰرِهِنَّ
وَيَحْفَظْنَ فُرُوجَهُنَّ ... ﴿٣١﴾

> "*Say to the believers, that they should cast down their eyes and guard their private parts; that is purer for them. Allāh is aware of the things they do. And say to the believing women that they should cast down their eyes and guard their private parts.*"
> [*an-Nūr* 24: 30–1]

A *ḥadīth* is related in which it is stated that whoever looks with lust on a non-*maḥram* will have molten lead poured into their eyes on the Day of Judgement.

8.10 Looking at One's Spouse

It is permitted to look at the entire body of one's spouse, but it is *mustaḥab* not to see the private parts. It is *ḥarām* to gaze with lust on a person other than one's own mate. It is likewise *ḥarām* to lay a lustful hand on a non-*maḥram*, or to make obscene gestures or suggestions to someone.

8.10.1 Looking at female relatives

A man may touch or look at the head, face, arms, and shins of a female relative, as long as he is free of lust when doing so. He may not [touch or even] look at her uncovered stomach, back, or thighs.

8.10.2 Looking at one's future spouse

It is permitted, even in the presence of desire, to look at [the hands and face of] the person one intends to marry. Likewise, a witness to matters of legal importance may look at a non-*maḥram*.

8.10.3 Looking at another's private parts

It is *ḥarām* to look at another person's private parts, *ʿawrah*, unless it is absolutely necessary to do so. People like doctors and nurses may look at however much they need to, and not more.

8.11 Ḥarām Sexual Practices

It is *ḥarām* to have:

- anal intercourse;
- and vaginal intercourse during the period of menstruation, *ḥayḍ*, or post-childbirth bleeding, *nifās*.
- Homosexuality is *ḥarām*. To deny this is *kufr*.

8.11.1 Permitted birth control

Birth control by use of the coitus interruptus method is permitted only when the wife gives her consent.

8.12 Muslim Dress

8.12.1 Purpose of clothing

It is *farḍ* to wear enough clothing as will cover the parts of the body which may not be exposed, and will protect the body from extreme cold or heat. It is *mustaḥab* to wear, in addition to this, as much clothing as will satisfy the Qur'ānic directive to adorn:

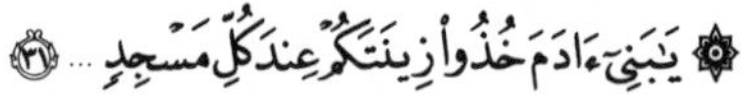

> *"O Children of Adam! Take your adornment at every place of worship,"* [*al-A'rāf* 7: 31]

or to display the beneficence of the Almighty, or to give evidence of one's thanks to Allāh. It is *Sunnah* not to wear the type of clothing which causes people to raise their eyebrows, [i.e. loud, trendy, or lavish clothes]. Taking excessive pains with one's clothing out of extravagance or vanity is *ḥarām* or *makrūh*; though if it is done for some reason other than these, it is permitted.

The hanging end of a turban should extend either all or half way to the waist.[11]

8.12.2 Wearing clothes with the colour red

It is *ḥarām* for men, but not for women, to wear red or saffron coloured clothing. Red, however, is not absolutely *ḥarām* for men, as they may wear it as stripes or mixed in a multicolour garment.

8.12.3 SILK CLOTHING

Cloth which is made entirely from silk is *ḥalāl* for women and *ḥarām* for men, except as a border not exceeding the width of four fingers. Cloth which is a blend of silk and another material, where the other material is dominant, may be worn by men at all times. Cloth which is a blend of silk and another material, where the silk is the dominant material, may be worn by men in war.

It is permitted to use sheets [bed coverings] and pillowcases of silk, according to Imām Abū Ḥanīfah [as well as Imāms Shāfiʿī and Mālik]. According to Imāms Abū Yūsuf and Muḥammad it is not permitted.

8.12.4 WEARING JEWELLERY

Women are permitted to wear jewellery of gold and silver. Men, however, may not wear any gold or silver jewellery except for a silver ring or a silver ring set with gold and precious stones. It is *ḥarām* for a small boy to wear silk or jewellery of gold and silver. Rings of iron, stone, and brass are not to be worn.

It is *Sunnah* for a ruler or *qāḍī* [or whoever else has need of it] to wear a signet ring. It is better that others [having no need of it] not wear one.

Silver braces and fillings may be used for the teeth, but not gold. According to Imām Abū Ḥanifah's two companions, Abū Yūsuf and Muḥammad however, gold may also be used.

8.13 Miscellaneous Rulings

8.13.1 SPORTS AND CONTESTS

Contests in archery, horseracing, and the like are permitted by the *Sharīʿah*. With regard to setting a prize for the winner of such contests, the following rules apply:

- If the prize is to come from one side specifically [for example, one of the two contestants says to the other, "If you beat me, then I will give you such and such. But if I beat you, then I will take nothing from you."], it is permitted.[12]

  Two students who differ on a question may assign a prize for the one who is right.[13] Then the one whose answer is right will [either] win the prize [or be absolved from his agreement to give it].
- If the prize is to come from either one of the two sides,[14] it is *ḥarām*, except that a third person step in and say, "If one of us finishes ahead of the other two, he will take so much as his prize."[15]

  If two people tie for first place [ʿUmar and Khālid], then the third person [Zayd] will not have to give anything; but the two winners will have to take their prizes from each other. In this way, this type of competition and awarding of prizes will be *ḥalāl*. However, the prize agreed upon for the winner does not automatically become his property [as heretofore mentioned]. Thus, he is not entitled to take it without the loser's actually presenting it to him.
- In the same way, an *amīr* [or any non-participant] may tell a group of his soldiers [or a group of contestants] that the one of them who finishes first [in a certain competition] will receive so much [from the *amīr*] as his prize.

Forbidden Games

Games like chess, backgammon, and dice are *ḥarām*.[16] To play such games with the understanding that the winner will take a certain amount in prize money is gambling, which is *ḥarām* and a major sin, *kabīrah*. To deny this is *kufr*.[17] Having amusement by pigeon racing, cockfighting and similar sports are also *ḥarām*.

Killing Animals

It is *ḥarām* to kill [without good reason] an animal whose flesh is *ḥalāl* if it is not going to be eaten [or preserved]. The killing of dangerous animals is permitted.

8.13.2 *Walīmah* – Wedding Feast

Walīmah dinner is *Sunnah* [and is best if performed within three days after the marriage ceremony]. Whoever receives an invitation should accept it. If, for no good reason, one does not then attend the dinner, one will be doing wrong.

It is improper [unless there was some kind of agreement beforehand] to take food home from an invitational dinner. One should not give such food to a beggar without permission from the one who is giving the dinner.

When a person knows that there will be loose talk and music at the *walīmah* dinner, he should not accept the invitation. If however, he did not know and then arrives to find such things taking place, he should either attempt to put an end to them, if he is in a position to do so without creating ill-will, or quietly finish his dinner. But if this person is a religious figure, a teacher, or an imām, he should leave quietly.

Imām Abū Ḥanīfah once found himself in such a situation and simply exercised patience. This event, however, took place in his youth, before he became a recognised religious personality.

8.13.3 Music

Music is *ḥarām* as it diverts attention from remembrance of Allāh and stirs the baser emotions. The Imām of Ṣufism, Shaikh Baha al-Dīn Naqshband, may Allāh be pleased with him, said, "It is not something which I myself practice, as it is not the *Sunnah*."

Musical instruments are generally agreed upon to be *ḥarām*; except war drums and drums used to announce weddings. It is *ḥarām* to take wages for wailing at funerals, or for playing music.

Poetry is rhythmic language. What is good in it is good, and what is bad in it is bad but to waste time in it is *makrūh*.

8.13.4 Hypocrisy

Hypocrisy in worship has the effect of nullifying the value of the worship and, furthermore, is a misdeed. In other words, whoever performs an act of worship so that people will see or hear him, will not receive any reward for that act from Allāh. The Messenger of Allāh, may the peace and blessings of Allāh be upon him, called this kind of behaviour a minor form of *shirk*.

The signs of a hypocrite, as explained in an authentic *ḥadīth*, are as follows: he will speak falsely, break promises, violate trusts, betray after swearing loyalty, and use abusive language in arguments.

8.13.5 Vices and Social Etiquettes

Ghībah – Backbiting

Ghībah [or relating fault with someone in their absence], even though it be true, is *ḥarām*, regardless of whether it is their practice of religion which is faulted, their appearance, character, or whatever. *Ghībah* concerning a tyrant, however, is not considered slander.

There is no *ghībah* except that it concerns someone in particular. To speak badly about the inhabitants of a certain city is not *ghībah*.

Namīmah – Scandalmongering

Namīmah or informing a person about the unpleasant things another said about him or her, so that relations between the two become strained, is *ḥarām*.

Abusing Another Muslim

It is *ḥarām* to use abusive language towards another Muslim [to curse or swear at him]. Similarly, abusive gestures with the hand, head, eyes, etc. are *ḥarām*. To grin in someone's face in a way calculated to humiliate is also *ḥarām*.

The Messenger of Allāh, may the peace and blessings of Allāh be upon him, taught that the inviolability of the wealth and honour of a Muslim are like the inviolability of his or her blood. He also once said to the Kaʿbah, "The Almighty has given you such a great measure of sanctity! But the sanctity of a Muslim and his blood, wealth, and honour is far greater than what you possess."

Cursing Others

If one person curses another who does not deserve to be cursed, then the curse will fall on the one who first pronounced it.

Lying

It is *ḥarām* to speak falsely except for bringing reconciliation between people or to keep one's family reconciled. In some cases an equivocal statement is better than an outright lie.[18] The use of equivocal language, however, is *makrūh* when there is no real need for it.

Spying

Spying on a Muslim in order to find out his faults is *ḥarām*. Furthermore, the worst kinds of falsehood are false testimony and false oaths when they lead to the separation of a Muslim from his wealth. Such falsehood, according to the Almighty, Allāh, is the same as *shirk*.

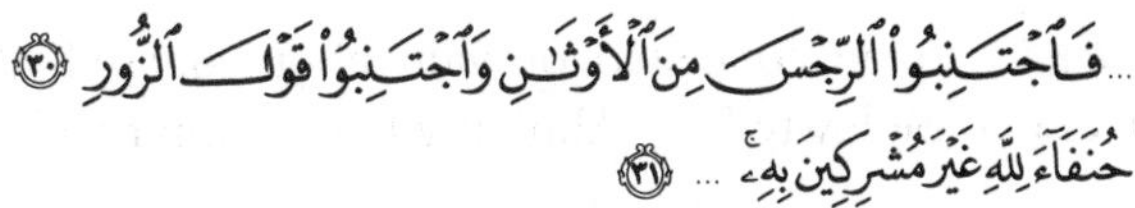

"So shun the abomination of idols, and shun the speaking of falsehood, being men who treat the straight way, not mushrikin." [*al-Ḥajj* 22: 30–1]

Bribery

Both the one who gives and the one who takes a bribe will go to *jahannam*.[19] Bribery is permitted only [after everything else has failed] in cases to prevent oneself from oppression or to obtain one's just right from a tyrant.

Praising Wrong

It is *ḥarām* to praise wrongdoers. In a *ḥadīth* it is written that the Almighty is displeased with such persons, and that the Throne shakes when they are praised.

Avoiding Bad Company

A Muslim should avoid the company of those who are habitually involved in what is unlawful. Failure to part company with such people will lead to one's becoming their partner in the punishment of this world and the next.

For good company it is best to sit in the presence of the *'ulamā'* and the pious. If this is not always possible, it is better not to socialise [with anyone but one's family].

Thanking Others

It is *mustaḥab*, and in some cases *wājib*, to give thanks and repay in kindness anyone who does one a favour. To deny someone's favour or to show ingratitude is wrong. Whoever is ungrateful to his fellow human being is ungrateful to his Lord.

Vanity

It is *ḥarām* to be conceited or vain about oneself, thinking everyone else to be lowly. The Almighty has commanded:

"*Therefore, hold not yourselves purified.*" [*an-Najm* 53: 32]

What is of importance is how one ends up when he dies; and no one knows how one is going to end up.

It is related in a *ḥadīth* that Allāh has decreed for someone to be a person of Paradise. It may happen that a large part of his life, he practices ill deeds which would eventually take him to Hell but he repents and performs good deeds and he enters Paradise; whilst for someone, Allāh has decreed to be one of the people of Hell. It may be that he continues for a long time to do good deeds which would eventually take him to Paradise but in the end he indulges in wrong doings and deserves the Hellfire [which was decreed for him]. Therefore one should not be proud of his deeds but should be conscious of and pray to Allāh to hold fast to the [righteous] way. Shaikh Sāʿdī says in his couplet:

> My wise master, Sheikh Shihābuddīn Suharwardī gave me two advices when we were travelling by sea: One about myself, that I should not be proud of myself, and another about others that I should not look for faults in others.

Boasting of One's Lineage

Boasting of one's ancestry is *ḥarām*, as is disputing for superiority in affluence or honour. It is written in the Holy Qur'ān:

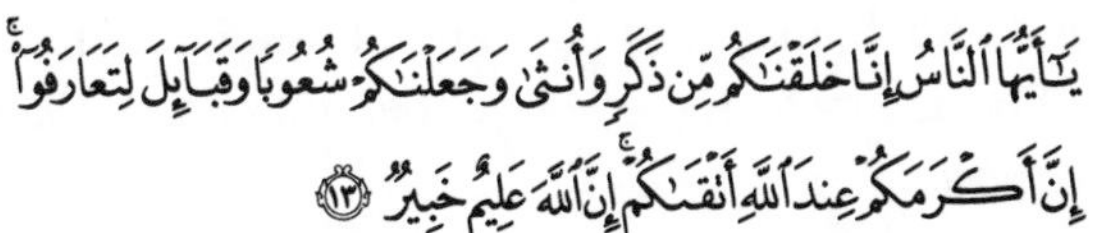

> "*O mankind! We have created you from a male and female, and made you nations and tribes, that you may know one another. Surely the noblest among you in the sight of Allāh is the most righteous of you, surely Allāh is All-Knowing, All-Aware.*" [*al-Hujurat* 49: 13]

The Responsibilities of One Muslim to Another

The responsibilities of one Muslim to another are six:

1. to greet him with peace, *salam*;
2. to bless him when he sneezes;
3. and to wish him well in his presence and absence;
4. to accept his invitation [to dinner];
5. to visit him when he is sick;
6. to attend his funeral.

Muslim Brotherhood

A Muslim must love for his fellow Muslim that which he loves for himself, and dislike for his brother that which he dislikes for himself.[20]

8.13.6 A MAN'S BEARD

It is *ḥarām* to trim one's beard to any less than a length which may be held in the fist. It is *makrūh* to pull the white or grey hair from one's beard. It is *Sunnah* to let the beard grow long, and to keep the moustache, fingernails, armpits, and pubic hair trimmed.

8.13.7 ASKING FOR BLESSINGS ON THE HOLY PROPHET ﷺ

It is *mustaḥab* to frequently make supplications (*darūd*) for the Messenger of Allāh, may the peace and blessings of Allāh be upon him. A gathering in which there is neither *dhikr* nor *Ṣalāh ʿalam-nabī* (*darūd*) is *makrūh.*

8.13.8 THE OBLIGATION OF A *QĀḌI*

Anyone giving legal decisions contrary to what is in the Book of Allāh is a *kāfir.*[21]

8.13.9 CONSULTING THE *SHARĪʿAH* FOR ALL THINGS

It is essential that all disputes and other legal affairs between Muslims be solved by having reference to the *Sharīʿah* [and its representatives, like *qāḍīs*, *muftīs*, and *ʿulamā*]. The ruling of the *Sharīʿah* is to be accepted by Muslims without rancour. To feel aversion for the ruling of the *Sharīʿah* is *kufr*, as the requisite for such a feeling is denial of the truth of the *Sharīʿah.*[22]

8.13.10 Wages for Islamic duties

According to Imām Abū Ḥanīfah, it is not permitted to take wages for making the *adhān*, or teaching the Qur'ān, or *fiqh*, or any other Islamic subject [But Imāms Mālik, Aḥmad ibn Ḥanbal and Shāfi'ī were of the opinion that to do so is permitted]. In our own times, the *fatwā* [given by the *Ḥanafī 'ulamā'* in view of the relative decline in interest among Muslims in the matter of Islamic duties] is that teaching of the Qur'ān and other Islamic duties may be performed for wages.

Qāḍīs, *muftīs*, *'ulamā'*, [imāms of *Masjids*, *ḥāfizs* of the Qur'ān] and *ghāzis* (soldiers) are to be given from the Muslim state treasury enough money to suffice them in all their legitimate needs.[23]

8.13.11 Imitating the opposite sex

It is *ḥarām* for a man to imitate [the dress and manners of] a woman, for a woman to imitate a man, and for a Muslim to imitate a disbeliever or wrongdoer.

8.13.12 Types of major sins

1. The greatest *kabīrah* is *kufr*.

   Next to associating others with Allāh is adherence to false doctrines.
2. The *kabīrah* which involves the rights of Muslims.

   This includes any kind of injustice done to the wealth, honour, or person of a Muslim. The Almighty may forgive a person who encroaches on His rights, but He will not forgive a person who encroaches on the rights of His servants. Imām Baghawī relates on the authority of Anas, may Allāh be pleased with him, that the Messenger of Allāh, may the peace and blessings of Allāh be upon him, said, "On the Day of Judgement a crier at the foot of the Throne will call out, 'Ummah of Muḥammad, your believing men and women are forgiven! Go now and settle your accounts with one another and enter the Paradise.' "

3. The *kabīrah* which involves the rights of Allāh alone.[24]

A Partial List of Major Sins Mentioned in Authentic Aḥādīth

1. *Shirk* [associating partners with Allāh].
2. Disobedience to one's parents.
3. Murder.
4. Taking false oaths.
5. Giving false testimony.
6. Falsely discrediting the reputation of a believing woman.
7. Devouring the money of an orphan for one's own use.
8. Taking, witnessing, or paying interest, *ribā.*
9. Desertion from the battlefield when *jihād* against unbelievers is going on.
10. Practising magic/sorcery.
11. Adultery/fornication especially with a woman of one's neighbour. It is stated in a *ḥadīth* that fornication with a neighbour's woman is more severe in sin than to fornicate with ten other women.
12. Theft.
13. Highway robbery.
14. Rebellion against a just ruler.
15. Suicide.*
16. Sodomy and homosexuality.
17. Consuming wine and intoxicants.
18. Leaving the five *farḍ* prayers.
19. Not paying *zakāh.*
20. Not fasting the month of *Ramaḍān* when one is physically able to fast.
21. Not performing the *ḥajj* when one is capable of doing so.
22. Lying about the Prophet, may the peace and blessings of Allāh be upon him [attributing to him *aḥādīth*, which he did not].

---

* Numbers 15 – 41 have been added by the revisers.

23. Breaking one's fast in *Ramaḍān* without reason.
24. Lying.
25. Imitating the opposite sex or unbelievers.
26. Eating pork, blood, or unslaughtered meat.
27. Leaving traces of urine on oneself.
28. Hypocrisy and showing off in acts of worship.
29. Spying on others to find their faults and secrets.
30. Eavesdropping.
31. Rejecting any of the beliefs of the Muslim majority.
32. Disobeying one's husband without Islamic justification.
33. Breaking the ties of kinship.
34. Hurting Muslims in any way.
35. Pride, arrogance, conceit, etc.
36. Men wearing silk or gold.
37. Pointing a weapon at another Muslim.
38. Arguing, quarrelling, and insulting someone.
39. Gambling and games of chance.
40. Backbiting and slander.
41. Scandal-mongering.

Among the greatest of the major sins mentioned in a *ḥadīth* is cursing one's own parents. The Companions asked incredulously how someone could curse his own parents. The Messenger of Allāh, the peace and blessings of Allāh be upon him, replied, "By cursing someone else's parents; thus causing the other person to respond in kind by cursing your parents."

8.13.13 Minor sins should not be discounted

To suppose a minor sin, *saghīrah*, to be a simple matter of no real consequence, and then to persist in it, is a major sin, *kabīrah*. To consider a *saghīrah* to be *ḥalāl* is *kufr*. Imām Bukhārī related that Anas, may Allāh be pleased with him, said, "You do things nowadays that you suppose to be less significant than even a hair. Whereas we, in the times of the Messenger of Allāh, may the peace and blessings of Allāh be upon him, used to consider those very same things to be fatal."

Notes

1. The important thing to note here is that Christians and Jews are required to use Islamic methods of slaughter. Flesh of an animal slaughtered by a Christian in a non-Islamic way, by electric shock for example, is as *ḥarām* as that slaughtered by a fire-worshipper, idolater, or atheist. (Trans.)
2. One may also use its equivalent, "In the Name of God," for example, or Jehovah, or Yahweh; but not, "In the name of the Father, Son, and Holy Ghost," as that would be *shirk*. (Trans.)
3. An animal is considered properly slaughtered when a sharp cutting instrument is used to cut,

   (a) the gullet, and

   (b) the trachea [or windpipe] of the animal, while mentioning Allāh's name by saying, "*Bismillāh, Allāhu Akbar.*"

   It is also recommended to cut the two major blood vessels on either side of the animal's neck, having the head of the animal face the *qiblah*, and to use a very sharp knife in order to lessen suffering to the animal. One should stop slaughtering once the obligatory organs have been severed, being careful not to cut off the head, as that would be *makrūh*. (Revs.)
4. The question of whether or not a *Ḥanafī* is permitted to eat shrimp revolves on the point of whether or not shrimp are fish. This is because Abū Ḥanīfah has interpreted the *Sunnah* as permitting the consumption of fish only. Thus, since a shrimp is technically a crustacean, it was the opinion of the Muftī Walī Ḥasan, former Grand Muftī of Pakistan, that the prudent *Ḥanafī* should not eat shrimp, unless it is for medical purposes. However, Imāms Mālik, Shāfi'ī, and Aḥmad were all of the opinion that the flesh of shellfish, like shrimp, is *ḥalāl*. With all due respect to the opinion of my teacher, Muftī Walī Ḥasan, I should like to point out that, on the question of shrimp in particular, the early *Ḥanafī* scholars were silent. Two later *Ḥanafīs*, however, who have written on the subject, Maulānā 'Abd al-Ḥayy of Lucknow, and Maulānā Ashraf 'Alī Thānwī, were both of the opinion that the flesh of shrimp may be eaten. Finally, a *fatwā* to that effect was issued by the muftīs at the *Dārul-'Ulūm*, Deoband. And Allāh knows best. (Trans.)
5. For this reason, fish caught by non-Muslims are *ḥalāl*. (Trans.)
6. According to Imāms Shāfi'ī, Mālik, and Aḥmad, it is *ḥalāl*. Imām Abū Ḥanīfah, however, opined that the horse is a noble beast used for *Jihād* in the way of Allāh, and should be respected. (Trans.)
7. In other words, since this is a matter which is mentioned with all clarity in the Qur'ān, a person who denies it is essentially denying the Qur'ān, which is an act of *kufr*. (Trans.)

8. To treat a cold with a glass of wine is *ḥarām.* To administer medicine in which alcohol is an ingredient becomes *ḥalāl* only when a substitute cannot be found. (Trans.)

9. It is the direct use of these things that is *ḥarām.* Thus, to drink from a golden goblet is *ḥarām.* But to drink from a glass goblet after filling it from a golden pitcher is not *ḥarām.* The use of gold or silver pens, inkpots, applicators, holders for *(kuḥl) surmah,* and mirrors is *ḥalāl.* Similarly, the use of utensils made from crystal or agate is *ḥalāl.* The use of utensils or plates into which silver has been riveted is *ḥalāl* on the condition that the silver not be worked into places which usually come into contact with the hands or mouth. (Trans.)

10. When in the company of non-*maḥrams*, out in public, or in prayer, one must cover one's *ʿawrah.* (Revs.)

11. A turban may also be worn without a hanging end. (Trans.)

12. Permission here is for the winner to take an agreed upon prize. This does not, however, mean that it automatically becomes his property. If the loser refuses to give the prize, and the winner takes him before the *qāḍī*, the loser will not be ordered by the *qāḍī* to give over the prize. Of course, if the loser wants to give the prize in the spirit of friendly competition, then, as it will be a gift, the winner will be entitled to keep it as his own property. (Trans.)

13. For example, Zayd says to ʿAmr, "If your answer is correct, I'll give you this much money. But if mine is correct, I will take nothing from you." (Trans.)

14. i.e., "If I win, then you will give me the prize. But if you win, then I will give you the prize." (Trans.)

15. Three people, for example, decided that if Zayd wins, then ʿAmr and Khālid will each get a dollar. Then, if Zayd does not finish first, he will not receive anything. The one among ʿAmr and Khālid who lags behind the winner will give the winner a dollar. (Trans.)

16. Imām Shāfiʿī, however, was of the opinion that chess in particular is permitted as long as it does not detract from the performance of one's obligations, or occupy one's thoughts and time unduly. (Trans.)

17. Gambling is specifically mentioned in the Qur'ān as *ḥarām.* See *Sūrah al-Mā'idah* 5: 90. (Trans.)

18. An equivocal statement is one which is capable of more than one interpretation. For example, when Abū Bakr, may Allāh be pleased with him, was asked who was ahead of him by the unbelieving people on the way of the *Ḥijrah*, he replied, "The man who showed me the way." (Trans.)

19. Bribery is a major sin (*kabīrah*); and the commission of a *kabīrah*, if it is not followed by sincere repentance, can lead to *jahannam.* (Trans.)

20. Obviously, this applies equally to sisters as well. (Revs.)

21. "*Whoever judges not according to what Allāh has revealed, they are the unbelievers,*" *Sūrah al-Mā'idah* 5: 44. [Imāms Abū Dāwūd and Ibn Mājah have related in their collections of *ḥadīth*, that the Messenger of Allāh, may the peace and blessings of Allāh be upon him, said, "There are three types of *qāḍīs* (Judges); one will go to Paradise and two will go to Hell. The one who goes to Paradise is a *qāḍī* (Judge) who knows the truth and bases his decisions on it. A biased (Judge) *qāḍī* who knows the truth but judges tyrannically will go to *jahannam.* An ignorant *qāḍī* who gives judgement but knows nothing of the *Sharīʿah* will go to *jahannam.*" (Trans.)

22. In the absence of *Sharīʿah* courts, a *muftī*, or religious scholar should be consulted either in person or through the mail. (Trans.)

23. In Muslim minority countries it is the responsibility of the Muslim community to provide for the needs of their *ʿulamā'*. (Trans.)

24. For example, non-performance of prayer, *ḥajj*, or fasting or any kind of shortcomings in acts of worship. (Revs.)

CHAPTER 9

Iḥsān

9.1 Meaning of Iḥsān

You should know, may Allāh grant you success, that it is the form of *Īmān*, Islam, and the *Sharīʿah* that has until now been the subject of this book. The reality, *ḥaqīqah* and realisation of these things should be sought in the company of the ascetics, who have devoted their lives in the way of Allāh, and His remembrance.[1]

It should not be supposed that this reality is in any way contradictory to the *Sharīʿah*, as that would be ignorance and *kufr*. On the contrary, all of these things are part of the *Sharīʿah*. For a person in the service of the righteous person who is able to free his heart of all emotional and intellectual ties to anything other than Allāh, who throws over the baser aspects of human nature, whose soul attains peace, and who is endowed with purity, for such a person the *Sharīʿah* takes on the further meaning of reality, *ḥaqīqah*. All tangible and apparent objects become transparent and the only thing one witnesses is the presence of the Almighty, watching and observing the deeds of His servant. The prayer of that person will take one to another kind of relationship with Allāh, and his two *rakʿats* will surpass in merit a hundred thousand *rakʿats* of someone below his or her spiritual station.

The same will be the case with his *zakāh, ṣadaqah, ṣawm, ḥajj*, and other acts of worship.

The Messenger of Allāh, may the peace and blessings of Allāh be upon him, said, "If you were to spend a mountain of gold the size of Mt. Uḥud in the way of Allāh, it would not equal a bushel or half a bushel of barley given by a Companion of mine."

The spiritual light of Islam or the Messenger of Allāh, may the peace and blessings of Allāh be upon him, should be sought in the breasts of the true ascetics so that that light may be kindled in your own heart. When this light enters you, you will be able to recognise, through your faculties of discernment, all good and evil. One becomes a stranger in this temporal world and is transported to the next world through one's constant remembrance of Allāh. One begins to seek the company of others who cause one's love for this world to decrease, and one's love for Allāh and the next world to increase. And Allāh knows best.[2]

9.2 A Word at the Close of the Book

A great deal has been written about *Sharī'ah* and *Iḥsān*. In these pages an attempt has been made to present the essentials of Islamic knowledge to common persons. Any further questions should be referred to the *'ulamā'* and scholars in your own community.

Notes

1. The reality of this existence is the life beyond the present. One must focus on this reality so as not to be deluded into loving this world and mistakenly accepting it as the reality of existence. (Revs.)

2. In the Introduction to his work entitled *al-Takashshuf fī Masā'il al-Taṣawwuf* (Urdu), Maulānā Ashraf 'Alī Thānwī writes:

   It is essential that all Muslims, having seen to the propriety of their beliefs and practice [of outer conduct], also attend to the propriety of their inner conduct. Countless Qur'ānic verses and *ḥadīths* prove conclusively that this is also essential, though many of those who attend only to externals are heedless of this matter. Certainly everyone knows that the Qur'ān and the *Sunnah* contain mention of the virtues of things like abstinence, contentment, humility, sincerity, patience, thankfulness, love for the Divine, acceptance of fate, trust, and so forth. Then, can there possibly remain any doubt as to the enjoining or prohibition of these matters by *Sharī'ah*? This is what is meant by the reformation of inner conduct; this is the primary goal of the Ṣufī way; and this is what happens to be an indisputable *farḍ* duty.

In addition, experience has proved, and indeed it is the way Allāh has approved, that the single most important factor in the process of inner reformation is that one's companionship, service, and obedience to those who have themselves been reformed. Wherever actual companionship is not feasible, abstract companionship even in the form of one's reading the biographies of the great sufis, can conceivably suffice in its place. This is the secret behind the frequent urging of the Qur'ān and *ḥadīths* towards companionship of the good, and their warnings against the companionship of the wicked. For this reason, too, the stories of Allāh's special servants are repeated throughout the texts of the Qur'ān and the *Sunnah*.

Another fact which has been borne out by experience is that one's companionship of the pious, whether it be actual or abstract, can only be of benefit when accompanied by conviction and attachment. Otherwise one may spend a lifetime with the best of people and never benefit from their company. Furthermore, in the same way that the companionship of refined people is beneficial, the companionship of corrupt people is detrimental.

In our own times, owing to the general lack of knowledge about Islam, and to the predominance of selfish desires, most people never consider reforming their inner selves. And then, even if they do think of it, and seek out the company of a spiritual guide, most of them are prevented, owing to imbalances between what they know and what they practice, from making any real progress on the Ṣufī way. The majority of such people are either too severe or too lax in their approach to Islam. Those who are too severe and narrow-minded often misconstrue the words, deeds, and states of the Ṣufī masters. Then, having decided for themselves that these things are contrary to the *Sunnah*, the narrow-minded ones shun the Ṣufī masters and thus remain deprived of their blessings. In fact, it sometimes happens, owing to their disrespectful and insulting behaviour toward the masters, that these narrow-minded people place their well-being in serious jeopardy. On the other hand, those who are lax or weak in faith often become the followers of ignorant Ṣufīs who subscribe to false doctrines. Then without weighing the words, deeds, and states of these Ṣufī pretenders on the scales of the *Sharī'ah*, they accept everything they tell them. In this manner, when they decide to serve and accompany ignorant shaikhs, they are actually throwing their religion away.

Shaikh Ashraf 'Alī Thānwī used to give anyone interested in taking up the Ṣufī way a booklet entitled *Haqīqat-uṭ-Ṭariqah* [The Truth About the Way]. In the interest of further clarifying this matter for sincere Muslims, the entire booklet is translated here.

The Essence of Inner Conduct

Neither *kashf* (visions) nor *karāmah* (minor miracles) are required or expected.

On the Day of Judgement no one [other than yourself] will be responsible for your salvation.

There is no promise that your worldly affairs will improve [as a result of your becoming a disciple of this Ṣufī order, or] through your tying talismans or charms around your necks, or that you will win court cases, or have an increase in income, or be cured of disease, or be granted knowledge of what is in the future.

Your behaviour will not be reformed merely through the attentions of your shaikh, nor will you cease to think evil thoughts. You will not automatically engage in worship without even having to resolve to do so. And your knowledge and understanding of the Qur'ān and Islam will not necessarily register any sort of increase.

There is no promise that you will attain any inner spiritual states, or even that you will find pleasure in the performance of worship or spiritual exercises, or that you will not be beset by alien thoughts while in worship. There is no guarantee that you will wash your sins away with your tears of remorse.

In your performance of spiritual exercises you need never see mystic lights or hear voices from the Unseen.

You may never have a sublime or meaningful dream or receive guidance from above.

On the contrary the real objective is to please the Almighty; and the way to achieve this objective is by complete adherence to the *Sharī'ah.*

Certain of the precepts of the *Sharī'ah* have to do with the believer's outer state, like prayer, fasting, *ḥajj*, *zakāh*, marriage, divorce, discharging marital responsibilities, oaths and their expiation, buying and selling, legal procedures and giving witness, bequests, inheritance, meeting and socialising, greeting and entertaining, and so on; knowledge of these matters is called *fiqh.*

Certain others have to do with the inner state, like one's love for the Almighty, awe of Him, remembrance of Him, acceptance of His decree, or one's decreasing love of the worldly, or lack of greed, or being conscientious in worship, or sincere in religious matters, or one's lack of contempt for others, or lack of conceit, or having control over one's temper, and so on; these matters are called *suluk*, or inner conduct.

Then, in the same way that a Muslim is to obey the rules of *fiqh* in his or her outward behaviour, he or she must also obey the rules of inner conduct. Moreover, it is usually as a result of some inner imbalance that irregularities occur in one's behaviour or practise of Islam. For example, a decrease in love for the Almighty might result in a lack of attention to daily prayers, or to one's saying them hurriedly. Likewise, as a result of avarice, one might not give *zakāh* or go for *ḥajj*. Or, owing to one's self aggrandisement, or to one's inability to check one's anger, one may commit injustice on another or usurp his or her rights. Even if one were to recognise one's fault, and then take care to correct it, the fact remains that unless some sort of inner rectification takes place, one will be sure to lapse in one's efforts to correct the problem.

Thus, for the above reasons, it should be obvious that the rectification of inner conduct is essential. Yet, the problem is that inner ailments are difficult to detect; and even if they are detected, it is no easy matter to prescribe a proper cure for them. In fact, even if the cure were to be known, the taking of the medicine is nearly always distasteful.

For these reasons an accomplished master is required; one who will be able to recognise and diagnose such spiritual maladies and then prescribe for them the appropriate cure. Moreover, the shaikh should have the power to create within the disciple the ability to rectify oneself. For this purpose, the shaikh will require the disciple to engage in certain spiritual exercises and disciplines, like *dhikr* which is in itself a form of worship.

Essentially, then, the disciple will have to do two things. The first is essential; and that is that he or she will have to adhere to the inner and outer precepts of the *Sharīʿah*. The second is recommended, and that is that he or she engage in much *dhikr*. The result of the first will be the attainment of Allāh's pleasure, and closeness to Him; while the result of the second, or *dhikr*, will be an increase in Allāh's pleasure and closeness to Him.

This, then, is the essence of the way to inner conduct, and of its objectives. The above endnote has been added by the translator.

Glossary of Technical Arabic Terms

A

Adhān – the formal call to prayer.

Ahl al-Bayt – People of the house. In his book, *al-Sayf al-Maslūl*, the *qāḍī* Thanā'ullāh counted the following people among the *ahl al-Bayt* of the Messenger of Allāh, may the peace and blessings of Allāh be upon him: the children of the Prophet, may the peace and blessings of Allāh be upon him, including Fāṭimah and her sons, Ruqayyah, Umm Kulthūm, and Zaynab; the wives of Messenger of Allāh, upon whom be peace, including 'Ā'ishah, Ḥafṣah, Zaynab, and all the others; the close relatives of Allāh's Messenger, may the peace and blessings of Allāh be upon him, including 'Abbās, 'Alī, Ja'far, 'Aqīl, and the sons of 'Abbās. These are the people whose spiritual purity is attested in the following verse of the Qur'ān.

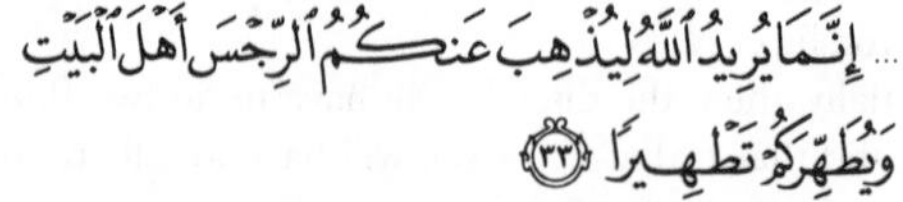

> "*Allāh desires to put away from you impurity, Ahl al-Bayt, and to cleanse you*" [*al-Aḥzāb* 33: 33].

Ajnabiy – 'Stranger', a non-*maḥram* male, see *maḥram.*

Ajnabiyyah – a non-*maḥram* female, see *maḥram.*

'Ālim – 'learned', a Muslim scholar of the Islamic sciences; pl. *'ulamā'*.

Anbiyā' – prophets, sing. *nabiy.*

Anṣār – 'helpers', the Muslim community in Madīnah who extended their help to the Prophet, may the peace and blessings of Allāh be upon him, especially after the *Hijrah.*

ʿArafāt – the place just outside Makkah where the most important pillar of *ḥajj* takes place: halting at ʿArafāt. Pilgrims halt there on the 9th of Dhu al-Ḥijjah from after the time of *ẓuhr* until after sunset; however standing at ʿArafāt is considered valid if one halts there, even for a few moments, from after the time of *ẓuhr* up until the true dawn of the 10th of Dhu al-Ḥijjah.

Arkān – the prescribed *farḍ* elements, 'pillars', of an act of worship.

ʿArsh – 'Throne'. Concerning the Throne of Allāh the Almighty, a Muslim believes it as a reality; Like the belief in other attributes of Allāh and the unseen, he must not delve into trying to interpret how the *ʿArsh* is according to his own opinions or letting his imagination free rein.

ʿAṣr – mid-afternoon prayer, one of the five daily *farḍ* prayers; see the section on Prayer (*ṣalāh* Time).

ʿAwrah – 'private parts'; those parts of the body which must be covered.

Āyah – a verse of the Qur'ān.

Ayyām at-Tashrīq – 'the Days of Drying the Meat' which is from the 11th to 13th of Dhu al-Ḥijjah. It is not permissible to fast during this period.

B

Bayʿah – the formal initiation to a spiritual order at the hands of a shaikh.

Bidʿah – innovation in religion; the invention of practices and forms which were unknown in the days of the Prophet, may the peace and blessings of Allāh be upon him, or his Companions and *Khulafāʾ*, may Allāh be pleased with them.

D

Darūd-aṣ-Ṣalātu ʿalan-Nabī – the invocation of divine blessings on the Messenger of Allāh, may the peace and blessings of Allāh be upon him.

Dhikr – also, *Dhikrullāh*: the remembrance of Allāh; *dhikr* may be performed in a number of ways, and it is universally recognised by all *Ṣufis* to be at the heart of all spiritual life.

Dhu al-Ḥijjah – the last month of the Islamic year in which the actual rites of the *ḥajj* are performed.

Du'ā' – a prayer of supplication.

F

Fajr – morning prayer; one of the five daily *farḍ* prayers.

Farḍ – an obligation; anything rendered obligatory by the *Sharī'ah.*

Fāsid – spoiled; legally null and void.

Fātiḥah – the opening *sūrah* of the Qur'ān.

Fatwā – a legal decision taken by a scholar on the basis of authoritative source or evidence from the *Sharī'ah.*

Fidyah – redemption for the omission of certain religious duties through material donations, or fines, or the performance of religious acts.

Fiqh – the juristical study of the *Sharī'ah*; the systematic explanation and interpretation of the two basic sources of all Islamic legislation, the Qur'ān and the *Sunnah* of the Messenger of Allāh, may the peace and blessings of Allāh be upon him, to explain the details of Islamic practice, understanding of *dīn.*

Fir'aun – Pharaoh, the tyrannical king of Egypt in the time of Mūsā, upon whom be peace.

G

Ghalīẓah Najāsah – gross impurities, see the section on *ṭahārah.*

Ghayb – the unseen, inscrutable.

Ghībah – backbiting, talking about someone behind his back in a way which, were he present, would displease him.

Ghislīn – the pus and corruption which flows from the bodies of the inhabitants of the Fire of Hell.

H

Ḥadīth – the deeds, sayings and silent approval of the Messenger of Allāh, may the peace and blessings of Allāh be upon him, as preserved by his Companions in the form of written or oral traditions which were then passed from generation to generation and collected.

Ḥājah – need, want, necessity.

Ḥanafī – of or relating to the school of legal thought developed under the guidance of Imām Abū Ḥanīfah.

Ḥaqā'iq – pl. of *ḥaqīqah*, see next.

Ḥaqīqah – truth, the underlying reality of a thing.

Ḥaqīqī – actual, as opposed to *ḥukmī* or legal. Thus, for example some substances are known by all to be impure. These are called *ḥaqīqī* impurities. But there are other substances whose impurity is known only by means of the *Sharī'ah*. These are called *ḥukmī* or legal impurities.

Ḥarām – unlawful, prohibited by the *Sharī'ah*;

Ḥaṭīm – the semi-circular structure located on the side of the Ka'bah that is between the Iraqi and Syrian corners which is actually a part of the Ka'bah and therefore must be included in one's *ṭawāf*.

Ḥayḍ – menstruation, the monthly period of menstruation.

Ḥourī – the name given to the maiden of the Garden of Paradise.

Ḥukmī – legal, see above at *ḥaqīqī*.

Ḥulūl – occupation of space; incarnation in something or someone.

I

'Ibādah – one's relationship as slave to Allāh, expressed outwardly in acts of obedience, worship, service and devotion.

Idṭibā' – during *ṭawāf* of the Ka'bah, it refers to baring the right shoulder by men in *iḥrām* while covering the left.

Ifrād – one of the three types of *ḥajj* where one takes up the intention of *iḥrām* to perform *ḥajj* only. It is typically performed by the residents of Makkah. The person who performs it is called a *mufrid*.

Iḥrām – the intention to enter a state where certain things are forbidden which were normally allowed by the person going on *ḥajj* or *'umrah*. The removing of one's regular clothes and donning two pieces of white seamless cloth, wearing sandals that do not cover the bone of the top part of the foot exposing the two ankles, uncovering the head, and reciting the *talbiyah*, with the intention of performing the *ḥajj* or *'umrah* is known as *iḥrām* and is *farḍ* for both the *ḥajj* and *ʿumrah.* The *iḥrām* for women is their normal Islamic dress, and does not require them to wear open sandals.

Iḥsān – the complementary inner state which gives depth and added meaning to the outer state of Islam. See the Book of *Iḥsān.*

Iḥṣār – prevention from performing the *ḥajj* or *ʿumrah* after taking up *iḥrām* which requires sacrifice.

ʿIlm al-Ghayb – knowledge of the unknown, an attribute possessed exclusively by the Almighty.

Imām – a leader; one who leads a congregation in *ṣalāh*; a leading scholar.

Īmān – faith in Islam, the state of being a believer.

Injīl – a book, like the Qur'ān and Torah, of Divine guidance. It was revealed to the Prophet ʿIsā ibn Maryam, upon whom be peace. The book however, was altered and finally destroyed by the enemies of true religion in the early centuries of the Christian era.

Iqāmah – the final call to prayer, and the signal for the people assembled in the Masjid to stand and form lines for the performance of prayer in congregation.

ʿIshā' – evening prayer; one of the five daily *farḍ* prayers.

Istighfār – seeking forgiveness; any supplication made in repentance.

Istisqā' – supplication for rain.

J

Jahannam – the Hell Fire.

Jā'iz – anything permitted by the *Sharīʿah,* allowed.

Jalsah – the sitting position in prayer which is assumed between two *sajdahs.*

Jamāʿah – a group of Muslims, especially a congregation for prayer.

Jāmiʿ Masjid – a large Masjid in which *jumuʿah* prayer is performed.

Jamrah – the stone pillars in Minā which pilgrims cast pebbles at during the 10th–13th of Dhu al-Ḥijjah. The pillar which is furthest from Makkah is the *jamrah al-'ūlā,* which is close to *Masjid al-Khayf,* the next pillar is the *jamrah al-wusṭā',* and the pillar nearest to Makkah is the *jamrah al-ʿaqabah.*

Janābah – the state of legal impurity which necessitates *ghusl*, having a wet dream or sexual intercourse.

Janāzah – a funeral; corpse.

Jannah – the Garden of Paradise.

Jizyah – a protection tax levied on the non-Muslim subject of a Muslim state and they are exempted from paying *zakāh* which is compulsory for Muslims.

Jumuʿah – the most blessed day of the Islamic week, Friday, the day of general assembly.

K

Kabīrah – an act of major wrongdoing.

Kafan – burial shrouds.

Kāfir – an unbeliever, non-Muslim.

Kawthar – a pool in *Jannah* from which the believers will drink.

Khafīfah Najāsah – light impurities; see the section on *ṭahārah.*

Khalīfah – successor; the title given to the four successors of the Messenger of Allāh, may the peace and blessings of Allāh be upon him, Abū Bakr, ʿUmar, ʿUthmān, and ʿAlī, may Allāh be pleased with them all. In Ṣufī terminology, one who, on the basis of his spiritual development, has been given permission by a shaikh to instruct others in the Ṣufī way. In the terminology of *fiqh*, a *Khalīfah* is a person who, having joined a congregation for prayer as a follower, is motioned forward by the imām during prayer [should his *wuḍū'* be broken or become unable to complete the prayer] to take his place as *imām* until the prayer is completed.

Khaṭīb – one who reads the *khuṭbah* in *jumuʿah* prayer.

Khatm – completion; a complete recitation of the Qur'ān, from beginning to end.

Khilāfah – office or rule of a *Khalīfah.*

Khuff – a particular type of tight-fitting leather stocking concerning which a number of rulings are listed in the section on *taharah.*

Khuffayn – the dual form of *khuff*, see above.

Khuṭbah – a discourse in Arabic delivered as part of the *jumuʿah* prayer or *ʿĪd* prayers.

Kufr – unbelief, denial of the truth of Islam.

Kusūf – solar eclipse.

M

Madhhab – a school of *fiqh*. As the four major *madhhabs* of the Sunnī orthodoxy differ only on points of procedure while agreeing to the last detail on matters of faith, they cannot be called sects. Nor can they be called *bid*ʿ*ah*, as a *madhhab* is no more than an informed and enlightened codification and clarification of the injunctions of the *Sharī*ʿ*ah* as they are found in the Qur'ān and *ḥadīth*.

Madrasah – any place where any aspect of Islam is taught more or less formally.

Maghrib – sunset prayer; one of the five daily *farḍ* prayers.

Maḥram – unmarriageable; thus, a relative so close as to preclude marriage, such as father, mother, sister, brother, son, daughter, etc. including close relatives of one's spouse.

Masbūq – latecomer; one who joins a congregation for prayer behind an imām after the imām has assumed the position for the first *rak*ʿ*ah*.

Mashāyikh – sing. *Shaikh*; spiritual guides.

Masjid – mosque.

Masnūn – in accordance with the *Sunnah*.

Minbar – the raised platform at the front of a *Masjid* from which the *khaṭīb* delivers his Friday discourse.

Mishkāt – a well-known collection of *Ḥadīth* compiled by the *Imām* Tabrizī in the sixth century of *Hijrah*.

Miswāk – a twig of fragrant wood cut for use as a toothbrush.

Mīzān – the scales will be used to weigh the deeds of mankind on the Day of Judgement.

Mu'akkadah – emphasised; the designation given to an act whose performance is encouraged by the *Sharī*ʿ*ah*.

Mubāḥ – legally permitted by the *Sharī*ʿ*ah*, *jā'iz* or permitted.

Mubārak – blessed.

Mudrik – one who has arrived on time; one who joins a *jamā*ʿ*ah* for prayer from before the first *rukū*ʿ.

Mufrid – see *ifrād*.

Muḥaddith – a scholar of *Ḥadīth*.

Muhājirīn – those who make *Hijrah*; those Makkan Companions who made *Hijrah* to Madīnah in the early years of Islam.

Muḥarram – the first month of the Islamic year.

Muḥdith – a person in a state of minor ritual impurity; a state necessitating *wuḍūʾ* [as opposed to *janābah*, which necessitates *ghusl*].

Muḥīṭ – All-encompassing, All-powerful, from the word *iḥāṭah* which means to surround something so completely as to make escape impossible.

Mujaddid – an inspired Islamic reformer.

Munfarid – one who performs prayer on his own, i.e. a single *muṣallī*.

Munkar – one of the two angels responsible for the questioning in the grave.

Muqīm – standing; one who is not travelling.

Muqtadī – a person is called a *muqtadī* when he is performing prayer behind an imām.

Musāfir – traveller.

Muṣallī – a person is called a *muṣallī* when he is performing prayer.

Mushrikīn – idolaters, unbelievers.

Mustaḥab – liked or praiseworthy; the designation given to acts whose performance is desirable.

Mutawaḍḍī – a person in the state of having performed *wuḍūʾ*.

Mutawātir – evidence which is indisputable owing to the frequency of its transmission. A *mutawātir ḥadīth* is a *ḥadīth* which is related by a great number of people at each successive stage of its transmission.

Mutayammim – a person in the state of having performed *tayammum*.

Muwālāh – to perform something in a continuous manner without break.

Muzdalifah – a plain outside of Makkah where pilgrims spend the night after halting at ʿArafāt. It is *wājib* for the pilgrim to be present at Muzdalifah at any time from the true dawn until sunrise on the 10th of Dhu al-Ḥijjah.

N

Nabī – The bearer of Divine Revelation, prophet; a person chosen by the Almighty to reveal, by means of *waḥy* or Divine inspiration, His Will or Message.

Nafl – any supererogatory act of worship.

Najāsah – impurity; see the chapter on *ṭahārah.*

Nakīr – one of the two angels responsible for the questioning in the grave.

Naqshbandī – of or relating to the Imām Bahā' ad-Dīn Naqshband or the Ṣufī order which he founded, may Allāh illumine his resting place and give him peace.

Niyah – intention; a mental acknowledgement of what one is about to perform in the way of worship.

Q

Qaḍā' – make up; compensation for an omission by performing the committed act at a later time.

Qa'dah – the sitting position in prayer which is assumed after every two *rak'ats*, and from which position prayer is brought to a close.

Qāḍī – Islamic Judge, an official of the Islamic state empowered to hear and decide cases brought before a court of *Sharī'ah* law.

Qawmah – the brief standing position in prayer between *rukū'* and *sajdah.*

Qiblah – the direction towards the Holy Ka'bah in Makkah which one faces in prayer.

Qirā'ah – recitation; esp. the recitation of the Qur'ān in prayer.

Qirān – one of the three types of *ḥajj* where the pilgrim makes the intention to perform both *ḥajj* and *'umrah* with the same *iḥrām*; i.e. they perform *'umrah* first and stay in *iḥrām* until they have completed *ḥajj*. The one who performs it is called a *qārin.*

Qiyām – the extended standing position in prayer in which *Sūrah Fātiḥah* and another *sūrah* or *ayāts* are read.

Qurbānī – the ritual slaughter of cattle as an act of worship.

R

Rak'ah – cycle; a component part of prayer which includes the *qiyām, rukū'* and *sajdah* positions.

Ramaḍān – the 9th month of the Islamic year, in which Muslims are required to observe *ṣawm*, fasting.

Ramal – to walk quickly in the first three circuits of *ṭawāf* of the Ka'bah when one has made the intention to perform *sa'y* afterwards. If *sa'y* is not to be performed, it should be left out.

Ramiy – to stone the pillars or *jamrahs* in Minā.

Rasūl – messenger, see *nabī.*

Rukū' – the bowed position in prayer; from the *qiyām* position, the *muṣallī* will bend down until coming to rest with the palms on the knee, and the back and the head on one level.

S

Ṣā' – a unit of volumetric measurement about 2 litres or 3.17 kg in weight. It is usually used to refer to the quantity of grain to be given as *ṣadaqah*, which is usually half a *ṣā'* or one *ṣā'*.

Sacrifice – Day of the 10th of Dhu al-Ḥijjah. The period of sacrifice is until sunset on the 12th of Dhu al-Ḥijjah, which is why this period is also called the Days of Sacrifice.

Ṣaghīrah – an act of minor wrongdoing.

Ṣaḥābah – the Companions of the Messenger of Allāh, may Allāh be pleased with them all.

Ṣaḥib at-tartīb – a pious person who has not missed five or less *farḍ* prayers since puberty, when the prayer had become *farḍ.*

Saḥīḥain – dual form of *ṣaḥīḥ*, authentic; the two most authentic collections of *ḥadīth*, *Ṣaḥīḥ* Bukhārī and *Ṣaḥīḥ* Muslim.

Sajdah – the position of prostration in prayer.

Salām – the closing words of prayer, "*as-Salāmu 'Alaikum wa Raḥmatullāh.*"

Ṣawm – fasting; the abstention from food, drink, and sexual intercourse from sunrise to sunset with the *niyah* of worshipping Allāh.

Sayyidinā – a title of respect; our sovereign.

Sha'bān – the 8th month of the Islamic year.

Shafā'ah – intercession.

Shahīd – a martyr; see the section on *janāzah.*

Shaikh – elder; a spiritual guide.

Sharī'ah – an open road; the body of laws taken from the Qur'ān and *Sunnah* which govern the faith and practice of the Muslim.

Shawwāl – the 10th month of the Islamic year.

Shī'ah – a heretical offshoot from the early days of Islam. The *Shī'ah* themselves are divided into a number of sects and sub-sects some of which hold beliefs contrary to the teachings of Islam.

Shirk – idolatry; association of partners with Allāh.

Sunnah – the way that has been walked in; the way of the Messenger of Allāh, may the peace and blessings of Allāh be upon him.

Sunnī – a Muslim who subscribes to the views and beliefs of orthodox Islam.

Sūrah – a chapter of the Qur'ān.

Sutrah – shield; a stick or rod which is placed in the ground in front of a *muṣallī* who is performing his prayer out in the open.

T

Ta'awwudh – seeking refuge; the words at the opening of prayer which are recited after the *takbīr* and *thanā A'ūdhu billahi minash-shayṭānir rajīm.*

Tahajjud – a *nafl* prayer performed during the last third of the night. See the section on Prayer (*ṣalāh*).

Ṭahārah – purity; the removal of impediments, themselves the result of impurity of one kind or another, to the proper performance of certain acts of worship.

Taḥiyyah – salutation; *taḥiyyah al-Masjid* and *taḥiyyah al-wuḍū'* are *nafl* prayers which are performed as a sort of salute to the Masjid and to *wuḍū'*.

Taḥrīmah – the *takbīr* at the opening of prayer. The words *taḥrīmah* and *ḥarām* are derived from the same root, which indicates that when the *muṣallī* makes *taḥrīmah*, everything outside of prayer becomes *ḥarām* until he has finished performing the prayer.

Takbīr – the words, one's saying the words, *"Allāhu Akbar"*. In prayer the opening *takbīr* is accompanied by a raising of the hands.

Talbiyah – the special prayer formula one recites during the state of *iḥrām*.

Talqīn – the chanting of the *kalimah* in the presence of one who is about to die. See the chapter on *janāzah*.

Tamattu' – one of the three types of *ḥajj* where the pilgrim performs *ḥajj* and *'umrah* with separate *iḥrāms* in the same *ḥajj* season, in the same journey. One first completes *'umrah* with the first *iḥrām* and then resumes normal life; when the Day of *Tarwiyah* arrives, *iḥrām* is taken up for *ḥajj* from their residence in Makkah. The one who performs it is called *mutamatti'*.

Tarāwīḥ – the 20 *rakʿats* of *nafl* performed in congregation throughout the month of *Ramaḍān* after *ʿishā* prayer.

Tartīb – sequence; the performance of *wuḍū'* or prayer in its proper or *masnūn* sequence.

Tarwiyah – the 8th day of Dhu al-Ḥijjah; the day on which the pilgrims begin the actual rites of *ḥajj* and leave Makkah for Minā.

Tasbīḥ – praise and glorification of Allāh.

Tashahhud – testifying to Allāh's oneness; in prayer, the recitation of *shahādah* while in the *qaʿdah* position.

Tasmiyah – saying *Bismillāh-ir-Raḥmān-ir-Raḥīm,* In the name of Allāh, the Most Gracious, the Most Merciful.

Ṭawāf – circumambulation of the Kaʿbah at Makkah. It consists of seven circuits performed counter-clockwise, with the Kaʿbah to one's left beginning and ending each round at the Black Stone. It is a pillar of the *ḥajj* and *ʿumrah.*

Ṭawāf al-Ifāḍah – see *ṭawāf az-Ziyārah.*

Ṭawāf al-Qudūm – the *ṭawāf* of arrival at the Holy Kaʿbah which is *Sunnah* for those coming from outside of Makkah.

Ṭawāf aṣ-Ṣadr – otherwise known as the *ṭawāf* of Farewell. The final *ṭawāf* one makes when leaving Makkah which is *wājib* for non-resident *ḥājies.*

Ṭawāf al-Wadāʿ – see *ṭawāf as-Ṣadr.*

Ṭawāf az-Ziyārah – the *ṭawāf* of visiting the House of Allāh, the Kaʿbah, in Makkah after the Day of ʿArafah which is a pillar of the *ḥajj.*

Tawbah – heartfelt repentance.

Ta'wīl – the attempt to give explanations for ambiguous or uncertain passages from the Qur'ān and *ḥadīth.*

Tayammum – a method of purification which, under certain prescribed conditions, may be used as an alternative to *wuḍū'* and *ghusl.*

Thanā' – praise; in prayer, the words which are recited immediately after the opening *takbīr* of *taḥrīmah* [also known as *istiftāḥ*].

Tilāwah – recitation of the Qur'ān.

Ṭuhr – purity; esp. a time of purity between two periods of *ḥayḍ.*

U

'Ulamā' – pl. of *'ālim*; scholars; esp. of the Islamic sciences.

Ummah – community; esp. the community of believers.

'Umrah – the lesser pilgrimage to the House of Allāh in Makkah which is *Sunnah mu'akkadah* to perform.

W

Waḥy – Divine revelation.

Wājib – an obligation; the major difference between *farḍ* and *wājib* is that in prayer if something *farḍ*, like *sajdah*, is left out, the prayer will become *fāsid*. Whereas if something *wājib*, like the *Fātiḥah*, is left out, the prayer will not become *fāsid* if *sajdah sahw* is made. See the chapter on Prayer (*ṣalāh*).

Walī – a friend of Allāh; a saintly person.

Waṣiyyah – a bequest; a will.

Wuḍū' – a method of cleansing oneself from the state of minor ritual impurity. See the section on *ṭahārah*.

Z

Zabūr – the Psalms of David, Prophet Dāwūd, upon whom be peace.

Zakāh – a payment levied on definite kinds of property and distributed among the needy. See the section on *zakāh*.

Zaqqūm – a tree in *jahannam*. See Qur'ān [44: 43].